THE INNER SOURCE

A Guide to
Meditative Therapy

Michael L. Emmons, Ph.D.

Impact 💧 **Publishers**
POST OFFICE BOX 1094
SAN LUIS OBISPO, CALIFORNIA 93406

First Edition, April 1978
Copyright ©1978
by Michael L. Emmons

Library of Congress Cataloging in Publication Data

Emmons, Michael L.
    The inner source.

    Includes index.
    1. Meditation.   2. Meditation--Therapeutic use.
I.   Title.
BF637.M4E47   615'.851   78-466
ISBN: 0-915166-47-X   ISBN: 0-915166-48-8   Paper

Published by   *Impact* &*Publishers*   POST OFFICE BOX 1094
SAN LUIS OBISPO, CA 93406

Cover Photograph by Shelby Stover
Printed in the United States of America

Contents

Part II
FOR THE THERAPIST

ACKNOWLEDGEMENTS

Perhaps the acknowledgements section of any book is the most joyous part -- first, because it is the last to be written, signifying completion, and more importantly, because it is filled with genuine thanksgiving. As I write these words I feel both feelings deeply, but especially those of genuine heartfelt thanks to all who have helped lighten the load along the way.

My highest accolade goes to my longtime friend, co-worker, co-author, partner, and now editor and publisher, Bob Alberti. Hannah More said, "Accept my thoughts for thanks; I have no words," which describes the depth of my feelings about Bob's contribution and dedication to this work. He has employed all of his multiple talents in helping to make this a finished product. Bob is truly a gifted editor and publisher.

I am especially grateful to all of my clients whose experiences I have reported here. They were willing to have faith in me at critical points in their lives.

Several have taken the time to critically read the manuscript and offer creative comment: Bob Barrows, Clara Froggatt, Carol Geer, Grant Miller. I am thankful for their helpfulness.

Anne Richardson deserves special thanks for copy editing work on the manuscript. It was always a pleasure to work with her.

Francee Rios completed most of the typing throughout the long history of the work. She has been faithfully cheerful, fast and accurate. I thank her for her dedication.

The efforts of Wolfgang Luthe and A. L. Kitselman have stimulated much of my thinking. Their pioneering works have been a treasure of information for me.

I appreciate the efforts of Heidi Howard and Lois Armerding who helped with typing at critical points.

The task of securing permissions is always a time-consuming one. Jan Bell, assistant publisher at Impact, helped a great deal with that task. She has also done an excellent job with early promotional efforts on the book.

Lynn Overholt, formerly an editor of Pocket Books, and Lach MacDonald, President of Padre Productions, both recognized the potential of the manuscript in its early, quite rough, stages. Lynn and Lach also offered creative suggestions for improving the work.

The talent of Shelby Stover is obvious by the evidence on the front cover, but he also was especially kind and patient, which I appreciated.

Kay, Brent, and Scott Emmons have been patient and supportive throughout the preparation period of the book. I thank them for making my load much easier.

Los Osos, California   M.L.E.
December, 1977

ACKNOWLEDGEMENTS

The author and publisher are grateful to:

Wesleyan University Press for permission to quote from *LSD, Man and Society*, by Richard C. DeBold and Russell C. Leaf (editors). Copyright 1967 by Wesleyan University.

The New American Library for permission to quote from *The Will to Meaning*, by Viktor E. Frankl. Copyright 1969 by Viktor E. Frankl. By arrangement with the New American Library, Inc., New York, NY.

Harcourt Brace Jovanovich, Inc. for permission to quote from *The Secret of the Golden Flower*, by Richard Wilhelm.

Harcourt Brace Jovanovich, Inc. for permission to quote from Carl G. Jung's commentary in *The Secret of the Golden Flower*, by Richard Wilhelm.

Charles C. Thomas, Publisher, for permission to quote from *Parapsychology, Frontier Science of the Mind*, by J. Rhine and J. Pratt, copyright 1957.

Psyche for permission to quote from "Deep Relaxation With Free Ideation," by Walter Frederking, Vol. 2, 1949, p. 211 + .

The International Society for General Semantics for permission to quote from *ETC: A Review of General Semantics*, Weller Embler, Vol. XXXI, No. 3, Sept. 1974.

Arthur Janov for permission to quote from *The Journal of Primal Therapy*.

Psychic Magazine, 680 Beach Street, San Francisco, CA 94109, for permission to quote from "Interview: Ingo Swann," Vol. IV, No. 4, April 1973.

A. L. Kitselman for permission to quote from *E-Therapy*.

The Viking Press, Inc. for permission to quote from *Psychosynthesis*, by Roberto Assagioli, and from *Realms of the Human Unconscious*, by Stanislav Grof.

Grune and Stratton, Inc. and Wolfgang Luthe for permission to quote from *Autogenic Therapy*, Wolfgang Luthe (editor), 1969. By permission of the publishers and the editor.

Harper & Row, Publishers, Inc. for permission to quote from *Letters of Aldous Huxley*, Grover Smith (editor). Letter "20 July, 1952" (pp. 646-650), Letter "14 August, 1952" (pp. 650-651). Copyright 1969 by Laura Huxley, copyright by Grover Smith. And for permission to quote from *The First and Last Freedom* by J. Krishnamurti, Copyright, 1975. Reprinted by permission of Harper & Row, Publishers, Inc.

DEDICATION

This book is dedicated to Karin Varner, Agis I. (Mike) Mahalakis and S. Gordon Simpson, friends whose lives were inspirational to my growth.

NOTE

Due to the nature of the methods described here it is very important to read the *entire* book before attempting to use these methods with oneself or with others.

The material in *The Inner Source* is based on experience with relatively healthy persons. No claim is expressed or implied for the value of these methods with individuals who are severely disturbed, emotionally, physically, or spiritually.

PUBLISHER'S NOTE

This publication is designed to provide accurate and authoritative information in regard to the subject matter covered. It is sold with the understanding that the publisher is not engaged in rendering psychological, medical, or other professional services. If expert assistance or counseling is needed, the services of a competent professional should be sought.

Part I

*All my best thoughts were stolen
by the ancients.*

Ralph Waldo Emerson

1

The Inner Source:
A Natural Help Within

> How he loved this river, how it enchanted him,
> how grateful he was to it! In his heart he heard the
> newly awakened voice speak, and it said to him:
> "Love this river, stay by it, learn from it." Yes, he
> wanted to learn from it, he wanted to listen to it. It
> seemed to him that whoever understood this river
> and its secrets, would understand much more, many
> secrets, all secrets.
>
> But today he only saw one of the river's secrets,
> one that gripped his soul. He saw that the water
> continually flowed and flowed and yet it was always
> there; it was always the same and yet every moment
> it was new. Who could understand, conceive this?
> He did not understand it; he was only aware of a dim
> suspicion, a faint memory, divine voices.
>
> —Hermann Hesse—

Hesse's "river" is a source that flows within each of us which people have sought to understand for centuries.

In the United States today we are in the midst of a great new excursion into comprehending our inner river in all of its completeness. We are stimulated with information about faith healing and spiritual healing; about death, near death and dying; about the functioning of our right and left brain; about meditation; and about holistic approaches to medicine and pain control. Dreaming, kundalini, est, balancing, primal therapy, centering, biofeedback, body healing energies, and imagery are all among the popular concepts and approaches for delving into the internal self.

3

Though the search is an ageless one, there is now a widespread heightening of this quest for knowing and using the full potential within.

A Natural Help Within

There is inside each of us a powerful source of knowledge, a self-contained system of help. This inner source is a natural, inherent, inborn process—a wisdom which some feel is God-directed and some feel is brain-directed. It has been given many names throughout the ages: the deep self, the overself, the superconscious, the higher self, the biological wisdom, the river, the subliminal self, the God-within, the oversoul, the not-self, the Christ consciousness. I have added yet another name to the list, perhaps the least confining; I call it simply "the Inner Source." The derivation of its power and the actual name given make no difference because the Inner Source will work to help us whatever we call it and wherever it comes from.

The tendency in the United States is to hypnotize the Inner Source, to biofeedback it, mind control it, seminar train it, guide its imagery, stimulate it with mantras, with music, with key phrases, with dance, with machines, with psychedelic drugs, with sensory isolation. It is rare to allow the Inner Source complete freedom of response. This is not to say that these other interventions are not valuable. Nevertheless, at the doorstep of wisdom, it is best to listen before speaking. There is an entirely *natural* way of getting in touch with the Inner Source and it is best to let *it* decide how to proceed before deciding how it should be influenced. If we can learn to trust the Inner Source, it will use a wide variety of systematic, often intricate and beautiful, ways to help us.

A Balanced View of Consciousness

People seem to view the unconscious from a negative stance, not realizing the presence of a more dominant, uplifting, positive aspect. They lean toward the Freudian position that the unconscious is a storehouse for repressed memories and feelings which are largely negative in nature. The unconscious is considered to be infantile, something to be distrusted and defeated. It needs to be cleaned up and shaped up, brought into control so that it won't cause problems with its misbehavior. Aldous Huxley (1972) portrays this limited viewpoint in the following delightful manner:

Is the house of the soul a mere bungalow with a cellar? Or does it have an upstairs above the ground floor of conscious-ness, as well as a garbage-littered basement beneath? Freud, the most popular and influential of modern psychologists, inclined to the bungalow-with-basement view of human nature. It was only to be expected; for Freud was a doctor and, like most doctors, paid more attention to sickness than to health. His primary concern was with the subterranean rats and black beetles, and with all the ways in which a conscious ego may be disturbed by the bad smells and the vermin below stairs.

The portion of our mind with which Freud was primarily concerned was the subconscious, whereas the "upstairs" Huxley refers to could be termed the superconscious. Contrary to popular belief, the superconscious, not the subconscious, is the dominant aspect of our unconscious mind. The tendency in the United States has been to focus exclusively on subconscious properties, failing to even recognize the existence of the more ingraining qualities of the superconscious. If the presence of the superconscious is known at all, it is often misunderstood and usually directed and manipulated instead of allowed to express itself fully. In the process of breaking us free from the limitations of our existence, the superconscious, or Inner Source, is continually striving for higher and higher levels of good or actualization.

The Workings of the Inner Source

Many of us have already experienced contact with the Inner Source in our lives. A client of mine spontaneously recalled attempting something similar as a child: "I remember lying in a place trying to do this even as a kid. It's weird, because nothing is coming now. As a kid when I would do this, it was like in your imagination you are there." Another reported that "the experiences were similar to what I had experienced often before, particularly when I would go to bed at night. They were then frightening, and I fought them, and thought of them as being similar to nightmares."

There are numerous ways this knowledge within—the Inner Source—shows itself. Have you ever witnessed your own mind at work during pre-sleep or post-sleep, that twilight state of half-sleep, half-awake? I recently asked a group of sixty-five incoming college students this same question. Although they came from a variety of ethnic backgrounds (American Indian, Black, Chinese and Japanese American, Mexican American, and Anglo), over sixty percent indicated that they had at times watched their minds at work in this special state of consciousness. These students reported a kaleidoscope of happenings, such as seeing colors, patterns, flashes of light, vast darkness, and feeling sensations like coldness, spirit presences, bodily elevation and lowering. In response to these occurrences, some found themselves feeling scared or weird or regretful, whereas others felt feelings of peace, pleasure, excitement, and enthusiasm.

As the book progresses, you will observe that the responses of these students are only inklings of an endless wellspring of purposeful events from within, and of the range of feelings one may undergo in experiencing these events. The Inner Source presents a wide array of mental, physical, and spiritual happenings which are designed to help us reach our full potential.

Dr. Wolfgang Luthe (1970), a Montreal psychiatrist and international authority on Autogenic Training, indicates that the responses of the "biological wisdom" are discharging or curing problem areas. He has identified a wide variety of responses. For example, one may hear words or music, experience tastes, smells, feel dizzy or lopsided, tremble or twitch or jerk, feel heavy, warm, experience anxiety, fear, euphoria, and have thoughts and memories. In addition, one may experience multiple images, unusual brightness, images of oneself, themes about life and death, pain-crying episodes, and sexual responses.

Not all of us will experience every single reaction catalogued by Luther. The Inner Source is extremely inventive in producing a unique set of responses for your particular needs. Depending upon the areas of your life that need attention, your Inner Source seems to know what to have you undergo. Even though one may never understand all of the phenomena produced by the Inner Source, one usually can detect the subject areas in which it is working. Psychological upsets may be the focal point. Death, childhood, divorce, childbirth, or mistreatment by a parent may be the topic. Physical problems may need to be reworked, from polio to migraine headaches, to head injuries, to malaria, to kidney disorders, to menstrual disorders. Areas of religious functioning such as spiritual experiences, the devil, angels, spirits, guilt, love of others, may need to be covered. No matter what subject area the Inner Source is presenting, our job is to trust and patiently allow it to unfold.

There are two basic goals of the Inner Source: a *Therapeutic or Healing Goal* and a *Creative Goal*. The therapeutic goal is achieved by experiencing five types of responses: (1) Discharging, (2) Extended Discharging, (3) Reinforcement, (4) Understanding, (5) Abreaction (re-experiencing pain). The creative goal is achieved through New Experiences presented by the Inner Source.

Below is a time-shortened representation of a "typical" journey of an Inner Source. The journey could take place in a single session but usually takes place over a series of sessions. All the stages illustrated may, but probably will not, take place for each person who experiences Meditative Therapy. The order of the stages occurs in various combinations. My purpose is to illustrate the components of the overall journey of the Inner Source. The experiences given have come from actual Meditative Therapy sessions of *several* individuals and were synthesized into this model. Actual content and sequence is unique to each individual.

Beginning	I hear noises outside, feel tense, see colors and different patterns. Seems to be a variety of colors, blending and bursting and blending into one
Discharging	another. My legs are hot and I get the sensation my hips are being rolled to the right and I am crooked. Some minor twitching under my left eye.
Extended Discharging	I just saw myself in bed jumping and moving a lot. The thought keeps coming in that I always

thought my mother acted like a little girl. I remember telling her, why don't you grow up—why don't you do things on your own instead of waiting for my dad. But he was never around. I used to get mad because she wouldn't take us to

Understanding do things without him. I'm mad at myself too because I'm falling into that pattern too and I don't like it. I'm really scared I'm going to end up like my mother (*stomach gurgles*).

Abreaction   She was mistrusting and snippy and never said what she wanted. Everything is all dark and black now, looks like cloud formations or something. I didn't like her, but I feel sorry for her now (*stomach gurgles*). I just got a flash of how much I hated my first husband, I just hated him and can't understand why it took me so long to get away from him. I made such a stupid mistake (*sobbing*). I didn't hate him as much as I did myself for making such a dumb mistake. God, my body is really cold and I get these waves or shudders starting at the top and going down. I feel like there are two little voices in my head, one on one side, one on the other (*sobbing*). Arguing back and forth, a little person. One says you were really dumb, the other says everyone's human, everyone makes mistakes. They've been shouting in there for seven years.

New   Oh well, maybe that's water under the bridge.
Experience Maybe I'm not such a bad person after all. I should just go on with my life now and take care of the things I can do something about. I'm beginning to feel a little dizzy and light headed and all of a sudden it seems to be lighter in here. I have a feeling of going inside of something, I don't know what or where it is, I seem to be aware of a light. The light is all around and very intense.

Reinforcement	Now that seems to be passing, but I feel like, like, boy, that was really something! Like, just for a second there, I completely lost contact or awareness, like my mind or whole self shut off for a second. When I went into it, it was like a total state of no motion at all.
Ending	It must be ready to finish up for the day. I just saw a train on the track and I could see the smoke from its brakes and it came to a stop. And I'm done.

Why Get in Touch with Your Inner Source?

Perhaps the best reason to get in touch with your Inner Source is because it knows more about you than you do consciously. It knows what experiences from the past still have residual pain attached to them and need to be reworked in order to set you free. It understands your doubts and fears and how to help overcome them. The Inner Source knows what physical difficulties bother you and how to deal with them. It understands your hidden or shut-down talents and how to release them. This inner advocate is in touch with your spiritual needs and what should be done with them. No matter what area of your life needs attention, your internal expert is available to help you, a constant companion who has great wisdom and power and love and will be of help at any time if you desire its benefits.

Since I am a psychologist, individuals come to me with what they think are psychological problems. When I explain to them about the workings of the Inner Source, however, I never attempt to point out specifically what the Inner Source will do to help. I cannot predict exactly how each person's Inner Source will proceed. Instead, I stress that the Inner Source is concerned with the complete development of a person, mentally, physically, spiritually, and that it is best to simply trust in its wisdom and allow it to do what needs to be done to help.

I offer this same counsel to anyone who desires to get in touch with the Inner Source, no matter what their own conscious reason for doing so. Whether one wishes to develop creativity, experience a closer relationship with God, be cured or healed, develop full potential, or live life more successfully, the Inner Source knows best how to deal with the unique needs of the individual.

Even for a basically healthy person, there appear to be good reasons for getting in touch with one's Inner Source. Insights may be gained in matters which one considered of little residual consequence. The Inner Source has the ability to lift us to new levels of creativity. The Inner Source often helps to cure hurts from past incidents which the individual may have thought cause no more physical or psychological discomfort or pain. I worked with a young woman who had polio fifteen years before, a man who had a fractured spine five years before, and a woman who had been through a divorce ten years ago. In each case, the Inner Source brought out "stored" physical and mental pain, doubt, and fear which were blocking the person's full development. Examples of creativity which have been stimulated include a new-found urge to paint and draw, a resurgence of interest in flying, and a new drive to write. Despite the reasons one has for allowing the Inner Source the opportunity to help, it knows best how to conduct the journey and often gives unexpected gifts along the way, beautiful experiences and outcomes we weren't even expecting.

Your Inner Source will begin working for you without any special inducements, such as drugs or hypnosis or special instructions from a therapist. With a competent mental health professional present you simply close your eyes and begin watching and describing out loud any type of experience that takes place. You are to pay close attention to three areas of response: your *bodily functioning*, your *inner visual field*, and your *thought processes*. That is all there is to it, just watch and verbally describe anything that is taking place in these three areas of response. By doing so, you will begin to experience the inner wisdom unfolding.

Analyze carefully what I have just said because there is a great emphasis in the therapeutic world today to focus on visual imagery alone, neglecting those workings of the Inner Source which focus on inner-directed thoughts and bodily reactions. The findings of Meditative Therapy point out that inner-directed thoughts and physical reactions are equally important. In fact, they are crucial to developing the full potential within each of us.

The Promise of Meditative Therapy

By patiently allowing the Inner Source to proceed, one may experience a wide range of positive outcomes. Potential results which often take place are as follows:

1. Relief from psychosomatic complaints;
2. Resolution of childhood conflicts;
3. Regulation of sleeping patterns;
4. Increased ability to relax;
5. Lessening of tension and anxiety;
6. Reduction of habitual fear responses;
7. Greater self-confidence;
8. Decreased physical pain;
9. Closer alignment to a spiritual source;
10. More frequent recollection of dreams;
11. Increased tendency toward inner direction;
12. More satisfying interpersonal relationships.

The reason that these results are given only as likely outcomes is because we each have our own unique set of outcomes, depending upon what areas of our life may need help. If you are already sleeping well, the Inner Source will not need to regulate that area of your life; if you don't have much physical pain, it will not need to work in that area. Some have had little childhood conflict, some already feel very close to a spiritual source, some may have no need to relax more deeply. The Inner Source knows where your life is in need of attention and will seek to help in those areas.

The Inner Source at Work: Four Case Examples

The Inner Source has the capability of producing exciting reactions within a short period of time. You may find it interesting to read about the experiences of others:

Sharon, a young woman, age 22, came to me with a problem of ammenorrhea (absence of a menstrual period). She had not had a period for over two years and had been under medical treatment for six months. In the process of medical analysis, a complete battery of medical tests, including blood tests and head x-rays, were administered. When she entered therapy she was undergoing additional testing because the hormone treatments she was receiving were ineffective. Although it is very difficult to establish an exact cause for a disorder of this nature, Sharon did have a series of upsetting events which took place very near the onset of her ammenorrhic condition. First, a romantic relationship in which she was involved was broken off by the young man, which caused her deep disappointment. Second, she had participated in one homosexual experience with her best friend as an experiment and found it to be very disappointing. Finally, she had lost twenty pounds, basically by not eating enough. Any of these experiences in isolation could possibly cause one to develop a disorder, but when all three take place so closely together the chances are greatly increased.

After two initial interviews wherein a history was taken, Meditative Therapy was started. During the week after her first session of seventy-three minutes duration, Sharon had her first period in over two years. Three months later, she reported that her periods had continued to take place regularly since her first Meditative Therapy session.

Jack was a 26-year-old Viet Nam veteran who was referred to me because he was suffering from recurring emotional upset in relation to a war experience which took place some three years before. In his words, ''I was a platoon leader in Viet Nam. During one mission, I sent a man out in front of me and he was killed. While he died I watched him bleed, but because of enemy fire I couldn't save him. After I found out that he was dead—I went crazy. I tried to 'charge'· but someone was on top of me and prevented it.'' Although Jack knew rationally that he could have done nothing to save the man, feelings of self-doubting guilt continued to haunt him. At some point prior to his discharge, he did consult a military psychiatrist, but was unable to gain much relief.

His present behavior was to cry, hyperventilate, and become emotionally upset when various stimuli which reminded him of the experience confronted him. In addition, he reported other difficulties which he maintained were with him prior to the Viet Nam experience, but had been worsened as a result of the trauma. Specifically, he considered himself to be a very nervous person. He would experience a large amount of anxiety before tests, he avoided giving speeches, and he was shy with people. Jack also reported physical symptoms of stomach trouble and periodic twitches in his body. Under stress he would experience palpitations and bowel disturbances. My initial attempt at relief was to employ the behavior therapy technique, systematic desensitization.[1] Although it was painful for him to talk about events that were reminders of the experience, we were able to jointly construct the seven-item hierarchy which follows:

1. (Least anxious) Looking through a magazine and seeing pictures that remind you of what happened.
2. Seeing someone on campus wearing a uniform from over there.
3. The nurse indicates that you can't give blood because you were in Southeast Asia.
4. Talking to me (therapist) and you have to think about what happened.
5. Walking along somewhere and you hear a loud explosion.
6. People you are with start telling war stories.
7. (Most anxious) Someone saying to you, "What was it like over there?"

Deep muscle relaxation was taught to him and he practiced for one week after which he was able to achieve good levels of relaxation. When he returned to begin desensitization, I told him I would relax him for about ten minutes and then present a relaxed scene where he would stay for a minute or so prior to being presented with the least anxious hierarchy item. He was relaxing well up to the point of relaxed scene presentation, but immediately

---

1. Systematic desensitization is a method invented by Joseph Wolpe, M.D. (1973) psychiatrist at Temple University. As the name implies, one is systematically (step by step) desensitized (made less sensitive) to a feared situation. Relaxation responses are paired with fear-anxiety responses which inhibit or unlearn the fear. The manner in which the technique is applied is usually through visual imagery, although there are methods where it can be applied in the real life situation. Any type of phobia, fear of heights, enclosed places, snakes, tests, speeches, rejection, can be treated with the method.

became emotionally upset and "came out" of the relaxing state when I indicated he shift to the pleasant place. The anticipation about seeing one of the hierarchy scenes evidently was unbearable to him.

At this juncture, I decided not to attempt a refinement of systematic desensitization or to establish other hierarchies relating to his present problems. Instead, he agreed to try Meditative Therapy beginning with his next appointment.

His initial two 1½-hour sessions were uneventful in relation to his main presenting complaint. During the third session after about forty-five minutes, he became frustrated and stated he felt we were getting nowhere, that the therapy wasn't working. I mildly intervened by asking if his Inner Source could give some hint as to what was blocking progress. Jack then saw two scenes in succession. First, he was standing someplace with a blanket entangling his head and arms. He was flailing his arms trying to get it off. Second, he was underneath a dark cloud bank which entirely blocked the sun, but at the same time, he knew it was clear and sunny up above. I asked him if he knew what was blocking out the sunlight and he said, "Yes, I know." When I replied, "What is it?" he was instantaneously crying, yelling, and writhing, vividly re-experiencing the event that had haunted him for three years. This lasted for two or three minutes and perhaps wasn't much different from drug-induced war neuroses' experiences most have read about or seen depicted in the movies. What transpired next, however, was particularly exciting. In his own words,

> Oh wow! It's like this huge blob of energy, just working its way down my body. I can actually feel it, it's going down my left leg now! Oh wow! It's unbelievable. Oh, I just feel so good!
>
> It's—how could there be so much—must be tons of energy! Now it's starting again, more is sapping out! It's just amazing! I'm just so happy, it's just amazing!
>
> Now there's another vibrating, really fast oscillation, my face and scalp are tingling! Arms and fingers too!
>
> It's all so clear, it's like all this fantastic energy, attacking my

heart, my stomach, it's so amazing! Still a great big charge in
my legs.
It's like a dam that just broke, comes pouring out!

After twenty or thirty minutes of this energy-draining experience,
he opened his eyes, we chatted for awhile, then the session ended.
When he returned one week later, he reported that he had felt
ecstatically relieved of his burden. Life seemed beautiful again. His
draining had continued on and off during the week, but not as
dramatically as during the actual session. We decided not to
continue the therapy, but to wait another week and see how he felt.
He returned and we tried Meditative Therapy for about fifteen
minutes, but he terminated it because he felt it was not needed.
That was the last I saw of him.

Approximately six months later, I sent him a follow-up evaluation
(See Appendix C). Results showed that he felt his main difficulty,
recurrence of the traumatic Viet Nam experience, was *Very Much
Improved* (the highest category on the scale), as was his general
nervous condition and his pre-test anxiety. His avoidance of
speeches was in the *Much Improved* category, and his shyness and
twitches showed *Average Improvement*. He reported *Little* or *No
Improvement* in his stomach trouble and his bowel disturbances and
palpitations under stress.

Lynne, a woman of 40, came to see me with a wide variety of
mental and physical problems. She had experienced a traumatic
history, which included an extremely difficult childhood, a series of
near-death auto accidents, and her own divorce and subsequent
attempted suicide. Prior to seeing me, she had been in therapy for
two years. Upon returning for her second Meditative Therapy
session, following a first session of ninety minutes duration a week
before, she reported the following experience. "While driving down
the road four days after the session, I heard a voice in my head say,
'You aren't alone anymore.' " She said it was a religious experience
to her and was very real and very peaceful. She had not felt alone
since the experience. One year later, Lynne still felt the experience
was a very significant, life-changing one for her.

Susan, the fourth of these case examples, was 34 when she came to see me. Three years before, she had undergone surgery for Raynaud's disease, a disease of the sympathetic nervous system. The operation involved severing certain nerves. During Susan's first session, forty-two minutes after the start, she started sobbing and wringing her hands, then reported: "My hands are sweating. That's funny because I'm not supposed to have any sweaty hands because of the operation. My hands have been dry for three years and now they actually feel sweaty. There's perspiration on my lips. These are things I haven't felt for a long time." Six months following this session, Susan stated that her perspiration response in the hands and lips had not returned on a regular basis, but had happened a few more times. She had undergone a total of five Meditative Therapy sessions and did report that her migraine headaches were gone, that she no longer felt as pressured as she used to, that she had much less tightness in her eyes, and that she no longer felt a tense urgency about her school and home life.

You may find what happened to these four individuals difficult to believe or to understand, especially considering that the events took place in such a short period of time. Not all results are as dramatic or happen as fast as those of Sharon, Jack, Lynne and Susan, but the Inner Source does not seem to be found lacking for profound experiences and outcomes. The experiences given in this chapter are only a glimpse of the range of responses inherent in all of us. Meditative Therapy is by no means to be regarded as a cure-all, but it seems to be consistently more thorough and powerful in terms of helping us reach our unique potential, mentally, physically, and spiritually, than other therapies.

It is worth noting that Meditative Therapy has thus far been utilized only with persons who are basically adequate in their functioning, although many were in considerable psychological, physical, or spiritual pain. These clients were not hospitalized, had not been labelled as schizophrenic, psychotic, or otherwise psychiatrically "classified." There is no experience at this time using Meditative Therapy with such severely disturbed individuals. Indeed, a psychiatrist friend of mine has speculated that perhaps such persons are so classified *because* they have been unable to make contact with the Inner Source. I am hopeful that this book will stimulate studies of Meditative Therapy with a wider range of individuals than I have experienced to date.

As you read on, you will be faced with other examples that may make you raise your eyebrows and wonder. Because of this fact, I have tried to be as objective and truthful as possible. I will not be able to provide all of the answers since there are Inner Source experiences that are beyond my own comprehension. What I have learned to do is to trust the Inner Source completely, to accept all its workings, whether dramatic, miraculous, parapsychological, or religious, because the ongoing and final outcomes are well worth the journey.

2

Synthetic Inner Therapies:
The Directed Path

Tonight I would like to hypnotize you as a group. Of course, this is purely voluntary, but I think that you will all find the experience a pleasant one if you decide to enter in. How do you all feel about it? Do you have any questions?

—*R. Leo Sprinkle*

With those words, Professor Sprinkle of the University of Wyoming introduced hypnosis to me and my colleagues in the doctoral program in 1967. After he answered a few of our curious questions, "Is there any danger?" "What if I don't wake up when you're done?" and "Isn't it true that people do things while hypnotized that they wouldn't ordinarily do when awake?" Most of us agreed to "take the trip." First, each of us took a pencil between the thumb and index finger of our dominant hand and began staring at the pencil. We were told repeatedly to: stare at the pencil without letting your eyes waver or blink. Your eyes will be getting heavier and heavier. Soon the pencil will drop from your hand, at which time you can close your eyes and enter a state of hypnosis.

It wasn't long before the sound of pencils hitting the floor could be heard throughout the room. Mine dropped after a few minues and I entered the hypnotic world of altered consciousness. Those of us who participated had a very pleasant experience. Our instructor guided us through a variety of experiences. We revisited a childhood memory, we went down a set of stairs, floated on a cloud, and felt our arm levitate from the desk up into the air. Upon being

19

brought out of the trance after twenty minutes, I still felt lazy, drowsy, and a little dazed. As we were being de-briefed, I even raised my hand and asked if there was a possibility that some of us were still a bit under. The instructor said yes, and indicated that it may take a few minutes before some of us awakened fully.

This experience with hypnosis was my formal introduction into the world of synthetically-altered consciousness. ("Formal" because, in prior years, I had done my share of altering consciousness with alcohol, and once had undergone sodium pentothal prior to a minor operation.) But for the most part, I had only participated in the natural state of altered consciousness occurring during sleep.

Synthetic and Natural Approaches to Altered Consciousness

Throughout recorded history, individuals have sought to alter consciousness in ways other than sleep. Most have done so because of the knowledge of some helpful force within, but some have done so just to feel good. Whether the purpose was for healing or therapy or for pleasure or for spiritual attunement, individuals have used such devices as fasting, spinning, drugs, chanting, deep breathing, sweat lodges, alcohol, sensory deprivation, hypnosis, music, and sleep deprivation.

Why should one go through all of these experiences when one's own Inner Source can alter consciousness without outside inducements? The Inner Source itself may produce spinning reactions, have you listen to music or watch flashing or stroboscopic lights, make you feel drugged at times, produce deep breathing. The difference between the natural way of the Inner Source and the synthetic way of outside agents is that the first is done with wisdom and is keyed to your unique needs, whereas the other is often guesswork and geared to the "average response." What should the dosage of LSD be for your particular needs? How much should you spin to alter your consciousness? What type of music is best to bring out the optimum response? The Inner Source knows how to use appropriate methods to help produce the best outcomes for you.

All of the methods listed above, plus a host of others, are synthetic or directive to some degree. The term *directive* is usually contrasted with the term *non-directive* when speaking of approaches to therapy. I am using these two terms to refer to the degree to which either the client or the therapist chooses how therapy should be conducted, rather than letting the Inner Source decide what to do. For example, you might decide to take a pill of some kind, or to do some of the other things mentioned above, such as fast or spin, which will "make things happen" or "accelerate the process." Such acts would be considered as synthetic or directive in nature, by my definition. Other examples: to close your eyes and visualize a beautiful scene; to take ten deep breaths; to say out loud the word "Mommy." The therapist, on the other hand, might be directive by telling you to take a pill, fast, visualize, or deep breathe.

You may have pre-set beliefs about what will happen once your consciousness has been altered. There are various theories about what should take place as the inner processes begin. The things you report in the process might also be subject to interpretation. Headaches may be seen as symbolic of hiding something important, or a snake may be interpreted as a sexual symbol. This *interpretation* of material is also directive, or what I call synthetic.

By contrast, non-directiveness or naturalness means to *allow the Inner Source* to conduct the process rather than the therapist or the client. If the Inner Source wants you to see colors, watch patiently; if it wants you to re-live an experience, do so willingly, trusting this inner intelligence to decide. Few of us are used to such a natural approach to our inner life. We have either been taught to ignore it, to allow someone to direct and interpret it, or to be in charge of ourselves. There will always be a plethora of synthetic ways of reaching and analyzing the inner consciousness. Individuals seem to be unwilling to suspend their own thinking and "wisdom" and allow the inherent pattern to come forth. This decision is most likely due to the fact that they truly are not aware that great results can be accomplished without being directive to any degree whatsoever. They have failed to understand that there is a self-contained wisdom that generally far exceeds their own inventiveness, their own originality, their own ability to help.

Both natural and synthetic approaches to the inner knowledge have long histories. Frank MacHovec, writing in the April, 1975 issue of the *American Journal of Clinical Hypnosis*, documents that there were techniques in existence in ancient times which were based on an altered state of consciousness. Ancient Greece, Egypt, India, China, Africa, and pre-Columbian America were the backdrop for methods of this nature. For example, the classic Yogic text, the *Yoga Sutras* (Mishra, 1973), dating from the third century A.D., and the ancient Buddhist text, the *Vissudhimaga*, (Goleman, 1977), fifth century A.D., both speak of a method of meditation similar to Meditative Therapy. In the therapist section of this book there is additional material on other natural/non-directive and synthetic/directive inner ways of healing.

Non-technical summaries of some of the synthetic ways which have been in the public eye are presented for your information in the order in which they were popularized. Each of these approaches limits the work of the Inner Source in some way. In the following chapter, a variety of natural approaches is discussed.

The contemporary scene of synthetic or directive approaches still includes the method of hypnosis to re-live repressed and traumatic memories. An early proponent of hypnosis and other directive techniques was *psychoanalysis* founder Sigmund Freud. An abundance of newer directive methods also flourish, most either direct replicas or offshoots of the earlier methods. Four of the most recent efforts are *Dianetic Therapy, LSD-Assisted Therapy, Primal Therapy*, and *Faith Imagination*. All have been highly touted by their main proponents: Dianetic Therapy is billed as the complete cure of all inorganic mental ills; LSD-Assisted Therapy is attributed with the potential to be as significant as the microscope and telescope have been for mankind; Primal Therapy is called *the* cure for neurosis, rendering all other psychological theories outdated and invalid; Faith Imagination is described as a way to know ''inner healing'' or ''healing of the memories.''

Traditional Psychoanalysis

I have selected Freud as a starting point in looking at directive approaches to inner experience because he ushers in the modern day era of psychology and because his name and influence continue to be ever present. Before he developed free association and psychoanalysis, Freud used mild *hypnosis* and *hypnotic suggestion* to help his patients. He and Breuer wrote of their method in 1895 in their book, *Studies in Hysteria*. They described how symptoms would disappear if disturbing memories were "thoroughly awakened," brought into consciousness, and verbalized with all of the emotion which originally accompanied them. (The case of Jack and his Viet Nam experience described in Chapter 1 is a good example of this type of reaction, even though hypnosis was not used with him).

Abreaction is the technical term for the re-experiencing felt by Jack and by Freud's patients in 1895. In addition, Freud used hypnotic suggestion in order to eliminate symptoms at times when the abreaction did not do so. Freud finally dropped both methods because he found that not all of his patients could be hypnotized. He moved on to the method of free association.

Free association is an eyes-open method wherein one lies down on the traditional couch, not facing the analyst, and says whatever comes into mind. The analyst takes careful notes in order to render interpretations of the content at some future point. The method does not involve closing one's eyes in order to observe the stream of interior images. Because it is an eyes-open method, free association will not be considered further here. Joseph Reyher (1963), a psychologist from Michigan State University, has developed a method called "emergent uncovering," which he describes as an eyes-closed free association. He has conducted experiments showing that the method is more powerful as an uncovering technique than Freud's psychoanalytic free association.

Dianetics-Scientology

Dianetics is the name of a therapy devised by an engineer and science fiction writer named L. Ron Hubbard, who wrote a best-selling book on the subject in 1950. In 1955 Hubbard started the "Church of Scientology" and indicated that, instead of being a therapy, Dianetics was more closely associated with a spiritual quest.

Scientology has been in existence since, and operates in many medium and large-sized cities in the United States and other countries. You may have been approached by one of their members while walking down the street. They often recruit potential members by handing out literature and by trying to draw you in for a "free personality analysis."

Hubbard and his organization have been surrounded by controversy throughout the years. You can perhaps imagine what kind of reception an engineer who claims to have found *the* cure for all inorganic ills would receive from the scientific community of medical doctors and mental health workers! In addition, Hubbard came into disfavor with a number of journalists, and disenchanted church members had a voice for their complaints. Several books, articles, and media programs have been critical of Hubbard and his church. Still, Hubbard often creates favorable impressions, as evidenced by the following statement from *Psychic Magazine*, made in April, 1973 by Ingo Swann, whom *Psychic* describes as an "unusually gifted sensitive:"

For me the most exciting thing is the experience that I have had that indicates that an individual can know more about himself as a spiritual operative being. And it's doubly exciting to find that there are men who are succeeding in communicating it to the public. I was very excited in 1962 when I read the works of a man who is, shall I say, controversial—L. Ron Hubbard. I was trying to find out if the human mind was capable of understanding itself. I was rather tired of everybody else understanding me but myself.

Our lives aren't as successful as we'd like them to be, and if we acknowledge that, and turn to a literature of the scope Mr. Hubbard has produced, we can find that we don't need to live at a level of ruin. We can take active steps to reclaim or rehabilitate ourselves toward a more successful life. I think this is a precursor to a new idea—that man can change himself for the better instead of confronting a future that seems to change him for the worse. So I think the work of Mr. Hubbard is extremely exciting. (p. 49)

My purpose here is to try to provide a basic summary of Dianetic Therapy, without dealing with Scientology or with the controversy surrounding Hubbard. I would only state that one should read other sources about Hubbard and his work if contemplating going through the therapy or joining the church.

Hubbard indicates that during periods of severe pain, one will go "unconscious" and the *analytic mind*, that part of the mind which is always in operation, will be blocked out. The *reactive mind*, the source of all disorders, takes over and records the painful event. However, this action, though protective, causes blanks in one's standard memory banks. These periods of "unconsciousness" are caused by a wide variety of instances, such as drug states, blows to the head, stupors during illness, childhood traumas with parents. The memories the reactive mind stores are not ordinary ones, as in the analytic mind's standard memory banks; these are "unconscious," painful memories and are termed engrams. An engram is a complete recording of all one's perceptions during a period of "unconsciousness." The engram is thought to have force attached to it because it is a powerful source of controlling the body in what Hubbard terms an "aberrated" manner. Because an engram contains both pain and painful emotion, it locks us into certain forms of reaction. Engram material is thought to be one's "crazy" material.

Dianetics uses the term "basic-basic," to describe one's first engram (usually prenatal): the primary moment of pain. In Dianetics it is thought that once basic-basic is reached and resolved, the entire case will clear up quickly.

The "therapist" in Dianetics is called an *auditor*. His/her job is to conduct "Dianetic Reverie" wherein one "re-lives" engrams. The auditor is in charge of guiding a return along one's own inner time track, a computer-like aspect of the mind. The auditor often uses an electronic device to detect traumatic areas through skin reactions to stimulus words. By returning one to the earliest moments of pain, to re-experience them as if they were in the present, one moves further along the path to being "clear," the original term for the final outcome of therapy.

The auditor is directive in the therapy process by having the individual repeat key phrases and by directing attention back and forth on the time track. For example, the auditor may say, "Today let's start out by going back to your fifth birthday." One in therapy who complains of a headache may be asked to repeat "my head hurts" several times. Doing so may evoke painful engrams. The auditor is non-interpretive in reference to the data that surfaces. The person alone knows the meaning. Auditors are not to engage in diagnosis or interpretation.

LSD-Assisted Therapy

Lysergic acid diethylamide, better known as LSD-25, was discovered by the Swiss chemist Albert Hoffmann in 1943, and was widely used as an aid to psychotherapy in the 1950's. LSD-assisted therapy has been surrounded by controversy from its inception, much of which has centered around the life of Timothy Leary, who popularized the drug. In addition, there were reports of deaths and near-deaths attributed to "bad trips" and flashback phenomena. These horrifying experiences are almost always traced to the use of LSD without proper supervision by a professional. The recent uncovering of the U.S. Army experiments, in which LSD was administered without the knowledge of the recipients, resulting in at least one suicide, re-kindled the stories and fears about the dangers of this mind-manifesting drug.

Amidst these major problems, there has developed a significant body of research centering around the therapeutic value of LSD ingestion under proper supervision. Highly respected scientists, researchers, and psychotherapists continue to laud the beneficial, often life-changing, outcomes of LSD-assisted therapy. Nevertheless, it is interesting to note according to the prestigious newsletter *Brain/Mind Bulletin* (November 7, 1977), a recent symposium on LSD concluded that "The drug is no longer an important tool of transformation for most of its best-known former advocates."

There are two basic approaches to the use of LSD as a therapy. The *psychedelic* approach relies on the administration of a large dosage of LSD which is taken for only one or two sessions and results in an intense, mystical experience. These high dosage sessions last from several hours to all day. The *psycholytic* approach is where LSD is administered in smaller dosages, once a week for ten to twenty weeks. Stanislav Grof, who began his LSD work in Czechoslovakia, has written extensively about the psycholytic drug experience. He and others show that a wide range of psychiatric disorders have been successfully treated with the aid of LSD to "deepen" the psychoanalytic process.

Grof's recent book, *Realms of the Human Unconscious* (1975), documents that LSD phenomena cover an extremely wide range and occur in almost all areas of mental and physical functioning. LSD events go beyond therapy into other realms of consciousness. He presents examples from ten areas of response:

1. Physical symptoms; 2. Perceptual changes; 3. Distortions in the perception of time and space; 4. Emotional changes; 5. Thinking, intellect, memory experiences; 6. Psychomotor changes; 7. Changes in consciousness; 8. Sexuality experiences; 9. The experience of art; 10. Religious and mystical experiences.

Grof's tenth category, especially the religious aspect, has been studied by other LSD researchers. LSD often produces a wide variety of religious content along with changes in religious attitudes. Masters and Houston (1966), in their book *Varieties of the Psychedelic Experience*, state that 96 percent of a group of 206 LSD subjects saw religious imagery of some kind during their sessions. Several other researchers have stated that up to 60 percent of their participants had significant changes in their religious attitudes after LSD sessions.

Most LSD researchers acknowledge that the individual's response to LSD depends upon what are called "set" and "setting" factors: the patient's difficulties or personality factors prior to taking LSD; the experimenter's personality; the goal of the LSD session; the physical location of the session; the instructions given to the patient; the quality and quantity of LSD received. All of these factors influence what psychological or religious benefit the individual might derive if involved in LSD sessions.

There are two key issues centering around these set and setting factors. First, Grof and Aldous Huxley (1968) hold that the drug brings out an inherent response regardless of the set and setting factors. The drug is viewed only as a catalyst to bring out the workings of a deeper self, according to Huxley. Grof feels that no two people respond exactly the same when taking LSD; that is, the effect of the drug doesn't *cause* one to react a certain way. The second factor involves how much direction and interpretation the therapist gives the client. Grof states that Freudian psychodynamic theories are "largely" supported by the outcomes of LSD psycholytic therapy, but prior to administering LSD, his patients have several weeks of drug-free psychotherapy. Between LSD sessions the patient is also seen. During these times the therapist, as described in Grof's book, works with the individual from a psychoanalytic, Freudian viewpoint. He states that transference problems (a Freudian concept) were worked on between sessions. Both of these issues are discussed further later in this chapter. First, let us analyze two other synthetic approaches.

Primal Therapy

If you think that a therapist who purports to have found "the cure" and at the same time tells other therapists that their own theories are outdated and invalid would cause a stir, you're right! Just as its two predecessors, Dianetics and LSD, had ruffled feathers, Primal Therapy also produced a good many "waves." Arthur Janov in his book, *The Primal Scream* (1970), made many claims that came under fire from other professionals. Add to this the fact that interested therapists can learn the therapy only at great expense (it is only taught at Janov's Institute), and you will begin to understand why Janov and his therapy have caused considerable upset.

Actually, what Janov hypothesized is similar to what others had said for years before. Janov sees mental illness as a result of repressing painful life experiences which center around interactions with one's parents. Unmet needs of the child begin to form a "Pool of Primal Pains" that causes a gradual shift from *real* and *feeling* to *unreal* and *repressing* (in effect, to "mentally ill"). Neurosis isn't a sudden event, but develops over a period of time as needs are not fulfilled by the parents. The culminating final blow is, according to Janov, an excruciating, painful event which seems to summarize the message that "mommy and daddy don't love me for what I am." This painful event is called the *major primal scene* and is viewed as the single most upsetting or humiliating event in the child's life, usually the culmination of a number of minor primal scenes, and typically occurring between five and seven years of age.

The common factor in mental illness, according to Janov, is tension. A system operating on repressed biological needs is a tension-bound system. Janov states that the stomach is one of the key focal points for tension. In order to overcome this pain, one must become "connected" with early unmet needs. By regaining full memories and feeling the intense pain associated with this full consciousness, one becomes cured.

Janov's therapeutic approach is to overthrow one's defense system. By breaking open the memory bank, the repressed pain can be experienced fully and become integrated into the system. The approach used by the primal therapist to get at the pain is stated only in general terms in Janov's book. Various methods are used to make one more susceptible to opening up. The therapist may have the patient stay awake all night, disallow personal vices such as smoking, or use psychological harassment to "ready" the client. Janov advocates such techniques as hyperventilation, having the client call for "mommy" or "daddy," and having the person hold a teddy bear to trigger painful experiences.

The real therapeutic benefit comes from within the person, according to primal theory. Interpretation by the therapist plays a minor role, whereas one's own insights, deriving from the primal process, are of great importance. The uniqueness of the individual is stressed.

Faith Imagination

Ruth Carter Stapleton, the sister of U.S. President Jimmy Carter, does not consider her approach, Faith Imagination or Healing of the Memories, to be a psychotherapy, but I have included it here because it *is* a psychotherapeutic approach which is very similar to the other directive approaches just discussed. Moreover, she has adapted a directive inner therapeutic approach and focused it specifically along religious lines.

Stapleton (1976) in her book, *The Gift of Inner Healing*, indicates that she is dealing with "root problems" or "old, sick memories" which cause the individual current problems. She patterns this belief after the work of physician Hugh Missildine (1963) in his book, *Your Inner Child of the Past*. She feels that if our subconscious minds have been fed "parental garbage," we will act that out as adults. Her purpose is to re-program the subconscious mind, or to erase negative material from our minds. In conjunction with the erasure of disturbing material, Stapleton seeks to replace it with positive material which is in harmony with the "love revealed by Jesus Christ."

The approach used by Stapleton is either to deal with upsetting memories of which the person is already consciously aware, or to try and bring out repressed memories. The client is to sit with eyes closed and re-visit a negative experience which has been held on to for years. Stapleton focuses heavily on the parents as a source of the problems. Several of the cases she presents center on the lack of a loving parent. In cases where one isn't fully aware of upsetting memories, Stapleton will recite a prayer, sometimes silently, which is designed to release repressed memories.

Once the person is visualizing a key scene, Stapleton brings Jesus into the visualization and guides His actions by having Him provide help for the troubled person. She has Jesus do a variety of things in the scene to heal the person's disturbing memory. These things often depend on what Stapleton feels needs to be done, but at times, she allows the individual to guide Jesus' actions.

Even though several cases are reported in the book where a one-time guided session will produce dramatic changes, Stapleton states that her approach is a process and rarely a one-time event.

From Synthetic to Natural

Each of these contemporary therapies is capable of producing valuable, and often dramatic, therapeutic changes. Each of the authors documents cases in which significant psychological problems are overcome using the particular approach. Despite this fact, I have objections to each approach in terms of *syntheticness* or *directiveness* at various stages of therapy. In the case of Dianetics, Primal Therapy, and Faith Imagination, the therapist is in charge of the therapy and focuses exclusively on negative subconscious material. Our minds are treated as computers programmed with garbage-laden memories. If the authors of these three approaches understand that there is an Inner Source, it is not readily observable from the way in which they treat the inner workings. The difference between the subconscious mind and the Inner Source is comparable to the difference between minimum and maximum, between lower court and higher court, between grade school level and college level, between part and whole. The lesser focus is not bad and it does produce excellent results at times, but it does not achieve all that is possible. The Inner Source does rid the subconscious mind of disturbing material, but it also has much grander purposes, dealing with the *whole person*. When a therapist is in charge of our inner workings, the synthetic way, we are limited to the therapist's knowledge. Where is the limit when the Inner Source conducts our journey?

In the case of Grof's LSD-assisted psycholytic therapy, the therapist allows the Inner Source to unfold more to its full potential, but only after using a synthetic drug as a catalyst. The Inner Source does not need a catalyst in order to get started. It can do that very well of its own accord. The Inner Source can also take care of other areas of which Grof seems to be unaware. Remember that the psycholytic therapist is directive before, between, and after the LSD sessions.

If the Inner Source wants any special knowledge imparted or any insights to occur, it knows how to accomplish the task. Interpreting one's inner content along the lines of any type of psychological theory, Freudian or any other, is not necessary. Neither is directing a person's thinking along any particular theoretical lines prior to LSD sessions. The Inner Source can produce beautiful insights if needed, but the great beauty of its workings is the fact that changes occur *naturally*.

In addition to therapist directiveness at various stages in LSD-Assisted Therapy, we must also consider what effect the synthetic drug has upon the natural workings of the Inner Source. I find it very difficult to believe that the drug only serves as a "trigger" to bring out the natural performance of the Inner Source. Despite what Huxley and Grof say, I believe that the drug itself *will* influence the person. At the very least, it may produce unconscious material too quickly. Also, because of the constant drug state, the Inner Source may not be allowed to finish the session when it wants to, since it must work within the existing conditions of the body. If allowed its natural way, the Inner Source will at times finish in a short period, sometimes as little as thirty minutes. The drug state may require the Inner Source to work beyond its desires. The Inner Source may also be forced to spend time neutralizing the problems caused if the body reacts poorly to the drug. Some may have side effects during sessions that must be dealt with by the Inner Source. There could also be after effects of the drug, like a "hang-over" effect. The Inner Source has more important things to do than to overcome the synthetically-induced problems caused by LSD.

I applaud the direction that Hubbard, Janov, and Stapleton take toward interpretation of content in their therapies. Each uses a minimal amount of interpretation of material which comes up from the subconscious. The difficulty I see is that the client has been geared to interpret in only one way, by the manner in which the therapist runs the therapy. All three of these therapies focus heavily on the parents as the prime cause of mental problems. That means that most of the material that comes up will be directly related to that theme. And, since these therapists focus primarily on negative memories, there needs to be little interpretation given. The conclusions are likely inescapable due to the previous focus on the parents being the culprits. Obviously, as mental health research and common sense tell us, parents cause a good many mental hang-ups. But to focus on them exclusively, *even primarily*, does not come close to covering the full realm of beneficial activities of the Inner Source.

You will remember that two of the many names given to the Inner Source over the ages are the God-Within and the Christ-Consciousness. From this one might assume that Stapleton's Faith Imagination would be looked at as a non-synthetic approach. However, she acts directively by "guiding the actions" of Jesus in her therapy, and otherwise directing the visualization. The Inner Source does not need to be guided or told what to do. It knows very well what our unique needs are and proceeds accordingly if we choose to allow it to work.

I do not know that the Inner Source can be said to be a God-within or a Christ-consciousness any more than I know it can be called a deep-self or a biological wisdom, or an Inner Source for that matter. Without a doubt, the Inner Source has a distinct religious and spiritual component, but you must judge for yourself what to call what I have termed the Inner Source. My only concern is that no matter what your beliefs are about the Inner Source, that you do not place any limits, any restrictions, upon its actions. Always allow the Inner Source to unfold its love, wisdom, and power in the natural way.

I do not wish to give the impression that I would like to eliminate all of the synthetic approaches to our inner workings. Meditative Therapy is not a cure all. There are times when other methods are needed, even synthetic inner methods. I personally use other therapeutic approaches in conjunction with Meditative Therapy, and some of those approaches are synthetic inner methods. My purpose in writing about the Inner Source is not to make us myopic, but to teach us to listen to our inner wisdom.

3

Natural Inner Therapies:
The Nondirected Path

*Behold I have set before you an open door which
no one is able to shut.*

—Revelation 3:8

Natural ways to healing require no drugs, no machines, no
interpretations. They are built upon the idea—demonstrated
repeatedly in actual experience—that there exists within the bounty
of each human soul a power that works without outside inducement.
This power—which I have called the Inner Source—resides in us,
knows how to help us, and works naturally, if we choose to let it.

Only a few have understood that the Inner Source can operate at
all stages of therapy in a natural, non-interfering manner. In this
chapter, I will briefly discuss four natural/non-directive approaches,
and then proceed in Chapter 4 to describe Meditative Therapy in
greater depth.

Active Imagination, the most widespread of the four natural
methods, is a technique of *Jungian analysis*, recently popular
among young adults, in part because of a renewed interest in
spirituality. Three other natural approaches, all relatively obscure in
the United States, include: *Deep Relaxation with Free Ideation*,
described only in a German professional journal in 1949; *E-Therapy*,
self-published by its author in a handwritten monograph which is
distributed only by him (As I recall my conversation with the author,

he had 10,000 copies printed in 1950, and still has not sold them all); and *Autogenic Abreaction*, written about in a highly technical and professional way, mostly used after several other methods of therapy have proved inadequate with the client, and primarily known in European countries. In the material which follows, you will recognize at least one similarity to the synthetic approaches: several of the authors have made some exciting claims!

Kitselman tells us that by undergoing E-therapy we will lose all sense of fear, hatred, grief, that we can become a prodigy in any field of our choice, and that we can become fully integrated. Luthe states Autogenic Abreaction is the "big gun" of therapy and is more powerful than psychoanalysis.

Active Imagination

Since we initiated our discussion of synthetic approaches with the early work of Freud, it seems appropriate to begin this section with Carl Gustav Jung, one of Freud's students. Jung eventually broke away from Freud and developed his own theories and techniques for helping others. One of the variety of methods he employed involved having the patient focus on a "stream of interior images." This process, which allowed "spontaneous visual images" to come forth, was called *Active Imagination* and, at times, *Visionary Meditation*. It was described by Jung as early as 1916.

Jung would instruct his client to use any fragment of fantasy, such as a dream fragment, as a starting point to trigger off the inherent imagery process. If, last night, one dreamed of a three-legged white horse, but was confused about its meaning, active imagination could be used to visualize the three-legged white horse the way it appeared in the dream. Soon, by watching the image, further fantasy material would add itself in a natural manner. Jung said that the process "relieves the unconscious and produces material rich in archetypal images and associations" and that it "brings a mass of unconscious material to light."

Active imagination is not totally natural because it starts with a mildly synthetic approach (visualizing a fantasy fragment) and because one is told to focus only on images. Thoughts and physical reactions are also equally important ways in which the Inner Source communicates. Despite these two limiting factors, Jung was headed in the direction of naturalness.

Other Jungian concepts which are important in the development of natural inner therapies are the *collective unconscious* (a universal, inherited aspect of the human unconscious which is common to us all according to Jung), and the notion of universal *archetypes* (pre-existent forms of the human spirit which help guide our innate drive for wholeness).

Deep Relaxation with Free Ideation

Walter Frederking, a German psychologist, developed the method of Deep Relaxation with Free Ideation from three approaches: psychoanalysis, psychocatharsis (Frank, 1913) and relaxation exercises. In addition, Frederking's work with the drug mescaline also contributed to defining the therapy.

The basic emphasis in the therapy is on the patient's inner experience as the key therapeutic factor rather than the analytic and intepretive capabilities of the therapist or patient. Frederking felt that there were inherent curative abilities in the visual and physical aspects of the inner process. He likens free ideation to the true dream, in that neither can be "arbitrarily influenced," that is, consciously determined.

A typical form of the creation of images, according to Frederking, is the "magic theater" described by Hermann Hesse in his famous novel *Steppenwolf* (1929). (Hesse was also referred to as the "poet of the interior" by some of the LSD experimenters mentioned in the previous chapter).

Deep Relaxation with Free Ideation is covered in more detail in the therapist section of this book.

E-Therapy

In 1950 A. L. Kitselman wrote a small book called *E-Therapy*, curious in that it is quite legibly handwritten, and is self-published. Kitselman had a good many copies printed at the start and still sells from the original printing at one dollar per copy. Even though the books have a musty odor, are handwritten, and have never hit the "big time," they are well worth the minimal cost.

Aldous Huxley (Smith, 1969) was interested in E-Therapy and sheds light on his thinking about the technique and about Mr. Kitselman in the quotes that follow from letters he wrote to friends in 1952:

. . . Therapeutic procedures should not be directive, but should rather be suggested by the deeper self, which can generally be relied on to come up with something of use to the organism, if it is politely asked to do so—e.g., some memory which requires to be talked out several times until there is no further emotional reaction to it, or else some symbolic image which may not seem significant at the moment, but will often turn out to make sense later on. This method of approach is, I believe, much better than any course of suggestions pushed in by the operator, or than a too busy probing of analysis. There is a part of the subconscious not-self which is much less stupid than the self and the personal sub-conscious, and can be relied upon to provide help if asked. In this context I am sending you under separate cover a pamphlet written by a [. . .] man [A. L. Kitselman] whom I first met some years ago when he was working on translations of Hinayana Buddhist texts from the Pali Canon and who has turned up again recently with something which, to judge by the results I have seen, is of considerable value. Essentially the procedure is a technique whereby the results of Buddhist meditation, as described in such books as the *Visuddhi Magga*, are sought and obtained by methods, not of solitary contemplation, but a collaboration between the person, who is trying to get out of the way as a self and establish contact with the beneficient non-self, and an observer who asks questions and otherwise provides help. [. . . .] So do read the pamphlet; it is blessedly short and explicit. Its findings are based in part on the author's findings as a practising psychologist, in part on his very considerable knowledge of the Pali texts, which suggested some of his procedures and described phenomena which subsequently displayed themselves in practice. . . .(p. 648).

First as to health. Maria has got over her operation very satisfactorily and is on the whole remarkable well. She has been much helped, I think, by a modified form of the 'E Therapy' described in the booklet we sent you. The value of this technique consists in the fact that it is a non-directive therapy, addressed to the central, axial consciousness with a request for help and enlightenment, which is very often forthcoming either in the form of some kind of intuitive answer to whatever may happen to be the most urgent problem of the moment, or sometimes in the form of symbolic imagery (a Reve Eveille expressive of the primordial Fact), or in the shape of repressed memories which it has become important to recall, or again in some physical release of tension. The procedure is actually a form of meditation, in which the meditator does not work alone, but is helped by the questions of an auditor. Why these questions should be helpful I do not exactly know. But the fact remains that they seem to assist the mind in its task of standing aside from the ego and its preoccupations, and laying itself open to the central consciousness. In a number of cases which I have seen the results have led to a remarkable increase in insight and improvement in behavior. (p. 650)

I have had the opportunity to personally meet with Mr. Kitselman on two occasions. During one of our visits he related that E-Therapy was discovered while he was working at the Dianetics Foundation in Honolulu. His work was offered to Hubbard (see chapter 2), rejected by him, and so Kitselman self-published it. Kitselman indicated that at the time he first wrote of the therapy he thought he had discovered something new, but found out later that it was referred to in *The Bhagavad Gita* (Stanford, 1970) which dates from about 750 B.C. It has been brought out a number of times in various forms since then.

The term "E-Therapy" was chosen because essentially that part of the mind that removes obstructions may be called by any name:

It has been called the 'examiner,' the 'integrator,' the 'purifier,' (a long list follows) . . . Since the name to be used depends upon the transient, we shall write "E" whenever this part of the mind is meant . . ." (p. 4)

Kitselman later speaks more specifically in spiritual terms:

So far as we know, it is quite accurate to refer to E as the father within, the holy spirit, the comforter, the witness, or the Messiah. If you regard God as an intelligent, transforming power within you, *praying* to *God* is equivalent to *asking E.* But if the God to whom you pray is a static picture of belief, you are hampering your E with fixed ideas. Most religious people pray to a God who is remote from them, an abstract product of tradition and belief, and such an inanimate deity is not very effective. A fortunate few, however, pray to a God who is a *live wire within*, and to such as these the Lord's Prayer is an *asking* of E." (p. 68)

In order to have "E" work there are two essential conditions to be met. First, there must be some kind of a request for action and second, one must be a passive observer of what transpires. The latter condition is helped by having another person present to make the request and to watch how things go. The individual attempting to obtain help from his or her "E" is more likely to be passively attentive with an observer nearby. In this therapy the observer also assumes a non-directing role.

There are seven activities of E described in the book. The E utilizes these to help the individual with personal difficulties. They take place at various times during the therapy.

1. Turn-off—a lessening of some tension or activity in the mind.
2. Fire—an especially pleasant feeling or experience.
3. Tremolo—a more or less violent agitation of the body or sense impressions.
4. Posturing—changing postures; body motions; facial grimacing.
5. History—incidents remembered or recalled either fragmentarily or in complete detail.
6. Strategy—a situation is presented in which the transient is apparently expected to do something.
7. Argument—if the transient says "why doesn't E start working?" or voices any other criticism or objections.

E has the power to play recordings of problematic past events and to "dis-identify" them for us. These events are often played back at amazingly fast speeds. Also, a whole series of events may be presented or processed at the same time. As indicated by the seven activities of E given above, E has many methods to help us become integrated. It is also important, according to Kitselman, that E knows what to do to help us, is smarter than any therapist, and will choose the particular process to employ.

On the first page of Kitselman's book certain claims are made for the ability of E-Therapy to help. It is said, among other things, that it will rid one of habits, overcome insecurities, allow the loss of all fear, hatred, and grief, and allow the development of supernormal powers. Additionally, E is said to have ten powers which are in all of us and therefore which may manifest themselves during therapy:

1. The power to recognize causes; 2. The power to judge actions; 3. The power to measure behavior patterns; 4. The power to understand structure; 5. The power to insight into character; 6. The power to measure tendencies; 7. The power to produce attainments; 8. The power to investigate history; 9. The power of extra-sensory perception; 10. The power of infallibility.

Hopefully your interest has been stirred to stimulate you to read *E-Therapy* because it really is a thought-provoking little book. I feel that at times Kitselman gets carried away and makes extravagant statements, but that is quite easy to do when observing the Inner Source at work. Anyway, please don't miss the treat. As Huxley said, "It is blessedly short and explicit."

Autogenic Abreaction

Autogenic Therapy is a series of therapeutic methods developed by the late Johannes H. Schultz, M.D. and Wolfgang Luthe, M.D., and originally derived from sleep and hypnosis research beginning in 1905. Schultz published the first edition of *Autogenic Training* in 1932. Luthe, who had been an associate of Schultz for years, has carried on as chief proponent and spokesman for autogenic methods since the death of Schultz in 1970. From 1969 through 1974 Schultz and/or Luthe wrote six volumes on autogenic training and therapy.

Although the major portion of the practice and experimental work on autogenic methods has been carried out in Germany and other countries, there has been recent interest in them in the United States. This interest has shown itself primarily in the areas of pain control, biofeedback, and relaxation training. Dr. Luthe, who presently resides in Montreal, has now presented several workshops in the United States, one of which I was able to attend in San Francisco in February, 1975.

The term "autogenic" means self-generating and is the clue to the essence of the therapy. These methods are designed to facilitate brain-directed mechanisms which participate in homeostatic, self-normalizing or self-integrating processes. The brain, through a wide array of psychophysiological discharges, aims toward re-establishing harmony throughout the system. Discharges follow self-regulatory principles, according to Luthe.

There are six basic autogenic approaches, but the major portion of experimental research has been devoted to the Standard Exercises. These six mental exercises, which are focused on allowing the body and mind to normalize themselves, are as follows: (1) heaviness; (2) warmth; (3) cardiac regulation; (4) respiration; (5) abdominal warmth; (6) cooling of the forehead. Therapy time for the largely self-administered Standard Exercises ranges from two to eight months. My emphasis is on Autogenic Abreaction, one of the autogenic methods falling under the category of Autogenic Neutralization. Autogenic abreaction evolved directly from the exhaustive work with the standard exercises. Luthe lists the starting date for autogenic abreaction as 1957.

A person who wishes to undergo autogenic abreaction must agree to certain rules. First, the individual must adopt a passive, spectator-like state of mind which Luthe terms *passive acceptance*. One must accept anything the brain wishes to do in order to help. This points up the second element, that one must not at any time interfere with the work of the brain. This is what Luthe labels as the *principle of non-interference*. Third, the individual must give an ongoing, *unrestricted verbal description* of anything that is occurring. One must simply watch the entire workings and report what happens. Last, it is necessary to allow the brain to complete its program, as it were, before finishing for the session, letting the brain unload to the point where termination is *brain-directed termination.*

The basic theory for all of the Autogenic methods is that one undergoes a self-induced shift to an autogenic state, one which allows self-regulating activities. The brain is thought to be directing the resulting curative process, treating mental and physical functions simultaneously.

The devices the brain chooses for its self-curative process in Autogenic Abreaction are in the form of autogenic discharges. These discharges are usually brief although there will be variable amounts of a certain discharge. Luthe identifies these categories of autogenic discharges (1969 b): 1. *Auditory:* speech, singing, laughing; 2. *Gustatory:* wide variety of tastes; 3. *Olfactory:* wide variety of smells; 4. *Vestibular Phenomena:* dizziness, floating, lopsidedness; 5. *Visual Phenomena:* color, patterns, filmstrips; 6. *Motor Phenomena:* trembling, twitching, tension; 7. *Sensory Phenomena:* heaviness, warmth, electrical sensations; 8. *Affective Phenomena:* anxiety, fear, depression, euphoria; 9. *Ideational Phenomena:* intruding thoughts, memories, planning.

As one progresses through Autogenic Abreaction there are special events or experiences one may undergo. These are, as given by Luthe: 1. *Multiple Images;* 2. *Unusual Brightness and Related Phenomena;* 3. *Images of Oneself;* 4. *Thematic Sequences of the Death-Life Cycle;* 5. *The Pain-Crying Mechanism;* 6. *The Pain-Aggression Mechanism;* 7. *Sexual Dynamics.*

Each person's brain is unique and will utilize the discharges and special phenomena alone or in a wide variety of combinations to accomplish its task.

If content analyses are performed of autogenic abreaction transcripts, specific themes of brain activity evolve. Because of individuality however, it is impossible to completely forecast what forms of approach any one brain will take. The patient must be open-minded and simply describe what is taking place while the therapist patiently and silently, for the most part, listens. The brain knows best how to handle its own system, its own disturbing neuronal material. Luthe states it in the following manner:

For the untrained observer, processes of brain-directed neutralization occurring during various forms of autogenic abreaction may sometimes appear to be an odd mixture of all kinds of
phenomena. Some of these brain-directed phenomena appear
to be familiar, while others seem to be strange. However, un-
familiar and odd as autogenic abreactions may look, one invariably discovers evidence indicating that the patient's brain apparently knew the reasons why it was necessary to proceed in
this particular manner. (1969b, pp. 182-183)

A great deal of comparative analysis has been undertaken by
experts from a variety of disciplines in attempts to fully explain the
magnificent results of autogenic methods. Pavlovian principles,
neurophysiological theories, psychophysiological approaches,
Cannon's work in homeostasis, Selye's work on stress, psychoanalytic theories, behavior therapy and hypnotherapy perspectives
are a sample of the viewpoints from which professionals have
attempted to explain autogenic therapy. The list goes on and is
certainly impressive, yet no one theory or combination of theories as
yet fully explains why this therapy works as it does.

The value of Schultz' and Luthe's classic work in autogenic
methods has only been partially experienced in the United States by
both the general public and the professional community. Once the
full degree of psychological benefit their therapeutic system can
produce has been discovered, I believe they will be accorded their
proper place among the great therapeutic psychologists of all time.

Most of the inner therapies we have just viewed have minor
amounts of directiveness: Jung has one select a dream fragment to
begin active imagination; Frederking begins with deep relaxation
exercises; Luthe employs the Standard Exercises prior to Autogenic
Abreaction. In the next chapter we shall see that *no* degree of
directiveness, no matter how mild, is truly needed to stimulate the
Inner Source to work. The therapies of this chapter are pointing
toward what I believe to be the ultimate method, the completely
natural journey of the Inner Source.

4

Meditative Therapy:
Getting in Touch
With Your Inner Source

That which is born with us and cannot die.

—Dante

We have explored the basic idea of a natural approach to the Inner Source. Now let us refine, clarify, and extend what is known by examining Meditative Therapy in greater depth. *Meditative Therapy is an inner-directed, eyes-closed process, in which the participant enters a naturally occurring altered state of consciousness and allows an inner source to engage in a self-unifying and self-healing process.* Simply described, the person closes his or her eyes and describes the events (thoughts, feelings, visualizations) that take place throughout the entire organism. As the inner workings unfold in this process, they treat the whole person in a *psycho/physio/spiritulogical* manner. That is, the Inner Source deals with aspects of mind, body, and spirit which may need attention. It is a part of us which seems to know everything about us and knows what to do to allow us to go beyond our present state of being, to transform our whole self, mentally, physically, and spiritually.

Meditative Therapy is not new. It was in existence long before Frederking, Kitselman, Luthe or I wrote about it. One of the reasons I did not select one of the existing names for the therapy is because

45

of the historical roots. (The earliest references I can find are those which are based in "mindfulness meditation," one of the basic forms of meditation). I also used a new name because I believe that mind, body, and spirit are intricately associated with each other in the workings of the Inner Source. To identify the Inner Source only with mind and body (Luthe) or only with spirit (Kitselman) might lead one to believe that the Inner Source is limited to those realms. It is in fact actively engaged with all three.

A Psychophysiospiritulogical Chart of Inner Space

In the chart given on page 47 I have presented a graphic characterization of the *psychophysiospiritulogical* workings of the Inner Source. These aspects of the three realms of human response are those which have been catalogued from the inner experiences of large numbers of people by such writers as Schultz, Luthe, Grof and Kitselman. My assumption is that each person has the potential to experience all of these reactions. For any one person certain experiences may or may not need to take place. I believe if the Inner Source were contacted and allowed to work regularly, the full range of responses would come forth as time progressed, and the need became apparent.

Any response occurring to a person in Meditative Therapy is individual and specific to that person. However, I have described psychological, physiological, and spiritual responses in general ways, in order to present an overall picture. Do not forget that each individual response is different from every other individual response. This fact is most clearly demonstrated in the area of physiological response. The heart rate does not always go down after undergoing Meditative Therapy. Blood pressure will rise for some people, lower for most, and remain unchanged for others. The same can be said for any physiological measure, and this truth extends to psychological and spiritual responses to Meditative Therapy. Although we can draw general conclusions about Meditative Therapy, these should not shroud the individual, unique response of each person.

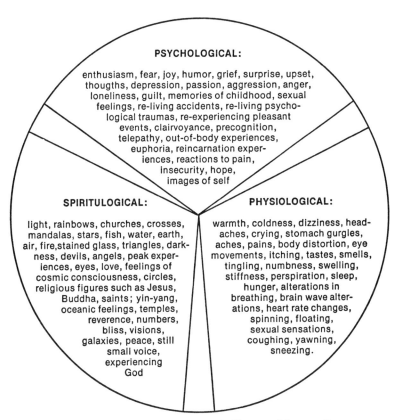

PSYCHOLOGICAL:

enthusiasm, fear, joy, humor, grief, surprise, upset, thougths, depression, passion, aggression, anger, loneliness, guilt, memories of childhood, sexual feelings, re-living accidents, re-living psychological traumas, re-experiencing pleasant events, clairvoyance, precognition, telepathy, out-of-body experiences, euphoria, reincarnation experiences, reactions to pain, insecurity, hope, images of self

SPIRITULOGICAL:

light, rainbows, churches, crosses, mandalas, stars, fish, water, earth, air, fire,stained glass, triangles, darkness, devils, angels, peak experiences, eyes, love, feelings of cosmic consciousness, circles, religious figures such as Jesus, Buddha, saints; yin-yang, oceanic feelings, temples, reverence, numbers, bliss, visions, galaxies, peace, still small voice, experiencing God

PHYSIOLOGICAL:

warmth, coldness, dizziness, headaches, crying, stomach gurgles, aches, pains, body distortion, eye movements, itching, tastes, smells, tingling, numbness, swelling, stiffness, perspiration, sleep, hunger, alterations in breathing, brain wave alterations, heart rate changes, spinning, floating, sexual sensations, coughing, yawning, sneezing.

A Psychophysiospiritulogical Chart of Inner Space

Psychological Response in Meditative Therapy

The psychological results which derive from undergoing Meditative Therapy appear to follow in the same direction as those given in the following chapter for meditation. The Inner Source is capable of eliminating or greatly improving a wide variety of neurotic complaints. (At this point, I have had too little experience to make a similar statement for the psychoses.) Examples of the specific types of psychological problems dealt with include depression, sexual complaints, phobias of various kinds, anxiety, psychosomatic disorders, problems with assertiveness. Generally speaking, Meditative Therapy has the potential to effect significant positive changes in all of these psychological areas.

Psychological response in Meditative Therapy also has been reported in general terms and discussed in the case study data in Chapter 1, and later in this chapter. Follow up questionnaires with my clients showed that 80 percent of the group of 36 felt they had more ability to relax and be themselves after Meditative Therapy. In addition, 69 percent gained a sense of relaxation and freedom from anxiety and tension. Other results showed that 50 percent felt they had gained a greater tolerance of others, and that those closest to them had noted improvement in their behavior after Meditative Therapy (See Appendix D).

Physiological Response in Meditative Therapy

At this point in time, there have been no physiological studies conducted on the completely natural Meditative Therapy approach to the Inner Source. There have been a large number of physiological studies carried out on Schultz and Luthe's Autogenic Standard Exercises discussed in Chapter 3. For example, the first exercise focuses on allowing heaviness to develop in the arms and legs. To begin, one simply assumes the recommended training posture, closes the eyes, and visualizes and repeats three times a formula (specific instruction) derived from the exercise. If the mental formula is "My right arm is heavy," one repeats this out loud and visualizes the words. The three repetitions are to take place in a 30 to 60 second span of time. One's *attitude* when doing these exercises is crucial. It should be one of passive acceptance, not active striving. One is not trying to force heaviness to come, but rather to allow it to develop of its own accord.

Although the Standard Exercises are simple and easy to practice, don't be deceived about their ability to produce powerful reactions. These reactions are the autogenic discharges mentioned in Chapter 3. Schultz and Luthe have determined that many of the discharges are unrelated to the particular formula being repeated. Their theory is that the brain, using the formulas as triggering devices, takes its opportunity to rid the client of disturbing material and to rebalance psychophysiological functioning. If, for example, you were using the autogenic standard exercises and working on heaviness, you might find your arm getting heavy, but also your body may twitch, tears may come to your eyes, you may perspire.

Physiological studes on these standard exercises are numerous. These studies have primarily been conducted in European countries and began as early as the 1920's. Results are very impressive and show in part that there are significant decreases in muscular tension, significant decreases in heart rate, marked decreases in blood pressure for hypertensive patients, significant changes in several measures of respiration, significant brain wave changes such as a return to a normal alpha wave pattern, and significantly decreased galvanic skin response (electrical conductivity—indicating reduced anxiety). All of these results are for those who have regularly practiced the standard exercises for three to six months.

I recognize that the autogenic standard exercises and Meditative Therapy are not identical. Nevertheless, since the discharges, or what I have termed the "workings," of the standard exercises and of Meditative Therapy are very similar, I feel that it is a valid assumption that Meditative Therapy would produce similar physiological outcomes. Going one step further, I hypothesize that when physiological studies are conducted on Meditative Therapy, the results will be more powerful than those for the autogenic standard exercises because Meditative Therapy is more intensive in both time and depth. This material is analyzed in more detail when meditation and Meditative Therapy are compared in the next chapter.

Spiritual Response in Meditative Therapy

One of my purposes in this book is to describe the spiritual response in Meditative Therapy. Let me first discuss the concept "spiritual" as I view it. Why did I choose the word "spiritual," and how does it relate to the word "religious?"

The word "spiritual" has more universal or global implications than the word "religious." I believe that the "spiritual" takes into account the "religious" (it does not avoid or disavow it), but also goes beyond it in terms of innate, inherent, incontrovertible, spiritual phenomena or symbols. Whereas religious material would be primarily focused on learned material and response, spiritual material and response would consist of both the learned and the innate.

The relationship between religious and spiritual I describe is similar to the relationship between the personal and collective unconscious of Jungian psychology. C.G. Jung (1958e) describes the personal unconscious as containing only contents of a subjective, individual nature whereas the collective unconscious components are entirely universal. Rather than being identified only with one specific person, the collective images are found everywhere, within each person.

My position is also closely aligned with that of the late Italian physician Roberto Assagioli, the founder of Psychosynthesis. In his book *Psychosynthesis* (1971), Assagioli refers to what he terms "spiritual psychosynthesis." He indicates that the word "spiritual" corresponds to the superconscious, and that psychosynthesis takes as basic in humans a spiritual self and a superconscious. Further, he states that, " . . . We are not attempting to force upon psychology a philosophical, theological or metaphysical position, but essentially we include within the study of psychological facts all those which may be related to the higher urges within man which tend to make him grow towards greater realizations of his spiritual essence." (p. 193)

Recently, Anthony Sutich (1973) has reported that Assagioli finally gave up on using the word "spiritual" and instead chose the word "transpersonal." Jung also referred to the collective unconscious as the transpersonal unconscious. No matter what word is chosen, the vital point is that we are concerned here with the question of what are the naturally occurring internal phenomena which have spiritual significance, including religious significance.

Let me further differentiate between spiritual and religious material in Meditative Therapy. Spiritual material includes such things as experiencing inner light, mandalas, fire, water, the sun. Religious material includes such visualized items as a prominent religious figure such as Jesus or Buddha, stained-glass windows, churches, temples, crosses, angels. There is crossover between the two categories. A person may have a learned response as well as an innate response to a spiritual item like light. A traditionally religious item such as the cross has an innate response to it which is exclusive of any learned response. It is neither my purpose nor do I have the knowledge to place all known types of phenomena into a spiritual or religious category. My purpose is to make you aware that both exist in Meditative Therapy. Although I have not conducted formal studies analyzing the frequency of spiritual response in Meditative Therapy, I have analyzed one particular aspect, the appearance of types of light experience (see Chapter 6). In addition, the chart presented on page 47 gave several examples of spiritual response in Meditative Therapy. Studies still need to be conducted which catalogue all the various types of spiritual response and their frequency of occurrence for different types of groups.

The questionnaires which I asked clients to complete as a follow-up to the Meditative Therapy experience had a series of statements dealing with spiritual response. Results showed that 66 percent gained a greater awareness of reality, but only 31 percent felt they now had a sense of knowing what life is all about. Close to 40 percent thought they now had a new way of looking at the world. In reference to whether or not the Meditative Therapy was a religious experience, 25 percent felt that it was. In addition, 31 percent had a greater awareness of God, or a Higher Power, or an Ultimate Reality.

There were also three questions which concerned spiritual outcomes in Meditative Therapy:

1. *Have your feelings on religion and what it means changed any as a result of your Meditative Therapy experience?* Thirteen (36 percent) answered yes to this question. Below are representative responses:

a. Closer to God. Traveling, but not knowing where. Frightened at times.

b. I am more aware of a spiritual need and belief.

c. I seem to have more faith in a Supreme Being. No longer the concept of heaven or hell or punishment for sins, but a good feeling and faith in a spiritual world.

d. Reaffirmed and made stronger (my beliefs). Belief in the existence of a higher order or general purpose, God. Established the belief that God exists inside everyone.

e. I found the source of spiritual power to come, paradoxically, from within and without myself. It's found by letting go rather than by trying to search out or find somewhere.

2. *Have your experiences with Meditative Therapy changed your feelings about death in any way?* Twelve (33 percent) felt that they were less afraid, more at ease, more positive about death now.

3. *Do you trust God or a supreme being or concept more than you did?* Eleven (31 percent) answered "yes" to this question. Most spoke about a positive experiencing of a higher force now, and felt much of this in the form of direct communication through dreams, inner promptings and intuition.

The Experience of Meditative Therapy

Undergoing the natural way of Meditative Therapy is not an everyday type of experience. Among other effects, it usually stimulates the client to wonder at the time that has so swiftly passed. The following comments were spoken spontaneously after client sessions of Meditative Therapy:

I tried to concentrate on trusting. I felt very vulnerable, felt shocked at one point. I just had to trust in you, the floor, etc. It scared me. I just had to shut off all fear and trust it. You know what, I feel good. You wouldn't believe it, but I do! It gets rid of layers and layers of stuff you live with. You live with them but you know they don't belong to you. You must trust." (session #3)

Boy, my body is really shaky. Back is wet, I must have been perspiring. Oh man, I feel like I have to work up to it (*getting up*). My legs feel flushed, like when I walk in the sun and feel tired. I really don't know if I should get up, my whole spine is extremely loose, not like when you get up in the morning when it's stiff. My fingers are softer, like there is something around them. Like there is more than flesh there. Yeah, physically it really feels good, like a transfusion, whatever transfusions do for you. (session #1)

That was heavy, so vivid, oh. That's a weird thing. Like those tingly feelings were over me, not in me. They would start at the top and move to the bottom of me. (session #1)

That's the best feeling I can remember ever having, drunk or otherwise. (session #2)

This therapy is really strange. I've never had anything like it happen to me before. (session #3)

That was stranger yet, that was really strange. I told my husband where I was and what happened, but he'll never believe this! I don't think I do. I feel now like it never happened, like it was just a dream for a second and went away. Because every time I come here I don't believe you, this guy's really strange. I'll never tell anyone 'cause they won't believe me (*laughs*). Huh? Wow! I just never thought of that at all. I thought about it to some extent, but never like that, it was so simple (*smiles*). If I would have talked for thirty years I'd never have figured that out, I know it. This is the strangest thing that's ever happened to me (*smiles*). (session #2)

That was weird, I could really feel myself hugging into a big teddy bear. I had one when I was a kid. (session #1)

This has got to be fascinating, got to be out of sight. I can't move my arms at all, they feel like chicken wings, but I can't move either. I'm surprised that I can do it. Just go to sleep and talk about it at the same time.'' (session #1)

What is the nature of an experience that prompts some participants to describe it in such exciting terms? How does Meditative Therapy work and why? Is the experience scary; does it hurt? What are the outcomes?

Allow yourself to pretend that you are one of my clients. It is your second or third session with me and I am discussing with you what types of approaches I feel would be helpful for your problems. I have told you that I usually employ a variety of methods but that I like to start with Meditative Therapy. I continue:

''Meditative Therapy relies on the principle that there is an Inner

Source of some kind inside each of us that knows all about us and knows what to do to help. How does that sound?''

You: ''That sounds good. How does it work?''

Me: ''What I have you do is come into my office, lie down on the pad I have over in the corner, close your eyes, and begin watching and describing outloud anything that comes into your awareness. You are to focus on visual images, bodily reactions and thoughts. You may see colors or patterns, your body may jerk or twitch, you may cry, thoughts may come in. Your job is just to patiently describe anything that takes place.''

You: ''What does this Inner Source do?''

Me: ''It depends on what needs to be done for each person, but usually, at some point, it deals with things that are bothering you. I can never predict exactly what it will do, I only know that it is out for your best interests. It seems to be smarter than we are so I have learned to just trust it and allow it to do what it wants to do.''

You: ''How long are the sessions?''

Me: ''Sessions can last anywhere from 20 or 30 minutes up to 2 hours. I have you set up a series of 2-hour sessions, once a week for 7 or 8 weeks. That way if we need the 2 hours we will have it. It is best to let the Inner Source start and finish on its own. It will let you know when it is finished for the day.''

You: ''How many sessions will this take?''

Me: ''It is really an individual matter, but most people get through the main part of it in 5 to 10 sessions. After that most can begin doing sessions on their own. We will know more after you have been through a few sessions. As I've mentioned, I use a variety of approaches. Let's just watch carefully how you're responding to Meditative Therapy and decide how to proceed as we go along.''

You: ''That's great. When do we start?''

Me: ''Let's begin next week. When you come next time, we can discuss any more questions you may have, then we will begin.''

Not everyone reacts in the same way ''you'' just did, of course. Some have other types of questions. Some don't like the sound of the Inner Source and decide not to undergo Meditative Therapy. Whatever the reactions, I deal with them as honestly as I can, but *I never try to force anyone to go through the process if they are not ready.*

What will your first session be like? Before giving several examples of the initial minutes of first sessions let me talk about the full range of possibilities.

The two most thorough presentations of Inner Source experiences are those of Luthe (Autogenic Abreaction) and Grof (LSD-Assisted Therapy). Autogenic Abreaction is non-directive/natural, whereas I have placed LSD into a directive/synthetic category.

Summaries of these two cataloguings of therapeutic experiences shows that the Inner Source has a great many ways of proceeding. Luthe speaks of *autogenic discharges* in the nine categories discussed on page 43: *auditory* (speech, singing, etc.); *gustatory* (wide range of tastes); *olfactory* (wide range of smells); *vestibular* (dizziness, floating etc.); *visual* (colors, patterns, filmstrips, etc.); *motor* (trembling, twitching, tension, etc.); *sensory* (heaviness, warmth, electrical sensations, etc.); *affective* (anxiety, fear, euphoria, etc.); *ideational* (thoughts, memories, planning).

In addition to these reactions, one may undergo what Luthe has termed special events or experiences. One may have *multiple images, unusual brightness, images of oneself, themes about life and death, pain-crying experiences, pain-aggression experiences,* and *sexual experiences.*

Grof (1975) writes from the *psycholytic* perspective: observing a series of LSD sessions over a long period of time, such as each week for 10 or 20 weeks. He speaks of: *physical symptoms* (heaviness, sweating, coldness, etc.); *perceptual changes* (flashing lights, geometric figures, people, etc.); *distortions in perception of time and space* (regression, loss of spatial perspective, etc.); *emotional changes* (anxiety, guilt feelings, etc.); *thinking, intellect, memory changes; psychomotor changes; changes in consciousness* (dream-like state, deep unconsciousness); *sexuality; the experience of art; religious and mystical experiences.*

I have presented below material from the first several minutes of the first session of six different individuals (3 female and 3 male):

Females

1. So, what am I supposed to be doing? . . . I see patterns of

light like I get when I first close my eyes. No color. Pinkish color now, with dark green lines on it. Just moving patterns and I'm getting a funny feeling on top of my scalp. I see a trike, a person walking down the street, a pair of hands.

2. I feel a little tension about opening up my mouth and getting started. Oh dear, is this an absolutely continual thing? . . . Sometimes I say things to myself like Jesus, Mary and Joseph and that came to me. I feel comfortable and actually a warmth along my back.

3. I feel like I'm going to fight it because I don't trust my own sanity or whatever. I fear losing control to a certain extent. Right now it just feels comfortable to lie on the mat. Feels like the blood is pulsing in my feet. Now my neck and shoulder area tends to be tense most of the time.

Males

1. I feel really tired, my eyes hurt, I'm fighting a headache. (His eyes open and I tell him to close them.) There is a thought in the back of my mind I'm trying to bring out, something my inner feelings have to tell me. My face feels like it is next to a fire. I feel rays. My head tingles.

2. Kind of like being in a psychiatrist's office, the classical one. Except you don't have one of those fancy couches (*laughs; takes deep breath*). My heart seems to be pumping a little harder than what it was before. Some minor twitching underneath my left eye.

3. My heart's beating kind of hard, an emptiness in my stomach, I'm very anxious, nervous, my hands are shaking. Seems to be a big blank area that's kind of enclosing me in a way. Kind of keeping things from coming through.

Referring back to the lists of Luthe and Grof you can see that the process was starting for the individuals. In the content of these six sessions were patterns, colors, visual images, bodily feelings, and thoughts. As each session unfolded many of these experiences were repeated or presented in varied forms. Other experiences were also presented, all of which fit into the categories of response given by Luthe and Grof.

Trust—Allowance—Patience

Some of the material you are about to read on physical and psychological situations dealt with by the Inner Source demonstrates some of the upsetting feelings and experiences in Meditative Therapy. It seems that we all must face unpleasant experiences if we wish to get better or grow. Throughout this book I will mention the words *trust*, *allowance* and *patience* in regard to painful experiences and also in regard to experiences one may not understand. Both experiences take place in Meditative Therapy. If we have trust, the Inner Source will put us through experiences that are necessary for our benefit. These experiences are not always easy in terms of pain or understanding, but if we can be patient and allow the Inner Source to do what it needs to do we will be far ahead. I believe that the Inner Source is acutely aware of our readiness level and never gives us anything which we cannot handle. At times we may find ourselves consciously rebelling about the pain or the seeming senselessness of an experience, but if we will only trust and patiently allow, we can proceed to new heights.

One of the most important functions I serve as a therapist is to teach those who are going through Meditative Therapy not to be afraid, but rather to allow, and trust, and be patient. Certainly it is scary when you are confronted by experiences that upset your equilibrium by being painful or difficult to comprehend. Such experiences have a tendency to throw off your frame of reference especially when pain and lack of understanding are combined. Going through an experience which is painful and whose purpose you don't understand is one of the supreme tests of trust. My clients who have experienced a good deal of "heavy" (painful and difficult to understand) material develop a healthy respect for the powers of the Inner Source.

Recently I asked a young client if she had benefitted from the 6 sessions of Meditative Therapy she had undergone and if she was ready to start again. We had switched to marriage counseling work with her spouse for several sessions. She lauded the therapy, noting many significant changes, but at the end of her "testimonial" said, only half kidding, that she wasn't sure she was ready to do it again. I smiled at the seeming incongruity of the matter, but she quickly stated, "Meditative Therapy has really been great for me, but I still don't have to *like* it do I?" One might call this the "visit-to-the-dentist-syndrome." You know you need to go, and you know it will help you, but, because there might be pain you resist.

Most of my clients have found that worry and anticipation about what might take place in Meditative Therapy is usually worse than anything upsetting that ever comes up.

In addition, the Inner Source has much more wisdom than the dentist, is uniquely keyed to each person's needs, and will do the job in the best possible way. Also, even when Meditative Therapy sessions do contain much upsetting material, most work through the bulk of it in 5 to 10 sessions.

The Therapeutic & Creative Journey of the Inner Source

In Chapter 1 it was noted that there are two basic goals of the Inner Source: a *therapeutic or healing goal* and a *creative goal.* The therapeutic process takes place more frequently in Meditative Therapy, and can be analyzed in terms of five categories: discharging, extended discharging, reinforcement, understanding, and abreaction. The creative process centers on new experiences. Briefly, these dimensions may be summarized:

The Therapeutic or Healing Goal: The Inner Source employs a variety of means to help the individual overcome psychological, physiological and spiritual difficulties:

1. Discharging: Experiencing momentary visual images, bodily reactions, thoughts, and feelings.

Examples: seeing colors and patterns; experiencing smells; twitching; feeling cold; feeling anxious; visualizing people, places, events.

2. Extended Discharging: Experiencing longer sequences of visual images, bodily reactions, thoughts, and feelings, but without abreactive intensity.

Examples: (see pages 59-62)

3. Reinforcement: Gaining a rewarding psychological, physical, or spiritual feeling during the meditative therapy process.

Examples: seeing a beautiful or relaxing scene; feeling deeply relaxed; feeling exhilarated; experiencing a humorous incident; having a "peak" experience.

4. *Understanding:* Realizing the causes of one's difficulties; gaining insights; arriving at solutions to confusing problem areas.

Examples: connecting the therapy experience with a past physical injury or mental upset; coming to new conclusions about one's upbringing; gaining personal answers about the meaning of life and/or how to live.

5. *Abreaction:* Re-living or re-experiencing various portions of disturbing or traumatic events.

Examples: (see pages 62-65)

The Creative Goal: The Inner Source presents experiences, often having spiritual and/or parapsychological overtones, which seem designed to awaken new levels of awareness, and/or to develop new dimensions of one's being. The ultimate meaning of these experiences is often not readily attainable.

1. *New Experiences:* Contacting a dimension of life or of one's being not previously experienced. The person is usually "struck by" or amazed at the experience, and it leaves a lasting impression.

Examples: (see pages 65-72)

Table 4-1 analyzes the categories of response of the Inner Source for the therapeutic and creative goals. The information for the table was derived from studying 423 individual Meditative Therapy sessions of 100 (54 female, 46 male) university counseling center and private practice clients. Although I have distinguished between the two goals, there is similarity in the processes by which the goals are reached. The primary difference between the therapeutic and creative goals are in content and accompanying feeling. The creative process may have discharging, extended discharging, reinforcement, understanding, and abreaction, just as the therapeutic process does. The content will be in terms of the unique and the feeling will be one of awe, great surprise, or intrigue.

Case Examples of Therapeutic Experiences
Extended Discharging: Physical Events

1. *Broken Bones*—This man had broken his right leg twice and

Table 4-1
The Therapeutic and Creative Journey of
The Inner Source, Based on 100 Participants*

THE THERAPEUTIC GOAL		THE CREATIVE GOAL	
Category	Percentage Occurrence	Category	Percentage Occurrence
1. discharging	100%	1. New Experiences	13%
2. Extended Discharging	95%		
3. Reinforcement	75%		
4. Understanding	71%		
5. Abreaction	20%		

* The 100 persons included here represent my entire population of Meditative Therapy clients at the date of this writing. Other samples noted in this book are drawn from this group of 100.

his left leg once. A surgical pin had been inserted into his right leg.

I guess my right leg is going to hurt this morning, the one I had surgery on. It sure hurts now. I just had a visual picture of just when I broke it. I skied down on it without assistance and went for two days on it and didn't know it was broken.

2. *The Dentist*—This man had undergone many hours of dental work.

My forehead feels smooth, but my head feels heavy and numb. I have a headache way down inside. My jaw is real sore like a dentist has been working on me. God knows I've had enough of that work done. I still have that headache and my jaw aches and my whole mouth. Now I don't feel so relaxed, I'm anxious. Feels kind of like just before I go to the dentist. I'm hot and sweaty and my palms are sweaty.

3. *Polio* — This woman had polio as a child.

I feel a real rush now and feel a little afraid. I keep seeing the house (*she describes it*). I feel energy going out of my arms and out of my head. I see myself when I was sick. My neck really hurts between my shoulder blades and I can see me soaking in the tub when I was sick. I felt a big rush in my body, almost like a gas. I see the backyard and an adult and kid. Kid being carried; kid is sick. I see the tub when I was sick with polio. My back is stiff. I feel an awful lot of weird energy in my body, like it's uncomfortable. Makes me feel kind of stiff and achy. I feel that energy or whatever all over, like I'm about to start shaking from being cold.

Extended Discharging: Psychological Events

1. *High School Experiences* — This man re-visited school experiences which took place seven years before.

I didn't drink much from then until high school, then it took a new meaning for me. We'd have a 6-pack stashed in the woods. Go out and freeze and drink then go back to the basketball game. It took the whole week to line up the 6-pack (*laughs*). One time we had a big party and got malt liquor and beer and everyone else had gone home. We stayed the night to party, but one of us got separated and later two got caught in the recreation room and the Priests kept telling us they thought more were involved. Later we sat on the hill, pretty drunk, concrete stairs and a Priest started coming up. I got so scared, my whole body was wired and I vomited (*stomach gurgles*). Not because I was sick, but because I might get caught. I was really terrified. Wasn't our Priest though and we all got to graduate (*gurgles*).

2. *Divorce* — This woman had gotten married at an early age, then divorced after several years. The divorce took place 10 years before and she had believed that it no longer bothered her.

Boy, getting married at 16 is the worst thing of all. I would have nightmares at night about my first marriage up until I got married the second time. It was the worst thing that ever happened. He would criticize me for everything I said and did; I could do nothing right. Yet, before we were married the things I did seemed O.K. There was no way I could be myself. R (present husband) blames me for being married before. I shouldn't be, there is no way I should be punished. Basically, those last two years we weren't married anyway (*dry crying—she starts making noises and motions as in crying, but without tears*). We only had intercourse three times and I got pregnant. I feel like I've paid enough, suffered enough, for being married before. It shouldn't matter anymore (*breathing heavily*). I would cry and cry, and I lost 15 pounds in less than a year. Our first child was 10 days old before he saw it. It's terrible being pregnant and having a baby with a person who's resisting.

Abreaction: Physical Events

1. *Doctor Visits*—This 50-year-old woman re-experienced visits to the doctor as a young child for a urinary disorder. The visits required dilation of the urethra.

I want to scream, but I can't, I never can. Even in my dreams I can never scream. Sometimes I wake up at night and scream, but not really. My throat closes off and I know I've been trying to scream because I'm (*breathing quickens*)—I feel like I'm being held down (*stomach gurgles*). (*Starts crying*). I feel like I'm being held down in that room. Oh God, I'm in that doctor's office! All these people, and my mother's there and I'm on this table and it's hard like the floor. Oh God (*gurgles, sobbing*). I can't even see it! I'm so ashamed! Put my feet in the stirrups, I can't believe it, and my mother was standing there. Everyone was white. Oh God. Told me to relax, that it wouldn't hurt. I hate them, I hate them. I think I'd kill them now. I don't want to kill them, but I feel like it. How could Mother have stood there and watched that? Why didn't she pick me up and hold me? I don't know, maybe when kids are six you don't hold them anymore.

2. *Childhood Disease* — This 26-year-old man had a bone disease as a child which was called Osgood-Schlatter disease.

My body feels crooked, doesn't feel aligned right. I don't feel straight. I'm aware of a pain in my left leg, muscles are twitching a little bit, tightening and loosening. I don't feel sad, but I have the feeling about sadness. My leg's still doing it — still doing it. It's shaking (*very observably*). Calming down, real soft twitching, boom, boom-boom, boom-boom, boom. It's getting harder and faster now, very vigorous, boom, boom! It's shaking from side to side.

3. *Miscarriage* — This young woman had lost a baby several years before due to a miscarriage. (Obviously miscarriage is both a physical and a psychological event. In this case, the physical ramifications were apparently more significant.)

. . . Color is like a spinning wheel, like fans you used to get when you were a kid, on a stick (*starts sobbing & coughing*). Oh, I don't understand that. We used to run with them (*sobbing*). All I can remember is just the spinning around, I don't see anything (*stops crying — starts crying*). I just feel sad. I just feel sad (*deep breath*). Baffles me about — I don't even know the name of them now (*stops crying*). My side still hurts and stomach still gurgles (*sobbing again*). I just don't feel like crying. Oh, oh, (*stops sobbing*) — I saw just white all around my eyes. My side is still hurting some. I just feel tired, not tired, just — I don't know, maybe kind of just accepting it (*crying*), just accepting it. Oh, (*sits up and cries*) I can't cry lying down. I feel like rocking back and forth (*rocks from side to side and around*). I want something to hold; I wanted that baby! I wanted that baby! (*sobbing and rocking — lies down — strokes and rubs her hair — still sobbing*). Oh, I guess, I'm feeling like, that baby beside me on my arm and the same walls and the same — ? — and thought about it for awhile — really just (*crying*), I don't know, I don't know. H (*husband*) didn't know how much I appreciated him. He didn't know it was real, he didn't know it. I just feel like, felt like a whole square of hurt just moved away — I can't have it anyway. Oh, (*sighs*) feeling cold again and can't (*crying stops*) keep thinking thoughts about that all the time—(*whispering, can't hear it—she laughs*). I don't feel anything, except cold, shiver again. There's something covering my eyes, nothing else going on—just as I said that I felt my heart beating very heavily, aware now that my head hurts (*deep breathing*). Sometimes my mind really makes me mad. I feel like I'm fighting myself. Right shoulder is tight, right side aches (*shakes her head*). I guess I didn't know that hurts (*crying*). She asked me how old the child was (*sobbing*). You can say things in your mind and that's O.K. and accept it, but that doesn't mean it's past (*stops crying*). I feel good—I don't feel bad. [*MLE: Do you think you are done?*] I really feel tired and I feel like going to sleep. (*End of session*)

Abreaction: Psychological Events

1. *Relationship with Father*—A 28-year-old woman in her first session re-visits her past relationship with her father.

Now I feel sad, not like striking at him, just feel sad. I've not done anything, but he doesn't seem to like me. No matter how hard I try it's never enough. But I can do well in school, but it doesn't matter, Daddy—I like school (*tears*). That's not enough—school's not enough (*sobbing*). Makes me feel angry, he won't tell me why, he won't tell me how to fix it. I just wish you'd tell me why you don't like me (*sobbing*). I've always tried to do what you wanted, but it's never been—Oh, Oh, my head feels better. Oh, I feel so hot and sweaty. If he would just tell me why, I'd feel better. I just can't bear not knowing why you don't like me.

2. *Suicide of Father*—This young woman's alcoholic father committed suicide when she was in her early teens. During the year following the incident she gained 100 pounds.

I'm looking into a broken mirror and I'm screaming. I feel as if there is a steel band around my chest. What I'm seeing upsets me a lot. I've never talked about it before. [*MLE: I feel that it is important to talk about it.*] I'm in a room where Father killed himself and I feel really sick. I feel really upset because there are small pieces of brain on the walls. I remember thinking I should do something about it because I was worried about my brother coming down, but I couldn't. So I went upstairs and got in bed and sort of curled up around this very bad feeling. Now I'm seeing my father sitting in a deep blue chair in the living room and I'm there watching T.V. And I feel, not exactly frightened, but apprehensive, like I might be scared. When I sit next to my father I always pull back a little. He's eating chocolate and drinking coke. When he sits there he looks very small and lonely. Whenever he drinks coke and eats chocolate, he's not as frightening; he seems less large. It's hard to explain, but I can tell when I'm frightened of Father. His eyes get fierce and kind of wild and he does crazy things.

Case Examples of Creative Experiences
New Experiences

Most synthetic theorists focus on the *therapeutic* quality of the Inner Source, which, as we have just seen, deals largely with upsetting experiences from one's life. There is also a *creative* quality of the Inner Source, to which writers give much less attention, perhaps because its meaning is not always readily understood. The examples presented below were selected in order to demonstrate this quality which I term *creative*. As you will notice it is impossible to separate the creative from the therapeutic. The creative quality can be as upsetting as the therapeutic quality. Also, you will observe that the creative and therapeutic aspects, when linked together, produce psychophysiospiritulogical material. You can observe psychological, physical, and spiritual areas being dealt with.

New Experiences

(30-year-old female, grade school teacher, third session, fifteen minutes after the session started)

(9:15 a.m.) I get the feeling that I'm going to have to go on with my life. I'm going to have to start my life. I just see these two hands behind me pushing me. I'm kind of bending at the middle, like a resistance thing. Now I see two praying hands (*stomach gurgles*). I can't understand why I don't trust my husband and I just saw that brick wall and door again (*starts sob-*

bing). It seems that if I'd ever get through that door somehow I'd trust or feel good, but I don't know how to get through the door. It's like I'm sitting on one side and trying to figure out how to get through it. I just got a flash. Why don't you just open it? Why try and scheme and connive to get what you want? Why not just go the direct way? Something is holding me back from opening the door or I don't know how to go the direct way. Something's holding me back. (9:30 a.m.) *(deep breath)* Well, now I walked over to the other end and there is a little crack of light. A little shaft of light there, but I'll have to open the door *(deep breath)*. My body is going back and forth and all of a sudden I think this is ridiculous. I'll either stay and open it or walk away. I know why I'm afraid, it's because there's not going to be anything on the other side *(deep breath—stomach gurgles)*. Well, I opened the door, I think *(deep breath)*. I don't remember opening it, but I'm looking on the other side. There is a light there, like a big expanse of nothing, but it's white. And clear, and a bright light there that's giving me light to work with. And a pen is writing on it. I just saw the word 'respect,' but it's not written on that tablet. The ones on the tablet are written, but there are no words. I just saw the word 'word' and I can see a little figure of a person on this great big white sheet, and it's walking toward these squiggly lines. (9:35 a.m.)

This session continued for another fifteen minutes. During this time she continued to see words of various kinds until she saw the word "stop," whereupon she finished the session and stated that she felt fine.

(22-year-old male, college student, fourth session, thirty minutes after the session started)

(1:30 p.m.) That area *(described before)* where it felt like I had pain in my back became a white line. Like I could see it became a white line and it bulged at the top and became a big bulge, and then it started to bulge at the bottom and formed into a, still a white line in a black background and then it, after it formed these two bulges, then it flashed over to a color, kind of, and it was a fetus still in the sack, still kind of floating, and it was looking at me with really black eyes. The whole thing was solid black, the eyes were. There was no white around them or anything. And it sounded like the voice of a really old, old man, and it was talking to me. And it said, "A whole powered man," as if it was asking a question, and it sounded like there was a choir that said, "It is good, it is good." Thousands of voices. Then it said, "A whole is a composite part of a unit," and the choir would sing, "It is good, it is good," again. Then finally it said, "Unite the being and you unite the verse," and it went, "It is good, it is good," and then there was this big flash of white light out of the right side across my visual field. The visual field turned really a soft cream color and then I saw a gun, the barrel of a gun sticking out, kind of looking at an angle down the barrel, and I saw a flash of yellow and I could kind of see the burning grains of gun powder and saw the bullet slowly moving out the end; it's really, really slow. And it hit somebody's forehead and it went in and kind of pushed its way in and the skin closed over behind it, and then the side of the head was completely cut open and I could, it looks like I was looking at a bunch of people, and as the bullet went through it was tearing them all apart and a lot of screams from all these people getting torn apart. And it worked its way towards the back of the head, the back of the head just exploded and all these bodies, these little tiny human bodies were all blowing around, and just shooting up and down (silence). Hmm. The head seemed to close back, the pieces came back toward the back of the head and fused over, kind of closed over. And the people remaining in the head kind of rearranged themselves into a huge kind of sphere of people. They are all sitting around in a circle, a concentric circle, but all around the inside of the head. Right in the absolute center there is a bright glow and all the people started clapping. I felt like I was at the top of the head looking down and all the people in the head were clapping, women and men together in there, all naked sitting around in there, and a, they started chanting, "en cha," "en cha," and it looked like a woman at first was all of a sudden spinning by this fire, like all I could see was long black hair spinning around, and when it stopped it was short and all I could see was two large eyes from behind the hair, and the chanting was still going on and all the clapping and everybody reached out and seemed to fuse together and the glow in the middle started to go out through everybody. Then the whole inside of the head was glowing; then all of a sudden it was just snuffed out and I guess kind of like a super (?) went down to a real dense black body and I realized that the person, whoever it was that got shot, was dead (*short silence*). I was kneeling down and had my head on a block and had my head chopped off, and I picked up my head, put it in my arm, and was standing up and it was on a platform in front of a large crowd of people. It was spraying blood out of my neck like a fountain at everybody and I said, ''Come all ye people, gather round,'' and my head down here was smiling. The blood would hit the people and hit them right on the chest right above the heart and then they would start smiling, and then he said something about coming to the end of the time, and so I felt I was sitting on this bluff above the sea looking out over the ocean and it looked like just the end of the sunset where the sky is getting really dark and still a few streaks of light, the clouds way out there, and I felt like I could see it with the head that was on my shoulders and I reached up and I couldn't see and it felt like I was looking in the mirror, couldn't see the head, but I knew there was one up there. So I took the one that was under my arm and threw it out in the ocean. Soon as it hit the water it started rising and all these clouds started getting lighter and lighter and it was just a big sun up in the air. (2:05 p.m.)

Shortly after this last sequence the session ended. He had one more session which followed the same approach by the Inner Source. He enjoyed all of the sessions and stated that his mind became more peaceful and less concerned about the things in life which he could do nothing about.

(18-year-old female, college student, fifth session, one hour and twenty-five minutes after the session started)

(4:45 p.m.) I saw an eyeball, open and shut and then disappeared. Now my stomach feels like an old, big, huge stomach. It takes up all my trunk, but it feels more normal than it did. I can see again, like before I'd look at a screen that's black and there is a difference between that and the backside of my eyelids. It is lighter. I'm back to my eyelids. Like I think about the screen. My body is taking on more depth. My eyes feel like they are stuck in one place. I'm conscious of my right eyelid being completely stuck, like I want to stretch it open. I'm conscious of breathing from my stomach again. I feel tired. If I let my eyes go back to the screen, they go right back to my eyelids again. I feel like someone is blowing me up again and I fill out the shape I'm supposed to be. I feel like some big speed is going to overtake me and I have to protect myself in a ball, and it goes faster and faster and faster and now one from behind swirling up and it's spinning and spinning. But it's fast, but I don't have to protect myself because I'm laying out in it now and it's fading away and it changed directions and now it is coming again. Lots of stripes and they come real fast, then curl up and spin and they just went the other way and I have to curl up too. Like being sucked up into a spinning whirlpool, but faster. This is happening all over on my left side. Makes me have to breathe shorter. And now I'm back, not curled up anymore. I'm prone. I'm not in a straight jacket, but my arms can't move. I'm like a mummy and I'm tilted and there is this vast, vast expanse. It alternates between being nothing and being lots of skinny little stripes. And the thing that was me is doing flip flops real rigid across. It's not a black background anymore, it is all those stripes. And that just flip flops into nothing and I'm not there anymore. And I'm back on my back on the mat. I'm swinging over to the left, but I'm not trying to. Because the left side of my neck is tired from pulling, but I'm pulling back and it is all clear. My body just rolls around. I have to hold my arms straight by my sides and tuck my chin in and I'm rolling around and also pivoting in a circle, like spokes on a wheel. I guess it slowed down. I can take deeper breaths and it is the only kind of breaths I can take. That's a relief to be able to breathe deeply. And my head turned back over to straight. I almost feel like I'm panting. I'm breathing with my whole lungs. (5:00 p.m.) I was seeing if I wanted to let myself on that side again. Goes to the middle, but the left side of my neck is still tense. I'm done.

At this point she sat up and I asked her how she felt. She replied, "I'm sure I'm done, but I don't feel good at all. I feel like a lot of turmoil, confusion, but not about anything specific. Like swinging back and forth, zinging back and forth." After this statement she began crying and said, "I've never felt that terrified and it wasn't even logical, nothing was familiar. My other sessions were okay because they were in my frame of reference, but this was terrifying. I don't feel quite safe and scared to do that again. But when I was doing it, it was like watching the movies, and if I didn't know that it was definitely inside of me, I would think that something was going screwy."

She went to her room shortly after this discussion. I called her later because of her reaction to the session and in order to make sure that she was feeling all right. She indicated that after she arrived home she curled up and was really panicky for ten or fifteen minues. Then her boyfriend hugged her and talked to her and "cleared her." Shortly after that, she went to work and felt fine, came home and slept well, and woke up wide awake at 7:00 a.m., which "never happens," and felt great. She said that the Meditative Therapy experience was "like a dream now." She continued having Meditative Therapy sessions with me for awhile longer, eventually learned to do it on her own, and is doing quite well.

(35-year-old male, college professor, sixth session, twelve minutes after the session started)

(1:58 p.m.) I'm beginning to feel myself sort of drop into a deeper sense of relaxation—a feeling of letting go, almost like falling. That feels very good just to let everything go. I notice that my breathing is very weak or shallow, but I don't need any more. Very good feeling just to breathe very little. I can't even feel my heart beating (*seven-minute silence—outwardly, it appeared as if he might have fallen asleep*). I feel like I'm sort of detached. For a short time I didn't have any real sense of where I was or what time it was. I saw a fish, very large, sort of lying on its side. It was on the beach, a pleasant feeling about it. I saw a very docile black and white dog. Very large dog with a thin face like an Afghan. A calm, very friendly dog, not asleep, but resting, Then I got such a feeling of being detached. Like I could go anywhere I wanted to go—sort of leave my body behind, just because I wanted to, and free myself of all physical limits and just be anywhere I wanted to be. And I sort of went somewhere—not sure where I went. I couldn't tell you how long. No sense of time or physical place. Just before that I was very aware of my breathing in that I couldn't feel myself breathing. Not sure that I was breathing. When I came back from wherever I went I was a little startled and a little disappointed to come back (2:16 p.m.). I feel so good about it that I would like to go back again. It's sort of like tapping a new resource that I've known was there for a long time, but I was kind of out of touch with. Now the fingers in my hands and the back of my neck feel very thick. It's a good feeling. Now my eyelids feel that way. Now it feels a little uncomfortable, like a, like the need to move (*opens eyes, moves hands and feet*). I guess that's it. (2:25 p.m.)

At this point I made sure that he was finished. He replied that he felt fine and then stated, "That feeling of being able to just transcend the physical and go anywhere I want to was really an exhilarating feeling. And it wasn't like dreaming, it was a real feeling. But it was sort of like I just tapped it, discovered it, didn't really use it." When he returned one week later he stated that he had thought about the experience all week long and it left him with a feeling that he could do anything, literally, not merely in a figurative sense.

(30-year-old female, college student, fourth session, sixteen minutes after the session started)

(8:55 a.m.) Gosh, I really feel dizzy, like I'm spinning around on a solid plane. God, it's like being on those tilty-type rides spinning and spinning around! (*Her head is shaking.*) I don't like that. (*Just try to stay with it.*) Uh, uh, I'm shaking apart! (*Let it happen.*) No, it's uh, oh, oh, uh, uh, oh, oh, oh (*starts sniffing*). (*Her arms are shaking.*) Uh, like I'm rocking back and forth, rocking, vibrating. Uh, oh, oh. Huh? A big empty space like I was breaking into thousands of pieces. Oh, oh, oh gosh, I feel like I've landed like a leaf when it falls to the ground. It kind of floats through. Oh, it feels good, oh. (*Her eyes open and close.*) Uh, oh, I see the house again. Seems even fuzzier than it did before. I can't even see their faces anymore. Moving farther and farther away. Uh—my mind felt all black, complete black. But it feels good. Feels very relaxed. (9:05 a.m.)

At this point the content of the session shifted to another area and the session lasted for another fifteen minutes. Right before she opened her eyes before finishing she said, "My body feels the way it should feel, not floating. Feels very, very solid, not like I'm going to fall apart again—never." After her eyes opened she stretched and said, "Oh, stretching feels good. My hair's all wet again, did I cry?" I replied that she had not cried much, but perhaps a little during the shaking. Her response was, "That was awful, I really felt like I was going to fall apart. I never felt like that before."

Non-Directive—Non-Interpretive

I consider the preceding experiences "creative" because of the unique way the Inner Source dealt with the content. Neither the clients nor I understood everything that took place. Surely we both had some insight, but at times the Inner Source works in symbolic language. I must remind you that *the greatest benefits of Meditative Therapy occur naturally*. Much of the history of therapeutic approaches has suggested that great insight needs to take place for a client to change. Usually these insights were gained from some dramatic interpretation rendered by the therapist. As a Meditative Therapist, I do *no interpretation* along the lines of any certain theory. I did not sit down with these individuals and state, or suggest, or lead them to any interpretation of their just-birthed experiences. There is no need to, because the Inner Source guides the therapy and "gets you better" of its own accord. I stress this same point to my clients, that they are to be careful about the conclusions they draw about their Meditative Therapy experiences. If any special conclusions need to be drawn, the Inner Source makes them very obvious.

Meditative Therapy Outcomes

The reason that most clients are willing to suspend judgment, trust the wisdom of the Inner source, and patiently allow it to work no matter what course it takes is because of the outcomes they experience. Rewarding feelings and experiences either take place during a session, immediately following a session or somewhere along the way as the person progresses through a series of sessions. In Appendix D I present findings from my follow-up questionnaire which illustrates some of these changes. Of 42 clients who had undergone at least 4 Meditative Therapy sessions, a total of 36 responded, 18 females and 18 males. The results for selected questions are summarized here.

When asked if their experience was a very pleasant one 91% felt that it was not unpleasant, 100% said that they were not disappointed. In judging whether or not the experience was one of insanity or did them harm mentally 97% replied no. (These are interesting outcomes when we reflect on our earlier discussion about painful and/or confusing experiences the Inner Source puts us through.) Only 16% felt that the sessions caused them physical discomfort or illness and only 6% that the sessions caused a frightening feeling which made them feel that they would "go crazy" or lose control.

Significantly, 88% said that Meditative Therapy was something they would try again; 80% felt it was of lasting benefit to them and that they now had more ability to relax and be themselves; and 70% gained a sense of relaxation and freedom from anxiety and tension.

Summarizing these results, we can see that Meditative Therapy was a good experience for the majority of this group. Indeed, 40% indicated that the experience was the greatest thing that ever happened to them!

The final question on the questionnaire asked, "Is there anything else you can tell of your experience that was particularly exciting, disturbing, unusual, etc?" This question produced a wide range of responses, mostly positive, describing increased trust in oneself and in the ability of the mind and body to work together. Two sample answers are given below:

It helped me work through 2 heavy relationships—that with my parents and that with Mel (boyfriend). Since my therapy sessions my parents and I, Mother especially, have grown so much closer together and I've realized that I used to "hate" her and now I'm feeling really close and understanding with our relationship. Also I worked out so much with Mel while going through the therapy, so that when I moved out yesterday it was an easy experience—scary and all, but I felt detached in a way, as I watched myself experience the whole thing. Life looks so damn good, Mike. Life is so good!

I keep thinking of things that have happened since I started therapy—one is that I bought drawing paper and I've been drawing. I've never had an art course so I always felt limited and defeated from the start. Now I just feel like trying and not judging whether I'm good or bad. I just draw and derive pleasure from the experience and I've been realizing that's a good indication of how freed I feel from past imagined hangups that limited me.

This therapy has allowed me to disassociate with many conditioned reactions and defenses. It has allowed me to clear my life of most of the repressed feelings and emotions of childhood, namely those most directly inhibiting physical, mental and emotional fulfillment.

I have, almost overnight (6 months), grown from being cold and unable to express or know love, to being warm and full of love and comfortable and spontaneous with its expression. I have become very sentimental, often crying when happy or seeing others happy. I'm able to see beauty and order in nature and have confidence that there's a reason for all and something to be learned in every relationship. Life is a growing process and all that we ever have is ourself; we're the key to our own happiness.

I believe that we are more than we know and that there are levels of awareness beyond our 5 senses and conscious comprehension.

I have also developed an inherent respect for my health. I feel better so I take better care, then I feel better, and I take even better care. I believe I even have the potential for self-healing and sickness prevention . . . .

The remainder of the questionnaire answers are found in the appendix. I find these questionnaire outcomes to be quite interesting, and instructive but I do feel that they "short shrift" each individual's unique outcomes to a large extent. The best way to find out about someone's personal experiences and outcomes in Meditative Therapy is to focus solely upon that person. I am unable to present each person's experience thoroughly because of space limitations. Keep in mind that we are all individuals, no two the same, so it is unlikely that we will respond the same. Arthur Janov makes an excellent point in this regard when he states that it is ridiculous to study five hundred homosexuals and come up with conclusions about the homosexual. Each case is idiosyncratic , so it is dangerous to apply group conclusions to an individual case. Meditative Therapy overwhelmingly confirms that we are all quite unique, and the Inner Source deals with the unique needs of each individual person.

In Summary—Ten Important Points About Meditative Therapy

1. Meditative Therapy is an inner-directed, eyes-closed process in which the participant enters a naturally occurring altered state of consciousness and allows an inner source to engage in a self-unifying and self-healing process.

2. The Inner Source deals with the person in a threefold, holistic, manner: psychologically, physiologically, spiritually. The inner workings reflect each of these three areas of content.

3. While allowing the Inner Source to conduct its journey, the participant gives an ongoing verbal description of thoughts, feelings, visual images, and bodily reactions.

4. Each person's Inner Source is acutely aware of his or her unique needs. There are some general trends when analyzing the workings of "the global Inner Source," but each individual Inner Source is intricately unique, geared to that individual's total development.

5. The workings of the Inner Source go beyond therapeutic or healing qualities alone. A creative component also exists and leads one into new dimensions of growth.

6. Any growth process may produce upset and fear. The workings of the Inner Source can be scary and difficult to understand. By trusting one's Inner Source, and patiently allowing its full realm of response, it will lead beyond upset and pain.

7. The Inner Source has the potential to produce dramatic results in a short period of time. Significant and lasting changes in problem areas take place in as little as five to ten sessions.

8. There is no need for the therapist or the client to be directive or interpretive of the workings of the Inner Source before, during, or after therapy. The Inner Source knows best how to deal with the inner realm of response.

9. It is important that one undergo an average of five to ten therapist-facilitated Meditative Therapy sessions prior to practicing self-Meditative Therapy. This book should be read in its entirety before attempting this method with oneself or others.

10. Most participants in a sample of thirty-six stated that Meditative Therapy was of lasting benefit to them and that they gained a sense of relaxation and freedom from anxiety. Forty percent called the experience the greatest thing that ever happened to them!

5

Meditation and Meditative Therapy:
Two Paths to the Inner World

Then he had fallen asleep, and on awakening he looked at the world like a new man. Softly he said the word Om to himself, over which he had fallen asleep, and it seemed to him as if his whole sleep had been a long, deep pronouncing of Om, thinking of Om, an immersion and penetration into Om, into the nameless, into the Divine.

What a wonderful sleep it had been! Never had a sleep so refreshed him, so renewed him, so rejuvenated him! Perhaps he had really died, perhaps he had been drowned and was reborn in another form. No, he recognized himself, he recognized his hands and feet, the place where he lay and the self in his breast, Siddhartha, self-willed, individualistic. But this Siddhartha was somewhat changed, renewed. He had slept wonderfully. He was remarkably awake, happy and curious.

—Hermann Hesse

What Is Meditation?

Meditation is an altered state of consciousness method wherein an individual seeks to develop a state of passive concentration or relaxed attention. Meditation has been in existence since ancient times and has been presented in a wide variety of ways. There have been several attempts to place the various methods of meditation into a framework. The ancient Buddhist text, the *Vissudhimaga*, presents a two-fold system: *meditative concentration* and *mindful-*

ness insight. Daniel Goleman (1977), in his book *The Varieties of the Meditative Experience*, describes the two basic ways of engaging in meditation given in the *Vissudhimaga.*

In the first category, meditative concentration, the task is to focus your attention or flow of thought onto a single object. The *Vissudhimaga* gives 40 objects (e.g., a flower, a tree) on which the meditator can concentrate in order to gain control of the mind through what is termed "one-pointed concentration." It is called one-pointed because once you are focusing on the object your mind will wander, but you are continually and gently to refocus on the same object. These objects can be external or internal. By repeatedly engaging in this process, you gain control of the mind.

John White (1974), in a book called *What Is Meditation?*, gives excellent examples of various methods of one-pointedness or meditative concentration. He speaks of three areas which fit into a category he calls silent meditation: concentration, contemplation, and mental repetition of a sound. Concentration is the focusing of attention on some internal image or object with the eyes closed. It may be a star, a cross, or the traditional "third eye" which corresponds to the spot in the center of the forehead. If the mind wanders, the meditative concentrator is to gently refocus attention on the image or object. In contemplation, the eyes are open and the person focuses on an external form or object, such as a candle flame, a picture, a star, a cross. The task is the same as in concentration only the eyes are open. White's third category of silent meditation is mental repetition of a sound. The sound can actually be any type of word or phrase. It may be a verse from the Bible or Koran or it may be a Christian or Buddhist prayer. In Transcendental Meditation (TM) for example, the meditator is given a "mantra" to repeat. Again, the purpose is the same as for the two previous methods; that is, to keep re-aligning the attention when the mind wanders.

The second category of the *Vissudhimaga* is called "the path of insight" and is based on mindfulness. In mindfulness, one pays attention to all of the sensations of the mind in a receptive rather than a reactive manner. The individual passively observes what takes place without reacting further. One is to note only what takes place and to go on. There are four kinds of mindfulness which are said to serve the same function while being different in focus. One can center on the body, the feelings, the mind, or on mind objects. In mindfulness of the body, the meditator is aware of each instant of bodily response such as movements or positions. Mindfulness of feelings focuses on one's inner sensations regardless of their content. Some feelings come from the senses, some are bodily feelings that take place in conjunction with psychological states, and some are thought to be biological reactions. Any of these feelings can be pleasant or unpleasant, but the meditator is to keep on going in spite of the valence of the feelings.

Goleman describes the remaining two categories of mindfulness as quite similar. In mindfulness of mental states, one is to center on moods, thoughts, or psychological states. In mindfulness of mind objects, the meditator is to again focus on the same objects as in mental states, but without noting their quality, according to Goleman. Evidently, the individual is to categorize these mind objects, by an intricate method, as helpful or harmful.

Lawrence LeShan (1974), in his book *How to Meditate*, does an excellent job of explaining and categorizing a wide variety of meditation approaches. In a chapter on the "How" of meditation, he describes several methods that appear to fit the mindfulness category from the *Vissudhimaga*. One of these is called "the meditation of the bubble," and "a structured meditation of the inner way." LeShan reports that one is to meditate on the stream of consciousness in a noninterfering but structured way. To begin the bubble technique, the meditator visualizes himself or herself sitting peacefully at the bottom of a clear lake. Just as bubbles rise slowly to the surface in a lake, one's own thoughts, feelings, perceptions, and other mind units also rise up in the mind. Each of these mind experiences is treated and pictured as a bubble. One is to notice them, watch them arise, and let them pass on, simply observing a mind unit for several seconds, then waiting for the next one. The meditator's task is not to analyze or make associations or interpretations of the bubbles, but only to let them come and go.

Over a period of time, as the meditator engages in any of the four methods of mindfulness, insights about the nature of the mind develop. When this takes place mindfulness unfolds into insight. "The practice of insight begins at the point when mindfulness continues without lag," according to Goleman.

Do We Really Know What Happens In Meditation?

Even though the practice of meditation in its various forms has been in existence since ancient times, scientific research on meditation is an infant. To my knowledge, there have been no studies which compare, first, whether all of the methods of meditative concentration are the same; second, whether all of the methods of mindfulness-insight are the same; third, whether the category of meditative concentration is the same as the category of mindfulness-insight. The most thorough research to date has been conducted on a relative newcomer to the field of meditation, Transcendental Meditation (TM), which was first introduced into the United States in 1959. Since the late 1960's, researchers have been centering their efforts on various outcomes of this meditative concentration approach.

I would like to see research conducted on a series of topics for each meditation technique. First, *the workings of the approach* could be tabulated. By the workings I mean the events that take place while one is meditating. Some researchers have made beginnings into this area of research. Edward Maupin (1972) reports on five different responses by subjects to a Zen Meditation exercise of concentration on breathing. The responses were as follows: (1) dizziness and fogginess; (2) relaxation and calmness; (3) pleasant bodily sensations ("vibrations" and "waves," body feeling "suspended" or "light"); (4) vivid breathing sensations ("filled with air"); (5) concentration and detachment (a "non-striving" attitude). Arthur Deikman (1972), in an article called "Experimental Meditation," describes the sensations encountered by those undergoing a meditation exercise of concentration on a blue vase. Here are a few of the reactions: (1) ". . . a great deal of agitation . . . but it isn't agitating . . ."; (2) ". . . at that point all sounds were obliterated . . . somehow everything was out of my consciousness . . ."; (3) ". . . and it was during this incandescent kind of radiating inner glow thing I could feel my pulse beating in my head . . ." Both of these studies of the workings of meditation focus on the meditative concentration category. Data still need to be gathered on the mindfulness-insight category.

Psychological Response in Meditation

As a second major area of research on meditation, I would like to see *psychological responses, physiological responses, and spiritual responses* measured. Several researchers have discussed the psychological responses of meditators. Three of the more important reports include: Lawrence LeShan, in a chapter from his book, *How to Meditate* (1974), called "The Psychological Effects of Meditation"; two chapters from Harold Bloomfield's book, *TM* (1975), respectively titled "The Psychological Effects of Transcendental Meditation" and "Meditation and Psychotherapy"; and a chapter from John White's book, *What Is Meditation?* (1974), titled "Meditation as Metatherapy," written by Daniel Goleman.

LeShan talks of two major psychological effects of consistent meditation which he evidently feels come irrespective of the type of meditative experience in which one participates. These effects are, first, a change in one's way of perceiving and relating to reality and, second, gaining greater enthusiasm and efficiency in one's everyday existence. Expanding on these two effects, LeShan indicates that personality organization becomes stronger, that one gains an inner peace and an increased self-confidence.

Bloomfield reports a variety of psychological outcomes resulting from regular practice, specifically with Transcendental Meditation. Such things as improved performance in one's job, increased academic performance, reduced anxiety, increased ability to handle stress, increased ego strength, improved spontaneity, improved capacity for intimate contact, and increased happiness are noted. In another chapter, Bloomfield presents a series of cases where TM has improved psychiatric problems of a more severe nature.

Goleman indicates that there is often noticeable improvement in one's general psychological state as a result of meditation. Specifically, he feels that psychosomatic disorders are often improved as a result of practicing meditation. One of the goals of meditation is to rid one of accumulated tensions, whether these have been generated from current day-to-day functioning, or from events of the past which produced tension build-up. In reference to the latter point, Goleman feels that the outcomes of meditation deal with a far greater scope and depth than psychoanalysis.

These presentations of psychological responses to meditation are quite encouraging. There is still a tendency to lump all of the different types of meditation together. In spite of this fact, we can say that the potential for significant psychological change exists. A great deal of experimental work is needed to verify whether or not psychological changes always take place, no matter what type of meditation approach is employed.

Physiological Response in Meditation

The most complete analysis of the physiological outcomes of meditation has come from the research conducted on Transcendental Meditation. This research is a good model for the much needed research on other types of meditation. Results have shown that during Transcendental Meditation there is a significant reduction in oxygen consumption, a definite decrease in heart rate and blood flow from the heart, decreased skin conductivity (galvanic skin response reading indicating lowered anxiety), increases in slow alpha, and in skeletal muscle blood flow. TM physiological studies have also shown that there is a decrease in blood lactate and in physical measures of overall anxiety. Also, brain waves tend to synchronize during TM and there is improved autonomic stability and consequent resistance to stress. These results are impressive and are an excellent beginning, but much more needs to be done. As mentioned, other types of meditative concentration approaches need to analyze physiological outcomes, and then comparisons can be made. Following that step, the mindfulness category of approach could be studied and those outcomes compared with the meditative concentration category.

Spiritual Response in Meditation

Sources on meditation talk little about spiritual response in meditation. Those oriented toward a religious approach will speak often of religious response in meditation, but usually not in terms of specific material. These sources will speak in general terms about a closer relationship with God, but do not present concrete examples of the naturally occurring spiritual events of meditation, such as seeing light and religious symbols. Those sources not oriented toward religion tend to downplay the spiritual response of meditation. I imagine that the reason for this is because of the fear of becoming involved in "religious" issues. Most psychologists have a tendency to avoid the spiritual area because they feel it is not amenable to scientific measurement as are the physiological and psychological areas. Hopefully, this problem will be partially alleviated if we will start by tabulating spiritual experiences in meditation and Meditative Therapy. I believe differentiation between "spiritual" and "religious" material (see chapter 4) will aid in this study.

The Relationship Between Meditation and Meditative Therapy

Meditative Therapy comes closest to being what I would term an advanced mindfulness-insight meditation as explained by Goleman in his interpretation of *The Vissudhimaga* (1977). Remember that mindfulness is different than meditative concentration and that mindfulness leads into insight by "continuing without lag." Continuing without lag seems to suggest that, after preliminary structured mindfulness methods, one is to focus on all impressions coming into awareness, to passively accept them, and to allow the flow to continue. Such a position is very close to the manner in which Meditative Therapy is conducted.

In the second half of *The Varieties of the Meditative Experience*, Goleman reviews several systems of meditation. Some of these contain approaches which fit the advanced mindfulness-insight category and appear to be quite similar to Meditative Therapy. Those most notable are *shikan-taza* (Kapleau, 1967), a version of *Zazen* meditation; *vipassana* (Trungpa, 1973), a practice of Tibetan Buddhism; *self-remembering* of Gurdjieff (Walker, 1969); and Krishnamurti's *self-knowledge* (1960).

Claudio Naranjo (1971), in his half of the book, *On the Psychology of Meditation* (co-author Robert Ornstein), has identified a branch of meditation called *the way of surrender and self-expression*. Certain methods described in this branch also appear to belong in the advanced mindfulness-insight category. In addition to placing Zazen, or Za-Zen as he has written it, into this category, Naranjo also includes a Chinese practice called *wu-hsin*. From his short description of it, wu-hsin appears to be similar to Meditative Therapy.

Throughout the ages there have been other forerunners to Meditative Therapy, like shikan-taza, self-remembering, vipassana. The problem we face is the inadequate descriptions of these methods given by writers in the discipline. Typically, the descriptions are vague and general rather than clear and specific. Exact working details are very difficult to search out, such as how to begin the method, what happens when you do it, and how long a session should last.

When I compare mindfulness methods with Meditative Therapy, I am speaking of what I have termed advanced mindfulness-insight. The category of mindfulness has "structured" (what I would term *synthetic*), and "unstructured" (what I would term *natural*), approaches. Only those which appear to be natural and non-interfering will be considered in this discussion, with the exception of meditative concentration, which, even though I consider it to be synthetic in nature, is included in the comparison because it has implications for a later discussion.

The Differences Between Meditation and Meditative Therapy

Reflecting on the material just presented and the description of Meditative Therapy in Chapter 4, differences between concentrative meditation and advanced mindfulness-insight meditation approaches and Meditative Therapy may be viewed in terms of two principal factors: 1) the verbalization factor, and 2) the time-depth factor.

The Verbalization Factor

In all of the descriptions of the concentrative meditation and advanced mindfulness-insight meditation approaches I have read, there is no mention of describing inner contents aloud. In Meditative Therapy, one of the essential requirements is for the participant to give a continuous oral report of everything which takes place. "Is this a crucial difference?" you may ask. I have no "hard data" to back me up, but my belief is that ongoing verbalization of material is extremely important. Things said out loud either lose power or gain power on a much deeper level than when they are kept inside. Has this something to do with hypnotic autosuggestion, altered states, talking to oneself, confession, "clearing" one's life? Whatever the reason, spoken words appear to have a healing effect. Because they are out in the open, not hidden, words take on new meaning. One of my clients stated it clearly during her first Meditative Therapy session, "Boy, when you speak out loud, it's just awful, the words are bigger than the thoughts. Words make thoughts seem really silly."

Words also make thoughts seem wise. The other facet of verbalization is that words said out loud can be reinforcing in a positive way. An example would be, "I feel good about myself, I am feeling a lot more self-confident." How many of us say this out loud to ourselves even with our eyes open? Seldom do we even allow ourselves to think it. When the Inner Source prompts us to realize certain positive factors and then they are stated out loud, they take on a new power.

The Time-Depth Factor

The second difference centers around the amount of time one engages in a meditation or Meditative Therapy session. Most types of concentrative meditation require a pre-set amount of time, usually 15 to 20 minutes per day, in which one engages in the exercise. In Meditative Therapy, the Inner Source is allowed to decide how much time a weekly session should last. The amount of time is not pre-set and sessions may last from 30 minutes to 2½ hours. Most sessions seem to be around 1½ hours, especially when sessions are first undertaken. As the Inner Source "works through" material, the amount of time needed often levels out to 45 minutes to an hour.

Meditative concentration and other methods which pre-set the amount of time at 15 to 20 minutes, restrict the Inner Source in its opportunity to help. The depth of response is less in 15 minutes than it would be in 1½ hours. The Inner Source doesn't have time to develop and unfold a lengthy sequence or segment of material. Even accumulated time over the week in meditative concentration will not make any difference in terms of depth of response. By meditating in a concentrated manner for 20 minutes per day, one will end up with 140 minutes per week, approximately the amount of time involved in a weekly Meditative Therapy session. I contend that the amount of time spent in concentration could be doubled and the process still would not reach the depth of response which is usual in Meditative Therapy. In addition to the limited time, repeatedly coming back to one's focal point, a mantra, a star, breathing, restricts the free flow of the Inner Source.

Most of the sources writing about the advanced mindfulness-insight methods are not highly structured, and their explanations remain unclear or ambiguous. The only mention of the time factor I could find related to advanced mindfulness was given by the Zen Master Yasutani, as quoted in a book edited by Philip Kapleau (1967), *The Three Pillars of Zen*. Speaking of shikan-taza, Yasutani indicates that the participant should not engage in the practice for longer than 30 minutes at a sitting. I consider this to be a limiting factor in terms of depth of response. Only in Meditative Therapy and in those advanced mindfulness-insight approaches which allow the Inner Source unlimited time can deeper responses take place.

Below is an example of the type of deep response that wouldn't be allowed to develop in any approach which limits the amount of time the Inner Source can work. Moreover, this is the type of deep response which would be unlikely to take place in structured approaches like concentration or beginning mindfulness.

Sounds like that lady outside (*someone walking down the hallway*) has high heels on. Mother used to wear them. We had hardwood floors and it sounded neat. I wore them too, and I didn't sound that way. It was kind of a disappointment (*fast walking now in the hall*). That sounds a little more like me.

Even though I wore them all the time, I didn't sound like Mother. She looked nice in them, but she looks nice in a lot of things I don't. She's just different than I am. Sometimes we are the same, but it doesn't seem like we are. This doesn't seem like me now (*laughs*). It doesn't seem like we are the same at all. She's really not cold, but she is cold. She's not emotional, but she is emotional. She's not emotional because you can't see it, but she is because you can feel it. I'm not quite sure how to relate to it. My sisters can sometimes, but I can't. They lived with her longer than I did. But I always tried so hard, so maybe I didn't pick up on it. It doesn't seem to bother them; it doesn't get in their way, but it does me. It's not so bad now because I'm trying to like her. Not like her, feel at ease with her; letting myself open to figure her out. 'Cause I like her, you know? (*sniffs*) It's just that somehow I passed her by, I don't know why. She seems kind of a shy, quiet type, but she isn't really, because you can feel the pressure inside and I just kind of never looked at it. Maybe I kind of skirted around it 'cause I didn't want to know, I don't know. Dad was so easy to talk to, easier to understand. He and I got along well. He'd get mad, but you knew. Now he'd be mad, really mad. That's okay 'cause I got mad too, all the time. Maybe he and I are alike and Mom and sisters are alike, but I don't think so. I don't know really, maybe I'll never know. I can see her in this green dress, pretty. She wore it so much that it was ratty, ugly, but still pretty (*clears throat*). I guess that's why I always wanted her to come when I was sick or didn't feel good, but I never asked her. I wonder why (*voice cracks*). I asked her in a whisper so she couldn't hear. I think I was afraid of her 'cause, that's dumb, 'cause it seems like I could with Dad, 'cause he got mad. But my mother never got mad. I guess that's why I never asked her. I kind of went around an inch away. I was with her, but I'd always stay away. But that was why (*whispers*), that was really weird. That's why, wow. That's too bad, really too bad. Hmmm, seems so simple now, but (*sniffs*) I just wonder why she did that. I wonder why (*sniffs*). I wonder why (*shakes her head "no"*). Just why (*voice cracks, starts crying*). I just wonder why she didn't say anything, nothing. She must have known. I mean, she could see me, she wasn't dumb (*still crying*). She did that all the time.

This segment began about 10 minutes after her Meditative Therapy session started and lasted almost the entire session (55 minutes). It is difficult to imagine her interrupting this sequence regularly to return to her point of concentration or to automatically arise after 15 or 20 or 30 minutes due to a pre-set finishing time. The Inner Source must be allowed to conduct the session as it needs to, in order to do its work thoroughly.

Are All Oranges the Same?

Most proponents of certain systems of meditation either feel their particular approach is the *only* way, or they use various types of meditative concentration, beginning mindfulness, and advanced mindfulness-insight in their systems. When they take the latter stance, even though it is more broadminded, there is still a tendency to feel that their way of combining approaches into a system is superior to others. Is there a more universal way of looking at the problem?

The three authors to whom I've referred throughout this chapter, LeShan, Goleman, and Naranjo, write from a more synthesizing viewpoint. LeShan states that all forms of meditation lead to the same place eventually. Goleman says all paths have the common goal of retraining attention and that all paths merge at the end. The final goal reached is the same regardless of the type of meditative approach employed. Naranjo provides the most thorough analysis of the diverse forms of meditation and concludes that there is a "unity within the diversity." He states that, in spite of the categories in which we place types of meditation, they are all "different forms of a common endeavor." From the standpoint of our discussion, Naranjo would state that the concentrative path, the beginning mindfulness path, and the advanced mindfulness-insight path have an essential core. This unity is to be found in an *attitude*. He writes that "the attitude, or inner posture, of the meditator is both his path and his goal." Naranjo seems to be saying that no matter what form or brand of meditation you select, it will lead you to the same place as any other.

From reading this discussion of unity, I must assume that these three psychologists, when they read of Meditative Therapy, will not view it as different from other forms of meditation. We can hypothesize that they will feel Meditative Therapy is a method which would also lead to the same final goal. It seems to me that these authors are saying that, in the end, all oranges are the same no matter under what conditions they are grown.

I believe that there is a hierarchy of meditative related methods and that the hierarchy consists of lower or basic methods and higher or advanced methods. If you focus exclusively on lower methods, you will never achieve the advanced results possible with higher methods. Because the methods of meditative concentration, beginning mindfulness, advanced mindfulness-insight, and Meditative Therapy are different, they lead to different outcomes. All oranges are not the same.

I am *not* stating that the deep methods are to be used *to the exclusion* of the basic methods, nor that they are ''the answer'' for all purposes. Each method is purposeful at its own level, but the most natural method is needed at some point in order for the greatest potential to be reached. We each need different methods ranging from basic to advanced at different points in our development. Depending upon our readiness, we may find a basic method the best place to begin. Others will find that the advanced methods fit their developmental pattern. Some will use a few, others all the meditation methods, in the stride toward enlightenment. Ultimately, the highest method of meditation, the one that allows the Inner Source its full realm of response, the one that trusts fully in our deepest knowing, will need to be chosen.

I believe that Meditative Therapy and perhaps other advanced methods of meditation are the master methods. These methods go beyond the abilities of the lower methods in leading one to the ultimate goal of full functioning. Used to the exclusion of other methods of meditation or therapy, none of the advanced methods will be complete, even though they will still produce excellent results.

All oranges are not the same. Soil conditions are different. Climatic conditions are different. There is not any reason to assume that they are all the same under varying conditions of growth. Perhaps there is one most important factor responsible for the ultimate orange, but if that factor is used in isolation, the orange will not be at the top when compared to oranges grown with all factors functioning. Meditative Therapy and advanced mindfulness-insight methods may be the ultimate methods, but used in isolation, they will never lead to full development as a person.

6

Light:
The Universal Source, Symbol, and Reality

Vain and unconscious men surrounded by the halo of science, under pretense that the spiritual light which guided humanity in the past was unreal, have raised opaque veils covered with obscure symbols, in order to hide the Light. They did not understand that what mattered was the human orientation which resulted therefrom, and that this reality could not be denied, whereas the Light itself was not of their realm.

—Lecomte du Nouy

A phenomenon of incalculable importance throughout human history, light is a central feature of the experience of Meditative Therapy for many persons. The presence of light is so powerful, so pervasive, so tangible, so symbolic that the subject demands further attention. This chapter explores the significance of light in relationship to Meditative Therapy.

Weller Embler, writing in the September, 1974 issue of *ETC: A Review of General Semantics*, stated:

And God said, Let there be light; and there was light. That was in the beginning; and ever since, of all the images of the spiritual life, light has taken a foremost place in the religions of the world, from pagan sunworship to the mystical philosophies of our own time. One of the four or five irreducible facts of human existence, light serves as the perfect figure of speech for a benign, abiding, and all-encompassing feature of the universe. In light there is truth, insofar as we can know the truth, from that which is shed by the faintest candle flame to the blazing splendor of a midsummer sun. And no other words seem quite as revealing of the mystical experience as those related to light: illumination, enlightenment, inner light, vision, radiant, burning, shining, dazzling, bright. Of all the English devotional verse of the seventeenth century, none is lovelier than that of Henry Vaughan. For Vaughan, light is the supreme mystical image, and he uses it in virtually all his poems. The first lines of "The World" are well known:

> I saw eternity the other night
> Like a great ring of pure and endless light
> All calm as it was bright.

Plato's Allegory of the Cave (in Book VII of *The Republic*) is the most famous extended figure of speech on the subject of philosophical enlightenment. The cave, it will be recalled, represents the world as a prison. In the cave, a fire at a distance behind the prisoners causes them to see only their shadows, which the fire has thrown on the opposite wall of the cave. The mouth of the cave, however, is open to the light of the sun. If a prisoner were released and turned toward the entrance, the glare of the sun would be so painful he would wish to return to the life of illusion to which he has been accustomed. But if he is compelled to ascend out of the cave and into the very light of the sun, at first he will be blinded and unable to see the realities of true existence.

Eventually he will become adjusted to the new light and his vision will grow ever clearer until he can behold the sun in its glory. Then when he remembers his life in the cave and the want of wisdom among his companions there, he will pity them and would rather endure anything than return to the den of shadows, ignorance, and error.

The Allegory of the Cave is a classic statement of Platonism, in the west the ancestral home of mystical philosophy. Among other meanings and interpretations, note that the fire in the cave is "like" the sun and even partakes of certain of the sun's properties; and so, too, the shadows of the inhabitants are similar to the prisoners themselves. Yet the fire is but the palest replica of the light of the universe, and the shadows but the vaguest abstractions of true being. All the furnishings of the world are mere appearance. At best they stand only for the ideal, which is seen darkly through them; but when, metaphorically speaking, we have found our way to the "light," we are vouchsafed a new vision, knowledge of the truth.

Is there more to the above statements than metaphor? "Raining cats and dogs;" "a mighty fortress is our God;" "music is the breath of our soul;" these are metaphors. Cats and dogs don't really come down; God isn't literally a mighty fortress; we don't breathe music. Embler seems to be implying that light is not a "real" internal event. How have others viewed internal light?

In *Visionary Experience*, a speech given in 1961, Aldous Huxley talks about methods used for aeons to induce what he terms *visionary experiences*. Such topics as hypnosis, sensory isolation, one-pointed concentration, breathing, fasting, sleep deprivation, self-torture, and ingestion of various mind-altering substances such as hashish, LSD and alcohol are discussed as methods of inducing the visionary experience. According to Huxley, the highest common factor of these visionary experiences is the light experience. He states that for all religions, light is the major divine symbol, and notes that light experience is quite often described in the Bible and other religious literature.

Huxley divides light into two forms, undifferentiated and differentiated. The differentiated light experience is in reference to objects, such as people or landscapes, which are aglow with a light of their own. The undifferentiated light experience is one in which everything envisioned is shining with light. All is surrounded by light no matter what the context. This all-encompassing light experience is the one most closely aligned with a genuine mystical or religious experience, Huxley says.

Gaskell's (1960) *Dictionary of all Scriptures and Myths* indicates:

In regard to the scheme of the symbolism, it will be found that in the sacred writings the activities which apparently are of the outer world of sense stand really for the activities of the

inner world of thought. The apparent sense-world of consciousness symbolises the real soul-world of humanity, in which we
become aware of all the emotions, faculties and activities of the
soul's experience of life.

If in the country on a fine day, we stand fronting a pool of
water, we may observe a prospect which beautifully pictures
the higher and the lower things of the soul and the cosmos, as
expressed in the Sacred Language of all Myths and Scriptures.

Sun-realm;	Light;	Celestial.
Sky-realm;	Fire;	Spiritual.
Air-realm;	Air;	Mental.
Water-realm;	Water;	Astral.
Earth-realm;	Earth;	Physical.

These ideograms are universal symbols of the Five Planes of
Existence, all in their proper order, that is, from the highest
(most inward) to the lowest (most outward) states of existence.
They are recognised in all the Sacred Books of the world, and
this Dictionary cannot be understood without regard to them.
Knowledge of the Five Planes and their symbols makes it easy
to at once make out the meanings of many other associated
symbols. In the Sun-realm is the Sun, a symbol of God-
manifest, or the Higher Self who passes through the whole
Cycle of Divine Life (zodiac) in a series of twelves stages (year).
In the Sky-realm are the higher emotions (bright clouds), and
the transmuting Fire of Wisdom (the lightning) which purifies
the human soul, life after life. In the Air-realm are the mental
faculties (people) and lower emotions (animals), also instincts
(plants), and aspirations (birds). In the Water-realm are re-
flected inversely the motives and things of the higher planes,
and these bring delusion and error into the soul. In the Earth-
realm are the outer conditions of mental activity (work) and progress (walking).(p. 14)

Later on in the *Dictionary* under the headings of *Light; Light,
Primordial; Light-Realm; Light-Treasure; Light-World; Lightning or
Lightning Flash*; are documented references to the light experience
from world-wide sources on religion and literature. Gaskell's

definition of Light-World is "a symbol of that state of consciousness which corresponds to an extension of spiritual vision which perceives the Truth and the Life within." (p. 453)

Summarizing the sources quoted above one can begin to observe that the *inner experiencing of light* is an event of ultimate importance. It has been accorded the highest place of significance as a religious and spiritual symbol and event throughout history. Let us further examine light from the perspectives of religious and mystical sources and sources on meditation and Meditative Therapy.

Light as Discussed in Religious and Mystical Sources

There are over fifty direct references to light in the Bible. Presented below are several of the most pertinent quotes, many in Christ's own words.

The Bible:

St. Matthew 5 (Christ's words):

14 Ye are the light of the world. A city that is set on an hill cannot be hid.

15 Neither do men light a candle, and put it under a bushel, but on a candlestick; and it giveth light unto all that are in the house.

16 Let your light so shine before men, that they may see your good works, and glorify your Father which is in heaven.

St. Matthew 6:

22 The light of the body is the eye: if, therefore, thine eye be single thy whole body shall be full of light.

23 But if thine eye be evil, thy whole body shall be full of darkness. If, therefore, the light that is in thee be darkness, how great is that darkness!

Essentially the same material from St. Matthew is given again in St. Luke, 11 (again these are Christ's words):

33 No man, when he hath lighted a candle, putteth it in a secret place, neither under a bushel, but on a candlestick, that they which come in may see the light.

34 The light of the body is the eye; therefore, when thine eye is single, thy whole body also is full of light; but when thine eye is evil, thy body also is full of darkness.

35 Take heed, therefore, that the light which is in thee be not darkness.

36 If thy whole body, therefore, be full of light, having no part dark, the whole shall be full of light, as when the bright shining of a candle doth give thee light.

St. John 1:

4 In him was life; and the life was the light of men.

5 And the light shineth in the darkness; and the darkness comprehended it not.

6 & 7 There was a man sent from God, whose name was John. The same came for a witness, to bear witness of the Light, that all men through him might believe.

8 He was not that Light, but was sent to bear witness of that Light.

9 That was the true Light, which lighteth every man that cometh into the world.

St. John 3 (Christ's words):

19 And this is the condemnation, that light is come into the world, and men loved darkness rather than light, because their deeds were evil.

20 For every one that doeth evil hateth the light, neither cometh to the light, lest his deeds should be reproved.

21 But he that doeth truth cometh to the light, that his deeds may be made manifest, that they are wrought in God.

St. John 8:

12 Then spake Jesus again unto them, saying, I am the light of the world: he that followeth me shall not walk in darkness, but shall have the light of life.

The Bhagavad Gita

This is the Hindu book containing the divine Krishna's words (Stanford, 1970).

He who finds his joy within
Within, his grove of pleasure
And the light of the sun within,
Merging with God, he gains God's bliss. (p. 45)

When the light that is knowledge
Shows in all the doors of the body
Then it may be known
That goodness is in power. (p. 103)

Books of the Dead: Egyptian and Tibetan

Books of the dead were thought to be written to prepare those who were ready to die for the afterlife. In actuality, they have much to say to the living also. The *Book of the Dead* (Budge, 1960) from the Egyptian hieroglyphics refers often to light, especially as contrasted with darkness. The Light-god, the Sun-god, and gods who dwell in the circle of Light are other items of interest. The Tibetan *Book of the Dead* (Leary, 1964) speaks throughout of the clear Light of Reality which one sees.

Edgar Cayce Material

Edgar Cayce was a psychic who would go into a self-induced trance state and give "readings" for people in reference to their concerns. Originally, the readings were geared toward physical body concerns, but later "life readings" were given. These covered a broad spectrum of topics related to all aspects of life. Throughout the readings there is a basic Christian perspective, although not a specific dogmatic approach.

The *Individual Reference File* (Turner, 1970), a compilation of extracts from the Edgar Cayce records, contains the following material on the subject of light:

Page 36. Nothing prevents—only self. Keep self and the shadow away. Turn thy face to the light and the shadows fall behind. (987-4)

Page 55. Question: What is the meaning of the white lightning I have seen? Answer: That awakening that is coming.

More and more as the white light comes to thee. More and more will there be the awakening. (987-4)

Page 63. For, as is given in the beginning: God moved and said, "Let there be light," and there was light; not the light of the sun but rather that of which, through which, in which every soul had, has and ever has its being. (5246-1)

Page 99. Know first and foremost . . . that the Lord thy God is one! Then know too, that thyself is one—thy ego, thy I Am. Thy purposes then, thy heart and thy life must be a consistent thing! For if thine eye be single (thy I AM, that is, the purposes the desires, and ye work at it!), then thy WHOLE BODY is full of light. (1537-1)

Page 180. These depend upon what the entity does with that mind seeking—ever seeking light. (1947-3)

The Cayce material speaks repeatedly of the light one is seeking through meditation. Penny Baker, in *Meditation, A Step Beyond with Edgar Cayce* (1973), holds that the ultimate goal of meditation is to see the white light which is symbolic of the "Christ consciousness." At certain times, this light will be a tiny speck, and at times it will be all inclusive, all enfolding "with a shining warmth of undescribable proportions." Elsie Seachrist also speaks from the view of the Cayce readings. In the tape, *Meditation, The Art of Listening*, she contends that through meditation comes the light, and that the voice of God is embodied in the light.

Jacob Boehme

Jacob Boehme, termed the Christian mystic, talks of light and the light-world considerably in his work written in 1620, *Six Theosophic Points* (1620). He refers to light as God's Kingdom and that the property of the white clear light is gentleness as contrasted to the dark world whose property is fierceness or hostility. Boehme speaks in terms of "an internal light," "the inward center of light," and "the inward light." Evelyn Underhill (1911) states that Boehme also called the inner light "God's light in thy soul" and "the Light of the Majesty."

The Secret of the Golden Flower

The Secret of the Golden Flower, an ancient Chinese text on meditation, translated and explained by Richard Wilhelm (1962) with commentary by the famous psychologist C. G. Jung, has been termed a "light religion" and speaks a great deal about the internal world of brightness and lightness. At one point the text states:

> The light is not in the body alone, nor is it only outside the body. Mountains and rivers and the great earth are lit by sun and moon; all that is this light. Therefore it is not only within the body. Understanding and clarity, perception and enlightenment, and all movements (of the spirit) are likewise this light; therefore it is not just something outside the body. The light-flower of heaven and earth fills all the thousand spaces. But also the light-flower of the individual body passes through heaven and covers the earth. Therefore, as soon as the light is circulating, heaven and earth, mountains and rivers, are all circulating with it at the same time. To concentrate the seed-flower of the human body above in the eyes, that is the great key of the human body. Children, take heed! If for a day you do not practise meditation, this light streams out, who knows whither? If you only meditate for a quarter of an hour, by it you can do away with the ten thousand aeons and a thousand births. All methods end in quietness. This marvellous magic cannot be fathomed. (p. 33)

In the second part of the book, Jung, in his commentary on the Golden Flower, quotes a description of an illumination experience of Edward Maitland in 1896. After the quote, Jung goes on to say that:

> This genuine experience contains all the essential symbols of our text. The phenomenon itself, that is, the vision of light, is an experience common to many mystics, and one that is undoubtedly of the greatest significance, because in all times and places it appears as the unconditional thing, which unites in itself the greatest energy and the profoundest meaning. (p. 106)

After quoting a description of another light experience of a woman named Hildegarde of Bingen, a mystic, Jung goes on to state:

I know a few individuals who are familiar with this phenomenon from personal experience. As far as I have been able to understand it, the phenomenon seems to have to do with an acute state of consciousness, as intensive as it is abstract, a "detached" consciousness, which, as Hildegarde pertinently remarks, brings up to consciousness regions of psychic events ordinarily covered with darkness. The fact that the general bodily sensations disappear during such an experience suggests that their specific energy has been withdrawn from them, and apparently gone towards heightening the clarity of consciousness. As a rule, the phenomenon is spontaneous, coming and going on its own initiative. Its effect is astonishing in that it almost always brings about a solution of psychic complications, and thereby frees the inner personality from emotional and intellectual entanglements, creating thus a unity of being which is universally felt as "liberation."

Evelyn Underhill's Mysticism

In her classic book, *Mysticism*, written in 1911, Evelyn Underhill has a wonderful chapter entitled, "The Illumination of the Self." She describes the experiences and writings of many individuals who have known the inner light. Included in the list are St. Teresa, St. Augustine, St. Francis of Assisi, St. John of the Cross, Dante, St. Hildegarde, and St. Catherine of Genoa. Underhill indicates that St. Teresa called the inner light "a light which knows no night." St. Augustine spoke of it as "the Light that never changes." Mechthild of Magdeburg referred to it as "the flowing light of the Godhead." Dante felt it to be "Light Eternal." St. Hildegarde wrote of it as "a special light, more brilliant than the brightness round the sun." Finally, Evelyn Underhill in her own descriptions of the inner light speaks of it as "the Uncreated Light," "the Divine Light," "the Inward Light," and "that Light whose smile kindles the universe."

Light in Meditation and Meditative Therapy

In the material cited in the preceding section, two examples from meditation sources referred to light: the Cayce material and the material on *The Secret of the Golden Flower*. In this section, we will observe that Luthe has noted bright light experiences in Autogenic Abreaction as being quite similar to those experienced in advanced stages of Zen and Yoga. We can see that light is an event recognized or a theme recurring in various meditation sources.

Of our three sources on natural approaches to the inner realm, only Luthe speaks directly about light. Writing in Volume VI of *Autogenic Therapy, Treatment with Autogenic Neutralization* (1973), he devotes an entire chapter to what he terms "Unusual Brightness and Related Phenomena." He has broken brightness down into three categories: (1) bright color phase; (2) bright light phase; (3) very bright light phase. In his sample of 100 patients suffering from neurotic and psychosomatic disorders, only 20% had an unusual brightness experience. All 20% had a "bright color" experience, 12% had a "bright light" experience, and only 5% a "very bright light" experience.

Generally, it has been found from observing Autogenic Abreaction process that as therapy progresses colors become lighter. Conversely, if therapy regresses (often due to resistance on an individual's part), colors become darker. Darker shades of color are also predominant when the inner-directed content is very upsetting, such as when dealing with death or anxiety-provoking situations.

Luthe explains further that the individuals who do experience unusual brightness phenomena do so on relatively rare occasions. He also points out that this brightness phenomena of Autogenic Abreaction appears to have some relationship to similar experiences noted in advanced Zen meditation and in Yoga states of ecstasy. Luthe's analysis of the very bright light phase appears to have implications along the lines of enlightenment or illumination often described in spiritual literature. In addition to the very intense brightness, the experience was found to be described as "boundless empty space and void of any structural, chromatic or dynamic components." During the experience one has feelings of euphoria, is very impressed by the event, and feels warm, relaxed, and heavy. After its completion, one feels liberated, as if the consciousness has been expanded, and feels calm, but full of energy.

I used a sample of 75 clients to evaluate light experiences. The sample contained 38 males, 37 females, with an average of 4.5 Meditative Therapy sessions. The number of sessions ranged from a minimum of one to a maximum of 18.

My approach to analyzing light experiences in Meditative Therapy transcripts was threefold. First, they were examined to see if any light experience of any type was present. Second, the recordings were looked at to see if any form of light-dark interaction took place. Finally, the material was analyzed in order to compare my results with Luthe's results in reference to bright color, bright light, and very bright light phenomena. All of this data is presented in Table 6-1. As will be observed, a total of 83% of the 75-client population reported seeing some form of light. Although a wide variety of examples were given, selected examples are presented in the table. The category of light-dark interaction shows that 60% of the group observed this experience. Again, typical examples are given. For these first two outcomes there is, to my knowledge, no previous data from the professional literature with which to compare. For the third set of outcomes, we do have the Luthe material for comparison. Before discussing this area, I will present one 40-year-old woman's extended experience with light-dark interaction. The following segments took place during her fourth session. The session began at 9:16 a.m.

I see like a paddle wheel slowly rotating. Black and white alternates on the paddles. I feel really scared and tingly all over, and I hear a motor and I don't remember hearing anything before. It is just droning. There is a light, like a meteor, with sort of an expanded tail. Like the tail has a lot of pieces. The light is heavy in the center and fading off. Black sky with thousands of white lights. A giant snail, white body in a black shell. A rainbow, white under and black on top, split in the middle. Unbelievably bright under it, white, all light. Florescent light, like neon lights, all white. Like the tip of the top is folding in and a lot of black liquid is coming down over the top. (*Starts sobbing*) I don't know why it makes me cry. (*9:20*) White rose spinning in black (*sobbing stops*), right in the middle. The leaves are black too, but the rose is beautiful (*takes a deep breath*). Light again, blinding white light, can't see the source. Over on the left looks like fans backwards, up and down whirlpool instead of on a flat surface. I'm hearing the dog (*outside*). There's the light again. I'm very dry, my legs feel really tight, been knotted up just terribly. I can't push them down enough — just pulled tight tendons. I see two little tubs of water, like footbaths, framework in between. Now it looks like a scale. White light is sitting on each one and now one has black on it. Black is weighing it down really heavy. Somebody is pulling on the sides of the weight parts, I can't see who. A lot of light around the one side, but not very heavy. A liquid white wave going over a black surface, like a wave moving fast over black sand. The black is all churning into hill forms, not flat, moving, flops over on the white trapping it. (*Starts sobbing*) (*9:25*)

These creative interactions between black and white continued to take place. At 9:45 she reported:

Such a war going on between white and black (*starts sobbing*).

Later she stated:

I'm so tired. It's all black, all black. (*Starts sobbing*) Psychedelic black shaking. I want to turn away from it.

At 10:20 she had the following experience:

A fan of blue light. Fan went backwards. White and black. Black and white. White fluffy cloud and a hole in the cloud. I'm looking through — a shaft. Grand Canyon. Feet, bare feet. A sandy beach, late afternoon. Sun's going down. (*She takes a big stretch*) (*At this point, she starts groaning, hitting her hands and feet on the mat, writhing all over, and yelling and screaming. It appeared to be like a temper tantrum.*) Oh God! (*Starts sobbing*) (*She rolls over on her stomach*) (*Coughing and sobbing—clears her throat and takes a deep breath)* On the train riding through a tunnel. Train is black, tunnel walls are white. A black river dried up with white. A white landscape. A black pinpoint in the distance.

At 10:38 she gave the following description:

Sun in the sky. Things are happening within the white light, but most I just see the white light. It's like being in the face of God. It doesn't stay, keeps getting away. I'm playing the piano. I'm on the wing of an airplane. Sun on my face. Big sunset, a lot of white clouds, but a big sunset behind it. I hear organ music. A big sunset all around the organ. *(Her eyes open) (10:45)*

This 1½-hour experience was quite confusing and obviously upsetting for my client, but she had learned to trust her Inner Source in therapy because of significant positive changes in her life to this point. As you can observe, her Inner Source brought her out of the session with a pleasant experience and a peaceful feeling. The necessity of this session became clear to us during her next session because the light personally guided her throughout. (This experience is given in the chapter to follow under the section, "Communication with Discarnate Entities").

Returning to Table 6-1, we can see that my group of 75 included 19% who experienced *bright color* at some point, 44% *bright light*, and none *very bright light*. The bright color experienced from the Luthe sample, 20%, and my sample, 19%, show close agreement. The bright light, Luthe 12%, my sample 44%, and the very bright light, Luthe 5%, my sample 0%, are not in agreement. The most obvious reason for this discrepancy is that Luthe and I are using different criteria to evaluate the two categories. Personally, I feel that the "very bright light" category is easy to determine because of the criteria Luthe presents. I feel that I had no cases in my sample. Another possible reason for the difference could be that our samples were not comparable; e.g., problem severity, different countries, different age groups.

Table 6-1
Manifestation of Various Types of Light
Experience Occurring in a Group of
Seventy-Five Counseling Clients

EXPERIENCE	PERCENT REPORTING	TYPICAL EXAMPLES
A. Any type of light	83%	"I keep getting flashes, like sheet lightning." "My eyes have a very light stroboscopic effect, have a light blinking, only on the left side though." "Like light radiating from concentric circles." "Picture the sun, feel the warmth of the sun." "All of a sudden it seems light in here (opens and closes eyes). I don't know if that was the cue (to finish the session) or not. Did you turn the light on? (No) Oh."
B. Light-Dark Interaction	60%	"There is a dark tunnel with faint light at the end." "Darkness and a few light spots in my visual field, kind of a sweeping motion to the right, like a windshield wiper wiping away. It got lighter." "Light and dark that swirls around like clouds, reminds me of Greek Mythology—in the beginning there was Chaos." "Almost like an entrance to a cave, there's a darkness and a lightness." "Something about dark and light. Darkness negative and

| (Table 6-1 continued) | | |
EXPERIENCE	PERCENT REPORTING	TYPICAL EXAMPLES
		evil, light is like good stuff. I'm wandering around in my mind between them.''
C1. Bright Color	19%	"Very bright red on the left" "A lot of bright blue light" "Bright colored foil"
C2. Bright Light	44%	"Like I'm waking up, real bright, like looking at the sun with eyes closed." "Feel like it's got a bright light on in there." "Hmmm, a real bright flash will come, so bright. If you were looking, you would want to turn your head."
C3. Very Bright Light	0%	(No individuals reported this experience)

Although my sample produced no one who experienced the "very bright light" experience, I had one individual who experienced Huxley's "undifferentiated light experience." Huxley (1972) described it as being a state where everything one sees internally is enshrouded with light. Light seems to be shining everywhere one looks in the inner experience. This individual's undifferentiated light experience came on two occasions: during his seventh session of Meditative Therapy and during his final (thirteenth) session. I have presented an analysis of his total experience along two lines, white light-golden light and spiritual material-religious material, in Table 6-2. Both are given because of their predominance and close correspondence. One will note that sessions 7 and 13 are the undifferentiated light experiences. This individual, from my own personal viewpoint, is the most completely spiritual person I know. Although not a minister, he is one who actively attempts to live spiritually in all phases of his life: diet, exercise, money, relationships with others, sex.

Table 6-2
A Presentation of one Individual's Meditative Therapy Experiences in Reference To White Light-Golden Light and Spiritual Material-Religious Material

White Light—Golden Light

I see you with a little flash-light looking down on me, like down on the floor with a flashlight - other than that the sky is filled with sparkly lights - like 2 balls of light connected together - there are a lot of these. (#1)

I see a path or road like in Biblical times, shepherds, boy is walking down - donkey with load - loaf of bread in a sack under his arm. A lot of light - the road funnels way down and light at the end - like there's - a central light and people worshiping it - like a saint with light rad-iating out of the head - really feel that light. Description is very inadequate. (#2)

Feeling of a lot of light (in-direct) shining up above - see light, but can't see the source. (#6)

See beautiful golden candel-abra with a dozen or so candles - everything golden - flame and candles, every-thing golden. (#7)

Spiritual Material-Religious Material

See a stained glass window and Saint-like figure up above. (#1)

Saw a green angel and a star right in the middle of my head. (#6)

See a big cross of light just above me, above my face. (#7)

See a, like a necklace, metal-white inlaid stones. In the cen-ter a figure resembling a Madonna holding a child. A very beautiful piece of jewelry. (#7)

I hear Christmas music now. (#7)

Also toward the end of number 7 he said: "I just feel very good about tonight, I just feel peace and contentment are going to be mine."

And at the completion his eyes felt puffy.

Just feel like saying, "We need to know that God is with us." (#8)

A medallion - stone in it - very

(Table 6-2 continued)

White Light-Golden Light	Spiritual Material-Religious Material
All night I have been feeling a great deal of light - almost everything I see has light attached to it in some way. See a young girl kneeling now - but behind her is a great deal of light. (#7)	brilliant - shiny-round-smooth. Keeps changing like from a Buddha to Virgin Mary to different things. (#8)
	Got words running through my head: ''Jesus is love.'' (#8)
See Jane (deceased wife) dressed in a light colored gown, carrying a lantern - very bright light shining from it - peaceful. She looks very young - very pure - holding the lantern up in front of her. (#7)	Cross in front of me - crucifix - Christ was on - lifted it up and He smiled. (#9)
	People going to a church - father all dressed in pure white-like an angel. A White, very bright Bible, trimmed in gold. (#10)
Feel a golden light up above my head and I am feeling kind of a glowing or tingling in my groin area. (#8)	Hear ''Ye are God's children - be of patience and be enduring.'' (#12)
See many people sitting and praying. A source of light is coming down. Back in time - feeling of the Last Supper. I know what they are looking at but I don't see it—the cross - crucifixion - too bright and brilliant to look directly at. See these different images of the crucifixion - head glowing like star in a halo. Some are getting the impression of ''Bless you,'' ''Bless you,'' - others - ''It's not so hard,'' ''It's not so hard.'' (#11)	Sensation of bells - don't hear - see them swinging, one above head, one in head, one in my chest. Faintly hear them, like the bells that ring at Mass when they say the Hail Marys and so forth. (#13)
	The song:"I can see clearly now, the rain is gone"- see Jesus standing in my forehead - arms stretched out - there was a beam of light and He was standing on that and a rocket came out of my head and then several birds, little white doves flew by his side. (#13)

(Table 6-2 continued)	
White Light-Golden Light	**Spiritual Material-Religious Material**
Bright light shining on my forehead over the left eye. (#12)	"I see a little angel playing a golden harp, sitting on a cloud, surrounded by light." (#13)
"I still feel that light in my forehead. It has stayed there pretty much, kind of a burning. Just—I see a Christmas tree, all lit up, star at top. A big, shining tree—big, shining, in the shape of a tree." (#13)	
"I see my sister kneeling and praying. Praying for me. I feel a lot of light in my head." (#13)	

One other case is of interest in our discussion of light. This 20-year-old woman wrote the following description after her second Meditative Therapy session. Her first session had been extremely "heavy." She had dealt with a good deal of severely psychologically disturbing material relating to her parents and to her own sanity. The reason I asked her to write the description is because at the end of the session she stated, among other things, "It was like somebody took a light and illumined my whole body. My body got so big and so inflated. I remember thinking why can this happen here and not when I'm meditating." Her written description is as follows:

It was as if there were a bright light encompassing my whole body. My body seemed to inflate and balloon out and "I", the "me-ness" of my body, seemed to be filled and carried with this light. The light moved through my body from the outer edges to the center, taking my "me-ness" with it and leaving a huge, inflated shell that I was aware of but not in. The light then narrowed into a stream of an intensity I would imagine a laser beam to have and focused deep down somewhere, no place physical that I can point to, just dep in my "me-ness." It kept getting brighter and smaller and it went back in time or my memories. I felt like I was reliving my life, yet not seeing any pictures or memories, it was as if the light was moving backwards in time at a fast pace and I was carried along with it. As it went it seemed to go back to the time I was born and even beyond that. This was only a feeling; I had no pictures in my mind but I felt as though my brain was taking me back past any conscious memory I could possibly have. The one picture I did have in my mind was of how vast my body got—it seemed to look like one of those gaseous genies in a bottle that are so huge when they come out—yet they are tied or united to their magic bottle by a thin trail of smoke. That's the picture I saw: my "me-ness" united to this huge form by a thin string of smoke. Meanwhile my laser light kept taking me back, back, and it seemed so cosmic and almost tied into the inner breath of life-type feeling. I felt like I'd stopped breathing and so at peace. I really got into enjoying the trip because my inconsequential thoughts that popped in every once in a while didn't disturb the feeling of going back in time. After awhile the light seemed to be focused on the lump in my throat where I'd tried to hold down my tears, and I came to realize that at any other time, I'd interpret the intensity of the light on my throat as intense pain. It focused on my throat for quite awhile until I felt restless and wanted to get up and move because I felt so much energy. The lump in my throat dissolved. A very cosmic "trippy" trip. I feel great.

Implications

The most remarkable implication of this chapter is that each and every one of us has the potential to experience the same light that most have thought only reserved for great souls such as Jesus or Buddha. The light may not appear much at first, or may only present itself in small amounts, but as one chooses to allow the Inner Source to work through the internal darkness, one becomes more and more filled with light. Gaining more and more light, each expresses that light differently. We can all be "Saints" in our own way, at our own level of development.

I am aware that the reports of light from my Meditative Therapy clients and the reports given in the various sources I have quoted are all quite subjective. At this point, there is no way of verifying the client's reports of content in Meditative Therapy, whether it is an experience of light or visualizing childhood.

Perhaps one day we will be able to physically measure the appearance of internal light and correlate the degree and quality of light with progress towards complete health and enlightenment. In his book *The Highest State of Consciousness*, John White (1972) speaks of the possibility that enlightenment may be a physical and measurable event in the brain. He was stimulated to take this view because of reading *The Divine Animal* by anthropologist Roger Wescott (1969). Wescott feels that consciousness may be "internal bioluminescence" or an actual form of light within one's brain. Interestingly, the sources cited in this chapter point in the same direction.

Experiencing light in Meditative Therapy is not the final goal. In fact, sources on meditation almost invariably state that we have to be very careful about becoming attached to any type of inner experience. Lawrence LeShan, in his book *How to Meditate* (1974), has a section called, "Great White Lights and How to Avoid Them," in which he relates a story about the Zen master, Dogen. One of Dogen's students was reputed to have come one day to report that during meditation he had suddenly seen a great white light with the Buddha behind it. Dogen's reply was, "That's nice; if you concentrate on your breathing, it will go away." The point LeShan is making, and which most other meditation sources stress, is not to get carried away by anything that comes up during meditation or as he terms it "the trap of exciting phenomena." Meditative Therapy requires essentially the same thing. It is important to stress, however, that one must simply accept what comes. In Meditative Therapy we are not trying to eliminate any experience if the Inner Source wants it to be there. For example, Dogen's reply might lead one to believe that it would be bad to see light in future meditations. My point is that, if light kept coming during subsequent meditations, the experience should be accepted rather than held on to or avoided or shunned. If the Inner Source wishes to present light, or anything else, it is best to allow it. Our job is to be patient and to allow, not force, things to come. One should not get carried away and wish for another white light experience or try to make it appear, but just keep allowing the Inner Source to flow.

Now I would like to add a personal comment that you might consider to be hedging on what I have just said. Perhaps I am caught in a "trap," but I am personally very thankful when light comes to me. Most of my experiences come during the night rather than during my Meditative Therapy sessions. After I have slept for a number of hours, I will at times awaken to a shining source. The source and degree of brightness vary in form: sometimes a bright sun or flashlight, and sometimes less bright patches or squares of light. As this is written, it has appeared seven times in the last six months. It comes at times of its choice, not mine. I have not been able to predict when it will visit me, or to tie its appearance to any specific acts or series of acts of mine. I try not to become smug or complacent or decide that that's all there is, but I still can't help feeling privileged to have been granted the light. The evidence in this chapter is too overwhelming for me. When I experience the light I look at that as one good example that I am growing in the right direction. To me, light is the highest signpost along the way.

In closing this chapter on light, I would like to share one short quote from an older woman during her first Meditative Therapy session:

People should be illuminous shapes of light. They are sometimes, but there's so much hurt shoved away inside that I guess it can't get out and so it dims all the light. The light is lost, such a shame. And you don't see it happening; you don't know it. It comes slowly, a little bit at a time, and all of a sudden, it's all gone.

7

The World of PSI:
Parapsychological Frontiers in Meditative Therapy

The B-region, then, is obviously the larger part of each of us, for it is the abode of everything that is latent and the reservoir of everything that passes unrecorded or unobserved . . . It is the source of our dreams, and apparently they may return to it. In it arise whatever mystical experiences we may have . . . our supra-normal cognitions, if such there be, and if we are telepathic subjects.

— William James

There are a variety of experiences that take place naturally in Meditative Therapy that are difficult to explain by ordinary means. I place these under the heading of parapsychological or psychic events (I am using the terms interchangeably). J.B. Rhine and J. Pratt (1957), in *Parapsychology, The Frontier Science of the Mind*, define parapsychology as "a division of psychology dealing with behavioral or personal effects that are demonstrably nonphysical (that is, which do not fall within the scope of physical principles)." Some of the experiences described in this chapter might not be categorized as "parapsychological" by a professional parapsychologist. Nevertheless, following the definition given above, all of the experiences listed here "fit" into that terminology.

Although parapsychological or psychic experiences are not as central to Meditative Therapy as is light, they are nonetheless significant enough to deserve a careful examination. As you will discover in this chapter, many Meditative Therapy clients experience psychic phenomena. This is an exciting, rather mysterious, and rapidly developing field which is an important element in our study of the workings of the Inner Source. I ask the reader to suspend judgement and merely consider these accurate reports of human experience, events for which usual explanations are inadequate.

Same Background

Parapsychology, also called "Psi" (psychic phenomena), has been in existence since ancient times, as has meditation. Psi's existence has always been surrounded by claims of the miraculous, allegations of fraud, and association with the occult, all of which add up to a stormy existence. Much of the ongoing controversy still exist exists today, but things may be changing for the "black sheep" of psychology. The August, 1977 issue of *The Reader's Digest* includes an article entitled, "What Do We Really Know About Psychic Phenomena?" Written by Dr. Laile Bartlett, a sociologist, the article tells that we are "amidst a great Psi explosion." She notes that part of the reason is due to the acceptance of the Parapsychological Association as a member of the elite American Association for the Advancement of Science in 1969. Dr. Bartlett also points to the Psi SEARCH exhibit, established by the Smithsonian Institution, as an example of the current upsurge of interest in parapsychology. The exhibit is touring the country and contains material documenting the scientific investigation of the field of Psi over the past 40 years.

The field of parapsychology includes the study of such phenomena as clairvoyance, extra-sensory perception, telepathy, precognition, and psychokinesis. These areas are those studied by the more traditional investigators. Depending upon the investigator, other phenomena which may be studied include: reincarnation; communication with discarnate entities; out of body experiences; mediumship; and psychic healing. Several of these types of psychic experiences take place naturally through the workings of the Inner Source. This chapter includes short definitions of those which concern us here, a discussion of their occurrence during meditation, and examples of experiences which have taken place in Meditative Therapy.

Telepathy—Being able to "read" someone's feelings or thoughts or experiences. It may be the result of another person purposefully trying to transmit the information, or it may be guessing what someone is thinking or doing without her/his knowledge.

Precognition—Predicting an event which has not yet taken place, such as an earthquake, illness, or death.

Reincarnation—The concept that our soul never dies and has lived at other times throughout history. An individual presently alive in the United States may have had past lives in Ancient Egypt, France, Medieval England, or other locations at other periods of time, according to reincarnation principles.

Communication with Discarnate Entities—This relates to the belief that spirit beings can communicate through visual appearance, words, automatic writing, ouija boards, and telepathy.

Out of Body Experiences (OOB's)—The belief that we each have a soul body and that it can "lift off" or rise up out of our physical body and travel around. During the OOB one's visual and thinking abilities are said to be intact.

Parapsychological or Psychic Experiences in Meditation

Many sources on meditation speak about the parapsychological or psychic implications of the practice of meditation. Joel Goldsmith, in *The Art of Meditation* (1956), refers to what he calls "psychic visions" and gives two examples to illustrate the term. First is the appearance of colors; second is the experience of seeing spirits (supernatural beings). In the book, *Concentration and Meditation* (1973), Christmas Humphreys indicates that experiences or powers of a psychic nature, such as ESP, out of body experiences (OOB's), and so on, will come when one's consciousness is raised to a sufficient level through meditation. Karlis Osis (1973) in an article, "Dimensions of the Meditative Experience," found that in certain subjects, ESP abilities were enhanced by meditation.

Penny Baker (1973) writing from the perspective of the Cayce material, includes an entire chapter called "Psychic Development." Baker states that one's psychic abilities will often develop with consistent meditation. Cayce defined "psychic" to mean the expression of latent "soul and spirit" forces. Baker implies, without giving any actual instances, that a wide variety of psychic abilities, including telepathy, precognition, premonition, and clairvoyance, may be manifested with frequent meditation. She also says that meditation is the safest and surest avenue to take in order to develop psychic abilities. LeShan (1974) also includes a chapter on "Mysticism, Meditation and the Paranormal," in which he speaks of the parapsychological powers which may develop as a result of meditation.

Perhaps the best overall analysis of parapsychological or psychic manifestations in meditation is given by Daniel Goleman (1974 b), writing in John White's book, *What Is Meditation?* He first documents a series of psychic feats performed by Maharaji-ji (who died in 1973) which Goleman observed on a trip to India. These feats were a result of Majaraji-ji's meditational abilities. Goleman goes on to give evidence that there is a direct relationship between skill in meditation and psychic abilities. This is also recognized in Patanjali's *Yoga Sutras* (Mishra, 1973), the classic work on Yoga, and in the *Vissudhimaga* (Goleman, 1977). According to Goleman, both sources document a full range of psychic abilities which result from facility with meditation, Yogic and Zen Buddhist respectively.

Most of these meditation sources give warnings about potential dangers in the development of psychic abilities or powers, some quite stern and all quite sobering. Before discussing these warnings, the psychic experiences coming forth naturally from the Inner Source will be presented.

Parapsychological and Psychic Experiences in Meditative Therapy

Although the sources I have given here on meditation give no percentages concerning the manifestation of parapsychological experiences in meditation, we are told that consistent practice meditating over some period of time will foster these experiences in all. It is my opinion that parapsychological occurrences in

Meditative Therapy follow a similar pattern: an opening up of psychic talents is inevitable if one faithfully undergoes Meditative Therapy on a regular basis. My clients had varying numbers of Meditative Therapy sessions. Many had only one or two sessions, and most only five sessions. The data from this group of 100 show that around 15 percent had experiences which can be defined as parapsychological or psychic.

ESP Experiences

Two days before the 1977 New York City blackout, Roge, a California magician attending a convention in Seattle, predicted the event. In a sealed envelope which he gave to the city editor of the *Seattle Post-Intelligencer* were the headlines of the banner story two days later.

None of the ESP experiences the Inner Source has produced in my work with Meditative Therapy are quite as startling as that of Roge and others which have been reported from time to time in the news media, but perhaps as one develops further, these natural talents can reach that magnitude.

Under the heading of ESP are included such experiences as telepathy, clairvoyance, and precognition. These happenings most often take place outside the actual Meditative Therapy session. Depending on the person, these ESP experiences may simply be an acceleration of similar experiences that have already taken place in their lives at other times before, or they may be an entirely new experience, something they may have scoffed at before.

Example: —Within an hour after his first Meditative Therapy session, this 25-year-old college student attended a movie. Afterward he told of an experience relating to the lines one of the actors said. He was quite perplexed when he discovered that he had heard exactly the same words shortly before in a sequence presented by his Inner Source during his first session. He had experienced this kind of thing before, to the degree that at times he would seem to know what his friends would say just before they said it. However, he felt he had never experienced something as dramatic as this precognitive experience.

Reincarnation Experiences

The topic of reincarnation is one which continually causes a great deal of controversy in our society. Did you live before in another lifetime? If it can be proved beyond the shadow of a doubt, what are the psychological and religious implications of such a finding? Those who believe consider such phenomena central to the entire nature of human existence. For those who don't believe, the questions about reincarnation do not matter much. Most of us are somewhere in between. Books like *The Search for Bridey Murphy* (Bernstein, 1956), and *Many Mansions* (Cerminara, 1950), can be quite thought provoking. One's interest may be stimulated when hearing of the research on past life regression conducted by Dr. Helen Wambach (1977). One may find inviting the notion of being a member of the group which she age-regresses beyond their present existences. The reader may be aware of the significant work done in reincarnation in the 1960's by Dr. Ian Stevenson and reported in his book, *Twenty Cases Suggestive of Reincarnation* (1966).

But where have all these efforts led, in the search to know if one's soul is older than the current body? Unfortunately, none of the sources listed above has yet been able to still the critics who feel that reincarnation is pure fantasy. I am not certain that the examples presented here will extend our knowledge any further, but these experiences did take place unprompted. I did not tell these individuals at any point during therapy that they might have a reincarnation experience. Of course, there is no way of telling at this point exactly what the Inner Source was doing by presenting these type of experiences and where the sequences were coming from. Perhaps they were "made up" from books previously read or stories previously heard, but those who have experienced them certainly accept the "realness" of the feelings involved.

Example One: A 28-year-old nurse, after about twenty minutes of her third and last Meditative Therapy session, related the following:

Some movement up in the corner, can't tell, a horse, very large head. Ah Ha! There He is, Mary and a baby on a donkey, traditional halo—now that's very relaxing (*sarcastically*). The baby seems to be older all of a sudden, 3 or 4, not Jesus, just a child. Donkey is more like a palomino now, mother and child walking by the horse, playing with a wagon in the back. Going across prairies, sort of see mountain range, trees to the right. A long way to go, walking, dusty, have thick heavy coats on, maybe it's cold. I'm getting a headache. Now it's sort of like split vision, now a wagon train on the right side, now something above similar to the Parthenon, but new. No connection between the two, not even the same country. Now more animals with the wagon train, a lot of cows. Kind of seems to be taking over on the bottom. Top could have been a monastary. A little girl with the woman instead of a boy. Not a Palomino horse anymore. No men, just women and children, dust, dry. I don't feel like crying, but I'm starting to tear up (*starts sobbing*) oh, it's dry, I'm so tired, I just want to go, oh, oh (*crying*). It's all dark now, just like night, seems like I can still hear the cows. I see the outline of the wagon and fire light, it's cold, (*breathes deeply*) feel like I am sleeping, under the wagon. Still see women out there cleaning, hear men laughing and talking. See an older woman now, 20 or 22, shawl. I feel warm, bed I'm in, feel like another body close to me. See her with long skirts swishing around, talking to me a little bit. Some soldiers riding up, quite a few, circling the camp, wagons too. Gee, looks like there are many of them, I'm getting scared. Girl comes back to the wagon now, she is comforting the little girl. Doesn't feel like me. Man on horse talking, everyone starts getting ready, we're supposed to go with them, don't know why (*crying*). I don't know what's happening. We're following, don't know where we are going. Oh, uh. [*breathing is heavy*] All I can see is blue night. No one's talking, everyone's quiet. I don't even think they are taking cows. See some men throwing spears on top of our wagons, killing our horses (*sobbing*). How did they get there? Fire. Oh, it's on fire. I can't get out! One next to me on fire, can't get out! uh, oh, oh, (*sobbing*). I feel like I'm being stampeded by horses and wagons. Oh, uh, someone is bending over me, like soldiers putting a blanket over me. Dead. Oh, feels like a relief, oh, uh, oh. I see soldiers and wagon, charred, not burnt to the ground. Woman's dead, he's laying her next to me, covering her with a blanket too. Digging some holes, only two soldiers. Where are other people? Put us in some grave, others on top of us, two others, three. Covered over with dirt and just dirt on and ride away. See lots of dead horses, burnt out wagons, everybody's dead (*takes several deep breaths*).

The above sequence lasted for twenty minutes. After it was completed, she went on for another forty-four minutes before she was apparently finished with the session. These remaining minutes were also very dramatic and overwhelming for her. For me personally, this was at the time the most powerful individual Meditative Therapy session I had witnessed. After it was ended she exclaimed, "Oh my God! I never experienced anything like that before! I don't feel like I have any energy left, I can hardly move. Oh, Christ, what was that all about? I feel exhausted."

At this point we talked for a few minutes and she eventually stated that her feelings were close to the surface and that she had a lot of anger. She started crying so I told her to lie down and close her eyes and to just let it come and to get it over with. She started sobbing:

Oh, I'm so bad, so bad. Oh, I wish I had long nails so I could scratch, oh, oh. (*hitting herself lightly with her fist, like tapping*) oh, oh, it's doing it when I'm even awake, my God, how consuming it is—. I think it's over now. Funny, I feel good about me now. I haven't felt that way for a long time, felt like I was cleaned out inside. Having a lot of positive things going through my mind now. I feel positive feelings toward my mind now. I feel positive feelings toward you which I haven't had. For helping me go through this. I wouldn't have tried desensitization if I would have known this was so all-consuming.

One month later we talked on the telephone and she stated that she had been feeling fantastic and that she was greatly moved by the experience. She asked, "Was it real? Little things that happen make me wonder if it was only my mind or did those things actually happen at some time?" Three months later she stated: "An inner sense of tranquility has persisted since my last counseling experience. I still get angry and tired, but this seems to be on the surface. There is an inner quietness now." Eighteen months later I called her and she said that this feeling of inner quietness and tranquility still was with her.

Example Two: The next case involves the experience of a 33-year-old woman, who provided the following written description for me. I remember the instance to be essentially the same as she has described it here.

My mind felt free and expanded, as though it filled the room or beyond. I was surprised to be standing at the edge of a forest clearing. I felt very large, unusually strong, serene, powerful and confident of my strength and status. I could feel my body changing in size and structure. I blinked my eyes and several Indian men were sitting in a group. As I walked forward they made way for me. I knew I was greatly respected. A voice inside my head said, "Iriquois." The scene faded. I was then inside a long structure with a rounded roof. The structure was made of things from the forest. A woman with long, black hair was cooking and tending a baby. I felt deep love for them and knew they were my wife and child. All faded into greyness.

I felt small and something was squeezing my waist and rib-cage tightly. I felt encased in binding and it was a little difficult to breathe. I felt like I was being bounced around and there was a clattering sound of wheels on an unpaved road and horses galloping. I felt familiar as a woman again. I looked out and I heard an echo in my mind say, "17th century France." The landscape was familiar. I felt anticipation. I arrived in a large city. Several young men opened the coach doors and were bowing and flirtatious. I felt very beautiful and in control of things. I noticed their powdered wigs and elegant clothes were of the latest style and they seemed somewhat acceptable. I was very tiny and they were all quite tall to me. The scene faded and I heard the noise of a party, shouting laughter, eating, drinking, and I realized I was sitting in a great stone hall at a table heavily laden with the richest foods and wines. I was enjoying the company of several men. I was sitting in the seat reserved for an important guest. I felt myself laughing, the feeling of pride and control and being appreciated for my clever talk and beauty—then I moved back from myself and looked at me while still feeling everything. I (she) was beautiful with a very fashionable powdered wig, a low cut powder blue heavy silk or satin (material) dress with a great deal of lace . . . the scene merged into dense black, green jungle.

I felt peaceful and close to the earth. A great love of the land and sky filled me. I looked down and discovered I was larger boned, black and softly rounded in figure. I was climbing a steep trail up the side of a cliff. I came to the top to watch a waterfall. It was huge and crashed down into foaming rapids. It was white and the river looked dark green with white rapids. I turned and walked back down to the village. All of the other women had to work. I did not. I felt at one with my world. I went to the edge of the river which was calm here and a dark green color. I got into a cut out log and sat on my knees and slowly paddled the canoe down the river. The scene faded.

The Negro lady was naked except for a small loin cloth and a metal arm band. Her (*my?*) hair was closely cropped and curled into tight little knots.

The Indian man's head was shaved and had a strip of hair down the center of the head. He was large and muscular, dressed in animal skins and had a fur robe. It was night.

Communication with Discarnate Entities

Interest in the United States on communications with the spirits of those who have already died has been stimulated by the current work of Elisabeth Kubler-Ross (1975) on death and dying, and Raymond Moody (1975) on near-death experiences. Such efforts are not necessarily new. Karlis Osis, Ph.D., collected significant information on this subject as early as 1960 in a work called, *Deathbed Observations by Physicians and Nurses.* I am sure that this type of communication has been in existence "among the people" for centuries. Many are unwilling to tell of their communication with discarnate entities because of the ridicule they have experienced. It seems that those who have not had similar experiences are very vocal about the "impossibility" of such a thing taking place, and may even question the sanity of the person telling the story.

In my Meditative Therapy work this type of experience has not happened very frequently. It may have something to do with the age level of the group with which I work. College-age students have usually not had very many "significant others" who have passed on. Of the two examples here of direct communication, one was aged 24, and had known his great-great-grandmother before her death. The other was around 40 and had a series of close friends and relatives who had died. Perhaps with a group of people who had several "significant others" who had passed on, the experience of communication with the spirit world would appear more frequently in Meditative Therapy.

Example One: Although I have no written record of the following incident, it was of sufficient uniqueness to cause me to remember vividly. This experience happened to a 24-year-old student toward the latter period of five or six sessions. He started describing the physical presence of his deceased great-great-grandmother moving around on his hip. He depicted the experience as a "funny feeling," but as a very real occurrence, as if she was doing some type of healing work on his hip.

Example Two: This report came from the woman in her 40's who had the intriguing black-white light experience reported on in the previous chapter. The sequence given here is from the session immediately following that session (her fourth). In this session (her fifth) there are several interesting points. First, about eight minutes after the session started, she reported, "I'm not in me. I don't know what it is, it's me, but not." Moments later she added, "The light is walking with me, has my hand, but I don't have one. I don't understand much of what's happening. Like there are a whole bunch of dead faces, past faces, not skeletons, just past dead faces." A few minutes later she stated, "There is a diamond, a diamond star sapphire with all the projections gleaming out in all directions. There is an opening right through and it's as if I'm looking through it. I see through to eternity. Oh, absolutely beautiful, I have chills all over, almost too beautiful (*her voice cracks*)."

These reports seemed to have special significance because her Inner Source was evidently leading her to a culmination point. This point as described in the sequence below, started about 20 minutes after the session initially began. As we will see from her report, the inner light was her guide throughout.

A great big flower just turned up. Not a lot of color, purple. Somebody in the middle of it. Like it is me when I was a happy child, a happy child I don't remember. Definitely a happy child. A coffin (*starts sobbing*). My mother, they won't let me see her. Mommie, oh Mommie (*sobbing*). She's in the box. Oh, Mommie! The box broke up into all kinds of cubicles, different shapes. The light is still around (*sobbing stops*). (*Sobbing starts*) I don't want to leave my mother, but the light says we have to go. I have one hand reached back. I don't want to move away. I can see my mother's face. I don't remember seeing her face before, other than in pictures. Incredibly sweet, smiling, holds her hand out and says it is okay to go (*sobbing continues*). I feel like I've never touched her. I hold her hand just for one minute. Oh, it would have been so nice to have you around, Mom. It's been lonely without you! She still says it is okay to go. She's okay (*takes a deep breath*). A big sunburst again (*coughs*). I'm really in a cold sweat, uh, uh, clogged up. It is light like at home, but it's not that light in here, no windows here. I still want to stay with mother, but her face is going out to the side of the picture. She says she'll be there though. Gone now (*two deep breaths and she starts sobbing*). There's still a shadow of light where she left me. A lot darker in the sky now, more stars, but still darker (*deep breath*). I'm having trouble giving up the coffin, I want to hold on to it (*deep breath*). I see a picture of me taken sitting on the grass by mother's grave. I know now why I looked the way I did. I must have understood a lot about it. I must have been 3 then, I couldn't have been 18 months. An 80-year-old 3-year-old. Black water on a white beach, waves roll up and mix. I'm really dry, have trouble breathing. Body is not as tight as usual. Now see a movie theater screen. Black heads watching a white screen. I'm looking at people from the front now. All people that are dead. Grandmother (*starts sobbing*), uh, I miss you! She says I'm doing fine, she's really pleased. She's sorry she had to go, she wanted to stay too. I want to put my head on her knee (*deep breath*). The light is very much around. Behind my grandmother. She's not smiling, but she looks peaceful (*deep breath*). She's happy (*deep breath*). Like I'm having a conversation with her, but she's not moving her mouth. I just hear it. Says she's not in pain anymore. She says I'm having some of my pain for her and I don't need to. Weird, she says she can rock as long as she wants to rock. The light is moving on, says we've got to go (*sobbing*) (*choking sound*). I see the sunburst again. My sister. I don't know her except from pictures, but she's grown up, not 3, looks like 3 but, I don't understand. She's very beautiful (*sobbing*). Oh, (*grabs stomach*) oh. She wants to know me too, but we'll never get to have that chance. Maybe some day. She seems like a wise, old woman. It's the eyes. It's just her head, I don't see her body. The light is very much right there too. Very beautiful. The light says we have to go.

This segment lasted around 20 minutes and the session continued for another 15 minutes. During the remainder of the session, she "talked to" a girlfriend, who had been like a sister, who had died several years before. She also visited a deceased grandfather. The light accompanied her throughout the session, and as she ended the session she stated:

A voice says I can let go with my hand (from the light), that I don't need to hang on to it, it will still be there. I feel like I'm waiting for a rainbow, all movement is going in that direction, but I don't see one. Sunrise, bright sun, no color, rainbow out in the middle of the sunrise. It is faint and little, all the way up to the top (*deep breath*). (*Opens eyes*) My eyes feel like they have been glued shut for the entire time. Wow!

She continued to talk about the experience she had just been through and, among other things, that she was afraid to ask if it is possible to talk to all those people, but that she sure heard them.

Example Three: During her fifth session, another woman client related the following description:

> There's a noise in my left ear. It's like, like no noise, no real noise. It's like a ghost of words, of voices. It doesn't sound like a voice or words. It's like a negative image, like a ghost of words. Comes in puffs, like puffs of smoke.

Although this example doesn't show a direct communication with spirit beings, I have included it here because it sounded like other descriptions I have heard in relationship to apparent communication from "the other side." During the same session, this woman reported the energy exchange experience given later under "Other Parapsychological Experiences."

Out of Body Experiences (OOB's)

It is very difficult to verify that someone has "left" the physical body, but Dr. Charles Tart, a psychologist at the University of California at Davis, has made some significant scientific inroads into the matter. According to Dr. Bartlett in her recent *Reader's Digest* article (1977), Tart has had at least one talented OOB subject who could "read off" a randomly selected 5-digit number put on a shelf far above her bed. Her spirit body, while traveling out of her physical body, could locate and correctly report the number. My approach to OOB's taking place in Meditative Therapy has been to record them. I have done nothing as sophisticated as Tart's experimental work in order to verify the spontaneous reports of my clients. Scientific proof of OOB phenomena must depend upon researchers like Tart. It seems that the naturally occurring OOB experiences stimulated by the Inner Source may be a fruitful testing ground, however.

The OOB is the most common parapsychological event taking place during Meditative Therapy sessions. Some individuals will leave their bodies between sessions, but this is rare. On occasion, an individual will have experienced an out of body experience prior to entering the Meditative Therapy experience. The first two presented below were basically unsophisticated about OOB's before experiencing them from the Inner Source. The next two were what I would call knowledgeable about the field of parapsychology and psychic phenomena, although neither had previously experienced an OOB experience.

Example One: This client is reported as a full-length case in the next chapter. She refers to the experience as "teletransportation — leaving the body and being elsewhere on several occasions." The only descriptions she had given during the sessions that might fit an OOB were in #5 where she said, "Part of me lifted off. Part of me on one side doing things, the other part on the other side doing things." Then early in session #9 she said, after a lapse of several minutes, "I was off someplace." Later in #9 she stated, "Hmm, I'm going somewhere else, I'll be back in a little while." Three minutes elapsed, she coughed and said, "I was flying around." In answer to the follow-up question concerning parapsychological changes in beliefs she reported:

> Having felt the sensation of being "out of self," I am more open to the theory. Meditative Therapy does increase awareness of separation of self and the other world; that is, a perspective of yourself almost independent of yourself — an appraising.

Later in the same follow-up when she was describing the events that happened to her during her sessions she said, "Soaring, just my 'being,' not my body."

Example Two: Another young woman client was about 10 minutes into her sixth session when she reported the following:

> . . . Cramping on the right side — hearing the pulse, the sound, a faint hum, reflecting the pulse in my head. And ovals in both eyes, alternate in brightness. . . . Still hearing that and I feel like, not crawling, but you're moving away. I don't know, it has an uncomfortable feeling, but I don't know what it is — really funny — almost like moving out of your body — can't describe it. I don't know if I ever felt that before — like a deeper part of you. Not detached, but withdrawn and shortly after that

the body lost its definition. I don't know, it frightened me, it felt neat at the time,but I don't know—it just—Then there is brightness—like the sun seeing through an eclipse—circle—very brightness coming from behind . . . .

After her session, which lasted another 35 minutes, she said,

When I felt that I was really aware of where my body was. I felt like I was still there, but moved away from that—lost the definition—started to move—scared me. Because I guess you don't know where you are going. It was like I stretched somewhere.

In the follow-up evaluation form in answer to a question relating to changes in parapsychological beliefs she stated, "Especially with the out-of-body experience. Before I *felt* these things could possibly happen, now I *know* they can. And feel, too, that they are not weird or freaky."

Example Three: This woman client had undergone six Inner Source-directed sessions in my office and was now doing them on her own at home. During her seventh or eighth session, she had an OOB experience which she later described to me in written communication in the following manner:

My out-of-body experience was very thrilling and exciting, especially because I had feared it so, but wanted to do it. It was very natural—like dreaming—only with a vividness not found in dreaming. I could feel the warmth of the sun, the pavement beneath my feet, even the cracks in the sidewalk. I could look down and see what I was wearing, feel the weight of my body, etc., as I walked along in the park.

Example Four: During her fifth and final session, another young client described the following sequence:

. . . I see the sun—see a valley. I'm looking across the valley to the mountains—I can feel the air out of my mouth and that air is cold now moving across my skin. I feel really long and I'm looking down and I see me laying down on the mat and I see the desk top and I see you writing—I feel some tension in my arms—like my skin is drawing in. I feel a cold breeze (*takes a deep breath)* — I feel really flat — my eyes opened. *(stretches, yawns) (end of session)*.

I then asked her how she felt when she saw the scene from above and she said, "It felt really separated from my body, then after I said it (described it), I felt a tension in my body, like on the outer side, like it was pulling something back."

Other Parapsychological Experiences

Some experiences which the Inner Source presents do not seem to fit into any of the existing psychic categories mentioned above.

Energy Exchanges: By the term "energy exchange" I refer to the occasions during Meditative Therapy when someone is either receiving energy from an outside source or energy from oneself is being drained off of the body to some unknown place. If you will remember Jack, the Viet Nam veteran discussed in Chapter 1, you will recall an example of an energy discharge.

An example of receiving energy from an outside source is given below. This was a 58-year-old housewife who reported this experience during her fifth session: "The minute I turn my hands up I feel a current coming through. Through my feet also today. I feel like a battery being recharged. Not from one little place, but from all over."

Traveling to the Astral Plane? A 28-year-old woman had undergone four previous Meditative Therapy sessions, all of which had been profound experiences for her. She had gained a great deal of insight by being able to detect and understand much of the content of the sessions. Her behavior also was changing rapidly as a result of the sessions. She considered that her sessions had patterns which made sense to her for the most part. During her fifth session she proceeded in much the same way as before except there was more of a "low keyed" approach to her verbal description of the experiences. After 50 minutes of continuous verbal description with pauses of no more than 10 seconds she stated: "I kind of don't feel I'm with it — feel like I'm floating in and out of it."

At this point she opened her eyes, sat up, and said: "Am I

coherent? I'm lapsing, I know I am, I don't remember things—I'm not coherent, I go in and out."

I questioned her a little bit about how she felt and she indicated she felt dizzy and "spacy" so I asked her to lie down for awhile and we would see if she was really finished. She then continued her ongoing description, again with only short pauses. This lasted for another 15 minutes when she stated: "I'm up again (*opens her eyes*). I feel very nauseated (*sits up*). I don't know what's happening—very strange—has no pattern—everything else had a pattern. I'm nauseated." At this point I indicated that it may not have a pattern to her, but that the Inner Source knew what it was doing so she should lie down and let it do what it wanted to do to help her. She laid back down and the session continued for another 20 minutes. Upon the completion she arose and was clear headed. Her excited comments were as follows: "I had long lapses where I was away. I had 5 major lapses longer than 10 minutes, 10 to 15 minutes if not longer. I fell asleep, but I could hear myself talking as I woke up. I know I wasn't here, I did, I was gone! I came back in and it was not my voice, when I came back in and it was not my voice, when I came back in it was a groggy type voice and it was not me!"

Part of the reason she became excited was because I maintained, and could document, that she had talked continuously and sensibly with only minor lapses of 10 to 15 seconds rather than minutes. She was incredulous that I could say such a thing when she steadfastly *knew* she had been "gone." Later, when I sent her the follow-up form, it appears that she considered this an OOB experience. She answered the question on parapsychological experiences as: "Definitely—leaving my body. I believe that people can become more in touch with the spiritual world and natural harmony. I feel that there is much more to life than just the old "five senses trip."

Stern Warnings

Earlier in this chapter, I reported that meditation sources generally recognize the appearance of psychic phenomena along the way as one meditates. Let's look at how various sources feel about these psychic events.

Humphreys, in *Concentration and Meditation* (1973), states directly that one should not try to develop psychic powers arising in meditation and that doing so is highly dangerous. He implies that one is only seeking to build the ego by developing psychic powers. The pursuit of psychic phenomena will not lead to wisdom. Psychic phenomena will be added to wisdom when and if the time becomes right. He feels that powers of this type will have a proper place later in one's meditational development, but in the meantime it is best to ignore them and treat them as illusionary.

Le Shan, in his book *How to Meditate* (1974), warns that it is possible to become too interested in psychic happenings that take place in meditation and forget the real goal, which is one's own development. His advice is to ignore psychic occurrences because on a practical, realistic level they are of no real consequence. He says that this psychic information is too unreliable and to make serious plans on it is "just plain kookiness."

Although not quite so harsh, Joel Goldsmith, in *The Art of Meditation* (1956), follows lines of thought similar to those of Humphreys and LeShan. He feels that these visions might have some importance, but reminds us that they have nothing to do with the spiritual world. They are completely on the psychic realm and urges that we are not to fixate on them, but to move on and go beyond these experiences to higher development.

The basic warning from the Cayce material regarding psychic abilities centers around choice (see Baker, 1973). That is, one must decide for what purpose he or she would use these talents. If it is only for material or other self-gain, then there would be danger in developing these talents. To be safe, according to Cayce, one must be only concerned with using psychic skills to help other people.

Goleman's sources (1974 b) seem to agree with the Cayce work. He reiterates the warnings about these psychic powers and states that they are not to be used to build up oneself in material gains. They should only be used to help people. One's motives must be pure. Psychic manifestations are not the final goal of meditation and are dangerous to self if used in this way.

My personal beliefs are close to the Cayce and Goleman recommendations. I feel that the approaches of Hymphreys, LeShan and Goldsmith are too restrictive and give the impression that psychic experienes are "evil." It seems to me that rather than being evil, out to trip us up, and nonspiritual, that these experiences are a natural part of the workings of the Inner Source and should be accepted and treated as such. In this regard, psychic phenomena are parallel to the phenomena of light discussed in the previous chapter. Surely one can get carried away and thrown off the track of growth by feeling superior to others who don't have these experiences. Nevertheless they seem to be signals that we are unfolding naturally. Fixation on *any* experience the Inner Source presents is not good, be it the commonly glorified religious experience or the commonly denigrated parapsychological experience. All are pieces of a larger fabric of personal development.

There is nothing crazy or evil about the appearance of Psi in meditation and Meditative Therapy. Once these inherent abilities appear, which I believe to be the signs of the beginning of the fulfillment of our fullest human potential, we should not neglect them or put them down. Our job is to trust the Inner Source and let it prompt us to further growth. One who feels led to develop these awakenings further on a conscious level may well do so, keeping in mind not to use the talents for selfish gain or harm to others. They are talents that can help others, so one needn't be afraid to proceed on, if such a path seems right. I believe each person should always work toward good with whatever talents he or she has. Allowing the Inner Source to guide our development, these talents or abilities will enhance our growth and the growth of others.

8

"Cleaning Cobwebs From My Mind:"
The Case of Kerrie

> *When the superficial, conscious mind is thus fully aware of all its activities, through that understanding it becomes spontaneously quiet, not drugged by compulsion or regimented by desire; then it is in a position to receive the intimation, the hints of the unconscious, of the many, many hidden layers of the mind—the racial instincts, the buried memories, the concealed pursuits, the deep wounds that are still unhealed. It is only when all these have projected themselves and are understood, when the whole consciousness is unburdened, unfettered by any wound, by any memory whatsoever, that it is in a position to receive the eternal.*
>
> *—Krishnamurti*

Although only 28 years old and quite attractive, Kerrie, the graduate student sitting in my office, told of multiple physical and psychological ailments. Imagine yourself being extremely fatigued. At the same time, you have an inner shakiness or trembling. You cry very easily for no logical reason. A wide variety of fears plague you, especially a fear of criticism. You are overly shy. Despite being constantly dragged out, you find yourself unable to relax. If you can imagine all of this, you will *begin* to get a picture of Kerrie.

Kerrie's initial reason for coming to see me was actually quite simply stated: "I want to learn to relax. A friend of mine who is also seeing you told me about systematic desensitization, and it sounded like I need it." As her story unfolded, however, she described all of the complaints mentioned above and, in addition, related a host of others.

She reported that she had been chronically ill as a child. Every winter she would have colds, strep throat, and swollen glands. Her father died when she was 16, and soon after she developed an ulcer which was diagnosed by x-ray. After treatment for two years she was cured as confirmed by x-ray, but presently, she had developed indigestion and a burning sensation. These reactions took place just prior to going to bed at night. At the age of 25, she was told by a doctor, who discovered it during her pregnancy, that she had a congenital kidney defect. The kidney evidently had a bump on it and would become infected periodically, at which time she would take medication. During her pregnancy, she also experienced a drug reaction of some kind and almost lost the baby.

Other current difficulties included getting the flu and colds easily and periodic allergic and asthmatic reactions. She found it difficult to get to sleep and hated to get up in the morning. She was very short-tempered with her 2½-year-old child. Kerrie had stiff necks, was short-winded, was excessively hungry, became cold easily, and had constant pain in her teeth. Finally, she experienced a sexual difficulty in that, if she had to wait for an orgasm, she would "automatically" scratch and bite her husband. This is not something that he found pleasurable, but painful!

How does a therapist approach treating someone with such a list of problems? Her case is atypical, of course. Most of us don't have this many complaints. People often do have more complaints than their therapists are aware of, however. You may have guessed that all of the information given above on Kerrie would not have come out unless I asked her about her *total* functioning. Professional mental health workers such as psychologists, social workers, and psychiatrists, are typically attuned only to their own fields. As you can see, Kerrie needed more than just psychological treatment. *This same statement is true of most of the clients I see.* Generally speaking, it is best to take an holistic approach, treating the whole person, rather than just a psychological approach.

Treatment Approach

Because Kerrie reported some complaints often caused by faulty dietary habits, I decided to check her eating patterns first. She had reported excessive hunger, extreme fatigue (could hardly climb stairs), crying easily for no reason, and an "inner shakiness." She was also somewhat overweight and had a history of gaining weight easily, which then was difficult for her to lose. These complaints signaled the likelihood of poor eating habits.

She reported eating instant oatmeal for breakfast with either Kool-Aid or juice. Lunch varied between sandwiches and salads, depending upon whether or not she was dieting. She would typically not eat much in the evening for dinner, but when she did the meal would consist of hamburger-based dishes. If she did not have an afternoon snack (usually crackers with peanut butter, or candy), she would begin feeling "uptight." In the evenings she would either have candy or smoke heavily. Typically, she would not smoke before noon, but by midnight she would be "practically chain smoking."

Because Kerrie's eating patterns were inconsistent and her diet low in protein, I suggested that she change to a high protein-low carbohydrate diet. Because she had come in for systematic desensitization and relaxation training, I decided to start with those procedures. (If I were to make this decision over again, I would have started with Meditative Therapy due to the wide variety of her problems. As we shall see, Kerrie began Meditative Therapy spontaneously before we had much of an opportunity to try the other methods anyway.)

You will recall from Chapter 1 that systematic desensitization involves deep relaxation, accompanied by imagined anxiety-producing scenes. The repeated association of relaxation and the anxiety stimulus works to reduce the anxiety to a manageable level.

After constructing a desensitization hierarchy of scenes related to fear of criticism (which she considered her most important fear), we started to proceed with relaxation instructions, a necessary first step in desensitization. We were approximately one-half way through the instructions, around 10 minutes, when her breathing rate noticeably increased. I asked her what was happening and she replied, "I'm dizzy." I said, "Okay, stay with your feelings and see if you can see anything coming into your mind. Try to describe any visual occurrences, thoughts, feelings, and any bodily changes." At first, she indicated that she saw nothing, so I decided to see if she could open her eyes. As she did so she stated, "I feel real heavy, I can't move out of the chair, my body is like lead." Later she told me that she had felt like something really heavy was on her legs, keeping her in the chair. To continue, I then asked her to reclose her eyes and again pay attention to and describe her complete functioning, encouraging her to passively observe and allow anything to happen that needed to in order to help her.

During the 55 minutes that followed, she went through a series of events, many of which centered around the death of her father over 10 years before. She was able to visualize these events with deep emotional feeling and involvement. Often she would cry as she related to me what she was experiencing. Also, her legs would hurt, and she would tremble and shudder at times. The central theme, in addition to death, was sickness, mainly her own past experiences with it. Her Inner Source worked extremely fast at times during this first session; as she put it, "like filmstrips being pulled past my eyes." In addition, she did experience pleasant reactions as well; for example, within 10 seconds of being involved in the circumstances surrounding her father's death, she found herself by the ocean sitting in the sunlight, smiling (within and in reality), and smelling the ocean smells.

In the weeks that followed, she went through eight additional sessions of Meditative Therapy. Doing so was not easy for her, and she was ambivalent about going through the therapy each time she came until almost the end. When she returned after her spontaneous session of Meditative Therapy we chatted for awhile about how she felt afterward, then I asked her if she would like to do it again. She replied "no," but instantaneously tears began to well up and roll down her face, signifying to both of us that she needed to proceed with Meditative Therapy. One might interpret this as her Inner Source pressing her to get well, or, in Luthe's terms, that her brain had found a way to normalize and was eager to discharge more disturbing material.

It is not unusual for strong feelings to "build up" prior to the start of a session. This tendency comes out in many forms, depending upon the person involved. This pattern repeated itself each time she came for counseling. It became almost uncanny in that as soon as tears started, as we talked, we both knew it was time to begin. Around the eighth session (our next to last), she no longer had tears come before we began. Also by then, she had no more conscious doubts about undergoing the treatment because she had been feeling tremendous.

Meditative Therapy Themes and Experiences

Table 8-1 presents a content analysis of Kerrie's Meditative Therapy experience (excluding the first session, which was not recorded). The primary themes she experienced during the therapy are given, along with a typical example of each theme. The themes are presented according to the number of times they came up throughout the therapy. It can be observed that experiences of her own childhood were predominant, but the experiences as a parent with her own child were nearly as frequent. Other important themes were her pregnancy and the birth of her child, and her own personal experiences with physical illnesses. Accompanying the visualizations, she would quite often experience physical reactions such as leg pains, headaches, teeth hurting, coughing and throat constriction and pain, crying and sobbing.

Of interest because of their recurrence, were Kerrie's feelings of spinning and the experience of seeing a flashing light. Examples are presented below:

Activity or Event	*Examples* [session number in ( )]
Spinning	I am spinning again (#2)
	I'm spinning—oh, it's in a centrifuge, oh— I'm trying to open my eyes and I can't—I can't stop it." (#4)
Flashing Light	There's some kind of a flashing light—(*she jumped*)—hurts my eyes—(*she jumped again*) (#2)

Table 8-1
THE CASE OF KERRIE
Predominant Meditative Therapy Themes
Plus Examples

Meditative Therapy Theme	Example/Session
1. Childhood	"In an elementary school - in a green and brown dress, 1st or 2nd grade, in the morning, I'm supposed to be writing, everyone else is finished - now we're trying to read, I can't read either, so I just make things up by the picture." (#6)
2. Parenthood: Playing with - Problems with her child	"I ask C to do something, then I decide she can't do it, then she want to try and can't, I get irritated, she's getting confused." (#5)
3. Pregnancy - Childbirth	"Oh! (*jumped*) Oh! I thought I was floating. It's a hospital room again (*breathing and sighing heavily*)—I can't talk— oh, uh, I can't see anything, my throat is all tightened up (*in obvious pain*)—I'm in the hospital when I was pregnant - can see the I.V. and they just gave me that shot and everything seems kind of confused, uh, uh." (#2)
4. Her own physical illnesses	"(*coughing*) I feel a choking [*Okay, stay with it*]. (*holds throat in pain, rubs chest*) - it's right after we were married, winter time, I'm real sick, oh, uh, (*breathing heavily, coughing*) oh, oh, (*sighing*) - It's grey, don't have car or money, no telephone, it's 10° below and I don't want to go outside." (#2)

> There's that flashing light again [*Does it have a color?*] — I don't know, it is like a strobe (#6) It's that light, that flashing light—a blue one—it's like in the ocean. (#9)

Other quotes of interest are as follows:

> I feel as if I've had a long sleep, but not really asleep. From time to time I will get messages on a blackboard telling me what to do or what not to do. Like it will say not to interfere like I did last time when it did something. (end of third session)
>
> When they started stripping me off, they hung me upside down and I started getting sick. Then it was like ghosts coming out of the body. (end of fifth session)
>
> I'm upset—it's going slow—[*just be patient*] not one of my virtues—I don't mean only slow—I mean *really* slow—my heart seems to have slowed down. (end of seventh session)
>
> It's a ball of ice—my head, wow, my brains were moving around and it hurt—it would click like one of those snapper things. (end of eighth session)

Kerrie's session transcripts showed that she had discharging, extended discharging, reinforcement and understanding in each of the eight recorded sessions. In addition she had abreaction in four sessions (2, 3, 4, 5) and new experiences in two sessions (3 and 5). The new experiences were messages on an inner blackboard telling her what to do or what not to do, and an out of body experience.

Results

In order to evaluate the outcomes of Kerrie's therapy experiences, I sent her follow-up evaluation measures at two different time periods, three months after she completed therapy, and again 18 months after therapy. These forms included a follow-up questionnaire on Meditative Therapy, a "follow-up of counseling" form, and two self-report measures which she had also completed when she first came in for counseling. (These can all be seen in the Appendices.) First, let's look at how she analyzed herself on the two tests at the various periods of time. These results are given in Table 8-2.

Table 8-2
THE CASE OF KERRIE
Fear Inventory and Willoughby Changes
3 Months and 18 Months After Therapy

Inventory	Pre-Therapy Score	Post Score (3 months)	Post Score (18 months)
1. Fear Inventory	94	13	21
2. Willoughby Personality Schedule	51	7	13

The Fear Inventory has seventy-three items which are to be rated for the degree of fear they cause the person. The scale for each item runs from zero (no fear) to four (very much fear). The highest total possible, if all items were rated a four, is 292. In a study conducted by F. Hannah, T. Storm, and W.K. Caird (1965), the mean or average response for 804 Canadian female college undergraduates was measured. The average score was 77.90.[1] As can be seen, Kerrie had an initial score of ninety-four and it dropped to thirteen at three months and then rose slightly to twenty-one at eighteen months after therapy. In brief, her reported fear level had dropped dramatically, and remained low.

For the Willoughby Personality Schedule, Joseph Wolpe, M.D. reports in his book, *Psychotherapy By Reciprocal Inhibition* (1958), that 80% of ''neurotic'' patients score above thirty on the test. Kerrie scored fifty-one before therapy commenced. This score dropped to seven three months after therapy and then rose slightly to thirteen at eighteen months away from therapy.

Both of these outcomes show that Kerrie's fears and doubts about herself diminished to well below the average.

---

1. **Technical Footnote**—The Fear Inventory which I administered to Kerrie contained seventy-six items rather than seventy-three as reported here. Assuming that Kerrie's three additional items averaged the same amount (1.30), her reduced totals would still show a similar relationship. Instead of 94-13-21 her scores would be 92.70-11.70-19.70.

Table 8-3 is a presentation of how Kerrie perceived herself as changed or improved on her most important complaints.

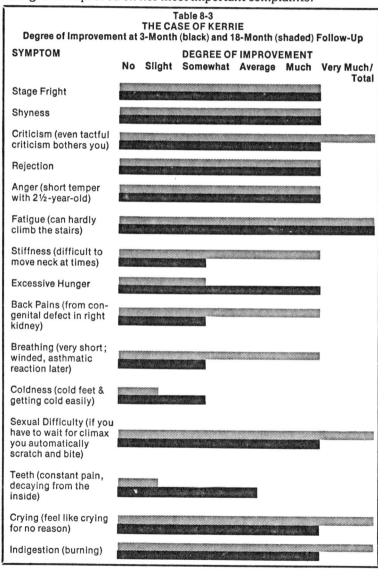

Table 8-3
THE CASE OF KERRIE
Degree of Improvement at 3-Month (black) and 18-Month (shaded) Follow-Up

SYMPTOM — DEGREE OF IMPROVEMENT (No, Slight, Somewhat, Average, Much, Very Much/Total)

Stage Fright

Shyness

Criticism (even tactful criticism bothers you)

Rejection

Anger (short temper with 2½-year-old)

Fatigue (can hardly climb the stairs)

Stiffness (difficult to move neck at times)

Excessive Hunger

Back Pains (from congenital defect in right kidney)

Breathing (very short; winded, asthmatic reaction later)

Coldness (cold feet & getting cold easily)

Sexual Difficulty (if you have to wait for climax you automatically scratch and bite)

Teeth (constant pain, decaying from the inside)

Crying (feel like crying for no reason)

Indigestion (burning)

As can be seen, 3 months following therapy she reported that 12 of the 15 complaints were either "totally" or "very much" improved. At the 18 month follow-up, 10 of the 15 were either "totally" or "very much" improved. Several individual items are of interest when comparing the 3 and 18-month outcomes. First, we notice that her stiff neck slipped from "very much improved" to "somewhat improved" and her back pains (from a congenital defect in her right kidney) also slipped from "very much" to "somewhat" improved. Her breathing (very short-winded, asthmatic reaction later) again changed by the same degree. On the positive side, we see a significant gain from "somewhat" to "very much" improved for the excessive hunger symptom. Overall, the excellent progress reported at 3 months was maintained at 18 months following therapy.

Evaluation of Results: Kerrie's View

In addition to Kerrie's ratings of improvement in the tables above, which were clearly very high, she contributed additional comments at the three month and 18 month follow-ups, and completed the "Meditative Therapy Follow-Up Questionnaire."

Kerrie's comments in the three month follow-up form were:

> I now have immense self-confidence, calm, high concentration powers, greater consciousness in speech, improved logical ability. Also, I have noticed a decrease in sexual desire (contraceptives, I think). And I can relax easily whenever I need to.

When answering the question, "What was the most outstanding factor in your counseling experience?" she stated, "The radical change in behavior patterns—self-confidence. Feeling that if I really want to I can do anything."

The 18 month follow-up didn't include these same questions, however, she attached comments to the follow-up form, related directly to her complaint picture:

1. For the problem of anger toward her young child she wrote: "Of course, I'm not with her all the time (work full time) and she is older."

2. For the problem of back pains: "I still have occasional pain, but drinking a lot of water seems to clear it up."

3. For the problem of coldness: "I still get cold easily, but it doesn't bother me as much."

4. For the problem of constant pain in her teeth, decaying from the inside: "I had the tooth that caused the most pain pulled. It was abscessed and infected the gum. Also, the dentist said the decay is caused by grinding my teeth especially when asleep."

Kerrie completed the "Meditative Therapy Follow-Up Questionnaire" at the 18 month follow-up period. The highest mark on the scale for this form is a "3" or "very much." She gave a "3" rating to:

— Greater Awareness of reality
— Feel it was of lasting benefit to me
— Like traveling to a far-off land
— More ability to relax and be myself
— Greater tolerance of others
— Sense of relaxation and freedom from anxiety and tension

Those marked "2" on the scale or "quite a bit" were:

— A very unpleasant experience
— Return to feelings of childhood
— Physical discomfort and illness
— A greater understanding of the importance and meaning of human relationships
— Improvement noted by people closest to me
— A better understanding of the cause and source of my trouble
— A set of new decisions and new directions for my life

As you will observe, she did experience some unpleasantness during the sessions. Kerrie stated that there were some pleasant experiences within the sessions; however, the "trips," as she termed them, were frightening to her. She did not find the experience one that was disappointing or that did her harm mentally or that it was an experience of insanity. It appears, however, that Kerrie was aware of the powerfulness of the therapy and treated it with distant respect. For example, she stated that she would be willing, but not eager to try the therapy again. Also she stated that:

It is frightening and apparently dangerous to "go under." I would not try it unsupervised simply because you get lost. By knowing someone is there, you can go further under without hesitation. Once I tried to do it by myself, but I had an eerie sensation of detachment, then fright—if someone who knows what's going on is there, you can really relax.

To the final question on the Meditative Therapy evaluation form, "Is there anything else you can tell of your experience that was particularly exciting, disturbing, unusual, etc?" she gave the following responses:

During recollections (another term she used for our sessions):

1. Frequently there is specific pain involved. Stiff neck, paralysis, numbing of legs and arms. At one point, my arms were neutralized, so I wouldn't move.

2. Also, a sensation of "going under, like traveling to a far-off land" or into the dark.

3. Soaring—just my "being," not my body.

4. Sensation of being lifted up, of being lighter.

5. Cleaning cobwebs from my mind—literally sweeping.

6. Movie of events—my lifetime—at fast and superfast speed—can smell specific things; sea, dust, eucalyptus, etc.

7. Seeing "halos" around people.

After sessions:

1. Ability to relax, into near trance, but not the same.

2. Confidence, ability to cope, more sex appeal.

3. Stimulation, can absorb fast.

4. I quit smoking with ease.

5. I occasionally get "special insight" into people's feelings or motivation.

Overall, I have had very good results in my career and I'm sure that your counseling helped me. In reading back over this, I see that I got a little dramatic, but the general info. is correct.

Evaluation of Results: The Therapist's View

Certainly I am quite pleased with the way Kerrie reacted to Meditative Therapy. Any time the methods I employ can produce such dramatic (and apparently permanent) changes in a relatively short period of time, I feel very good! Of course, I know that Kerrie had a great deal to do with the outcomes she experienced beyond the methods chosen. One of the tendencies of the Inner Source, which I mentioned in conjunction with the appearance of Kerrie's tears, is to start "building" feelings a few days prior to a session. My theory is that the Inner Source knows that the person has an appointment and so prepares in advance to release or "work through" upsetting material. There were many times that Kerrie dreaded coming to her sessions. She would often, on the day of the session, have to force herself, drag herself, up the stairs leading to my office. In addition, Kerrie found the sessions frightening, but was willing to trust her Inner Source, in spite of this fear. Kerrie also consistently stayed on the diet recommended to her. Breaking any habit is not an easy task. What this all adds up to is that Kerrie's outcome had a lot to do with her personal attributes of courage, trust, willingness to work, and perseverance.

Kerrie's attributes would have been an asset no matter what methods were chosen, but don't let this give you the impression that *any* methods chosen would have produced these dramatic results. Both the dietary approach and the Meditative Therapy approach are powerful ways to change behavior in their own right. The main problem in analyzing Kerrie's results is: To what degree are they "pure?" Did Meditative Therapy or the change in diet contribute most to the outcomes? From a practical standpoint, the question makes little difference to me, because I am thankful that she was able to improve so much. From a scientific viewpoint (although scientific and practical aren't *always* incompatible), I am very much concerned about what therapeutic approach leads to what outcomes.

For two reasons, I believe that Meditative Therapy was the key to Kerrie's response. First, Meditative Therapy was the primary treatment approach. She had nine sessions of MT out of a total of 12. Most of her changes took place by the end of her counseling experience. Although we both felt that dietary changes helped Kerrie a great deal, changes of the nature Kerrie experienced usually would not take place in such a short period of time if diet was the major factor.

My second reason relates to the breadth and depth of psychological and physical responses her Inner Source dealt with in therapy. A simple change like diet usually won't affect such a wide range of complaints. Much of the Meditative Therapy material concerned problems centering around her past psychological and physical problems. The harboring or storing of residual conflict and pain can often come out as current physical or psychological problems. Once these are resolved or discharged, the complaints improve greatly. In my view, Kerrie's very first session, wherein she dealt with her father's death and several episodes of her own hospitalization, was the key sign of what led to her excellent results. The remainder of her sessions followed this same pattern.

On the three month follow-up form is a question, "Which therapy do you feel was the most beneficial to you?" Kerrie answered in the following way: "I can't decide. Without the diet, I'm not sure Meditative Therapy would be possible (wouldn't relax or concentrate)." Although I still will stay with my choice of Meditative Therapy, Kerrie's comment shows that it is impossible to ascertain which approach produced her major changes. Hopefully, future research will help clarify the issue.

As demonstrated here by Kerrie's outcome, Meditative Therapy has the potential to produce significant and long-lasting changes in a short period of time. Not every person reacts as well as Kerrie did, of course, but her experience shows the excellent potential of Meditative Therapy.

9

Holistic Health:
The Inner Source and
Psychophysiospiritulogical Wholeness

It was interesting to note also that Cayce saw a person as a whole, with mind, body and spirit as a single unit, all so closely tied that it was not possible for one aspect to be diseased, either physically or mentally, without the whole person suffering the consequences.

—*James C. Windsor*

In 1969 I became very intent upon being the best therapist I could be. I decided that the way to accomplish this was to find the ultimate method, the method that would cure all psychological ailments. To be the best therapist I felt that I needed to find *the method* that would help people the most. Because I was so desirous of this goal I began to pray that I might be led to discover or locate this highest method of helping others. At first, my search led me into many areas of endeavor in the field of psychology. But soon I looked elsewhere into spiritual, psychic, and physical healing areas. I remember my wife, Kay, "raising her eyebrows" each time I embarked on a "new kick." I was like a child with a new toy, each time I thought that I had discovered *the method*, and would react as if I had finally reached my aim.

I didn't understand the true value of E-therapy and Autogenic Abreaction for several years. Instead of trying the methods in their pure form, I mixed in the synthetic approaches such as hypnotic suggestions, hyperventilation, having the client repeat key phrases, and applying pressure to body parts to stimulate reactions. When I finally decided, through a long process of trial and error, to allow the Inner Source to operate in a completely natural way, I believed for certain that I had found *the method*. Meditative Therapy seemed to be the answer. I even considered giving up all other methods in order to devote myself to this method that must surely be the ultimate one.

The Disease in "The Cure"

Fortunately, I decided to wait a little longer, and analyze Meditative Therapy more thoroughly, before dropping all other methods. Had I written this earlier, and announced Meditative Therapy as "the cure," the book would have suffered from my diseased thinking. *There is no one cure for all that ails us psychologically*, and to say so constitutes therapeutic narrow-mindedness. There is "disease" in thinking of any one method as "the cure." Meditative Therapy is the most powerful meditative and therapeutic method I know of, but there is much more beyond any one method.

My logic, thinking that the search would be complete upon the "discovery" of one method, was faulty. There is something beyond believing that there is *one* answer for anything. In therapy, the "something beyond" is *using a combination of psychological, physical and spiritual therapeutic methods to treat the whole person*. It was a shock to me when I finally came to the realization that the result of my journey suggested a *total* treatment method or system, rather than a single psychological treatment method or system. I settled on an holistic-eclectic approach to complete health.

Eclectic

The idea of the eclectic outlook is basically like a melting pot theory of psychological therapy. *Eclectic* methods are those which select freely from a variety of methods in a certain field, such as medicine, education, religion, or psychology. We need to gain an understanding that no one *method*, such as assertiveness training or guided imagery or free association, will be thorough enough to treat someone psychologically, and that no one *system*, such as behavior therapy or psychosynthesis or psychoanalysis, will be complete enough either. If you as a client go to a therapist who only uses one method or one system you may gain a great deal of help, but I propose that a psychotherapist who is thorough selects from a wide variety of methods and systems. I believe that an eclectic psychotherapeutic system broadens the chances of helping each client, who has a cluster of unique needs.

Therapists would be more helpful if they would select methods which meet client needs according to the following three bipolar criteria: (1) *directive—non-directive*, (2) *inner—outer*, and (3) *talk—non-talk*. Since my purpose is to stimulate your thinking I have not categorized all therapies into these three bipolar areas. In my own personal approach to the psychological aspect of helping others I have my own favorite methods. My choice of a non-directive method is the client-centered method of Rogers (1961). My directive method is assertiveness training, first developed by Salter (1949), then Wolpe (1968), and later by Alberti and myself in the books: *Your Perfect Right* (1970, 1974) and *Stand Up, Speak Out, Talk Back!* (1975) which we co-authored. For the inner method I have chosen Meditative Therapy. The outer method could be a talk therapy, such as the client-centered or assertiveness training approaches.

My selection of three methods (client-centered, Meditative Therapy, Assertiveness Training) fulfills the six bipolar choices. There are a multitude of other methods which could be substituted, and there are a wide range of combinations possible. The three methods I have selected are not the only psychological methods I employ, but they form my basic framework. I try to search all systems of therapy rather than focusing myopically on the methods of only one system, such as Gestalt, Behavior Therapy, or Analytic Therapy. I am always looking for new methods which will help people in their stride toward self-fulfillment.

Holistic

The word *holistic* derives from the Greek word *holos* which means whole. Holistic includes all realms of our being. When referring to the word holistic we are thinking of taking into account the whole person, mentally, physically, spiritually. To me, as a psychologist, this means responding to all aspects of one's health, not simply psychological or psychosomatic health. Typically, even those who treat psychosomatic disorders aren't thorough enough along physical lines. Spiritual problems, and methods to treat those problems, are areas that are not traditionally considered by most mental health or physical health workers. There is an inseparable interrelationship or intertwining between the mental, physical and spiritual and it is vital to treat ourselves as a unit. Although it is essentially impossible to separate ourselves into distinct units of diagnosis or treatment, it is crucial that all areas be taken into consideration.

It is not sufficient simply to refer to a medical doctor, a minister, and a psychologist and let it go at that. Specialists should endeavor to be knowledgeable about *all* of a client's problems, and be familiar about what areas their own eclectic psychological, physical, or spiritual system may not be adequte to treat. Knowledge of methods in all three major areas of endeavor which might be helpful to a client is an important criterion to apply in selecting a professional therapist.

Meditative Therapy naturally treats the person on a holistic level. The Inner Source will work with psychological, physical and spiritual areas of functioning. However, the Inner Source needs "outer help" in many instances. Philosophically, I believe that the Inner Source wants each person to learn how to take care of his or her inner *and* outer life. If all of one's psychophysiospiritulogical difficulties could be taken care of by the passive (inner) method of meditative therapy, that may sound delightful, but that is not the *reality* of life. The converse is also true: if one's total functioning could be taken care of by active (outer) methods that may sound delightful, but that is not the reality of life either. One must learn to live life successfully inwardly *and* outwardly. Inner methods will be helpful to our outer functioning and outer methods will be helpful to our inner functioning, but *both* are needed to develop ourselves fully.

Complete Health, Psychophysiospiritulogically!

Complete health is a term I have chosen for the goal of an holistic-eclectic therapy system. If one is at the height of mental-physical-spiritual functioning, complete health exists. From my viewpoint, one who is truly "self-actualized" or truly "enlightened" (or truly whatever-word-is-used) necessarily needs to be completely, *psychophysiospiritulogically*, healthy.

Complete health has to be different for each unique individual. I believe each person knows inherently what his or her personal complete health is. Even though the ultimate goal may not be clear at certain points in time, the initial steps to take to begin the journey are known (although perhaps not in conscious awareness). As more and more growth takes place, new steps will be apparent and the ultimate, complete health goal becomes clearer. Progress along these lines is quite tangible and can be judged by symptom removal or the appearance of mental, physical, and spiritual traits of self-actualization, enlightenment, cosmic consciousness, and/or liberation.

My efforts to facilitate complete health follow the psychological, physiological, and spiritual paths I have noted. The following material will make my procedures more clear.

Psychological Approach

If you, as a client, step into my office with a problem I try to create an atmosphere that will allow you to tell me all about the problem, including ideas about what is causing the complaint. Since most people who come to a psychologist think that their problems are psychological, I would let you explain the problem in those terms first. Then we explore beyond the basic introduction of the problem, into a more thorough psychological analysis, and finally into an holistic approach.

The way I look further psychologically is by asking more questions about what is presented and about what is not presented. Some statements will need more explanation and, if you failed to describe a certain area, such as your parents, I will check that out. In addition, I may ask you to keep a psychological journal, which involves a record of what causes you psychological problems during the week. I also have clients complete several forms that give me more psychological information. Typically I give a fear inventory, a personality schedule, and an assertiveness inventory.

After the journal has been kept for a while, and the psychological inventories are completed, I will go over the information with you, asking more questions—what is meant by a certain statement in the journal or response to a question on one of the inventories. My purpose is to gain as complete a picture as possible of your psychological functioning.

Physical Approach

If you were my client, at some point during your first or second session with me I might say, "Would you mind if I ask you some questions about other areas? I like to be as thorough as possible and check everything out. I may ask you some questions you wouldn't expect a psychologist to ask, if that is okay." Once I get permission to proceed, the first line of questioning I typically employ is in the area of physical functioning. I might say, "Imagine you are talking with a medical doctor, and simply describe anything that bothers you physically. Start at the top of your head and go down. I want you to tell me about everything, including head, ears, eyes, teeth, and neck. Your back, chest, including heart and lungs, and on down the line should be covered. Sleeping patterns, bowel movements, and sexual functioning are other areas to be considered. If you get stumped along the way I will ask questions to help out."

A thorough examination of diet and exercise patterns is incorporated into the analysis. I would take an initial "typical day" sample of food intake, and then usually request that you keep exact track of your diet for one week: a log of everything eaten or drunk, including snacks, meals, vitamins, alcohol, and medications. The type and frequency of your physical exercise is also determined. If you jog, lift weights or whatever, I ask what actually takes place in terms of time per exercise period, the strenuousness of the workout, and how often you engage in exercise each week.

In addition to this line of questioning I check out your past experiences with any form of physical illness or injury. Once again, my approach is to be as thorough as possible. If you have been involved in any auto accidents, falls, or any other type of stressful "physical" experience I need to know about it.

More and more I have come to the conclusions that an individual arriving for psychotherapy should be medically screened. I believe clients should be given an initial battery of medical tests—a *thorough* analysis of current physiological functioning. A recent example will illustrate the reason for this statement: The case involves a young woman, age 22, whom I referred to an M.D. with this complaint: she had been off birth control pills for two years, had not used any birth control method during that time span, and yet she had not become pregnant. In addition, she had abdominal cramping during and between her menstrual periods. The first physician, because of preliminary findings, sent the young woman to a gynecologist who diagnosed endometriosis. Presently, she is being medically treated to see if surgery can be avoided. (Two other women clients who decided to go off birth control pills altogether subsequently lost several of their anxiety symptoms.)

I have become more careful about appropriate medical referrals also because of experience in cases where referrals were not made by me, but in which the individual decided to seek medical help independently. I treated a 26-year-old woman for a period of three to four months, using a variety of methods. She continued to complain of excessive fatigue. Finally, she decided to go to our University Health Center where, after appropriate testing, a diagnosis of mononucleosis was made. In another case, a young man who experienced dramatic mood swings, uncontrollable junk food "eating binges," and headaches, decided to be checked out medically, and it was discovered he had very low blood sugar. Needless to say, a therapist could treat someone psychologically for years and never make a dent in these disorders! Now, rather than allowing such cases to slip by me, relying on "chance," I try to be as thorough as possible with each person.

Spiritual Approach

Along with an assessment of your physical and psychological functioning I also like to look at your spiritual functioning. I take a history of religious upbringing in terms of home and church and also involvement after leaving home. Other areas covered include how you feel about God, about guilt, about prayer, about meditation, about sin. The area of spiritual concern seems to be more touchy to deal with than diet and exercise or psychological functioning, but as mentioned above, it is crucial to treat the person as a whole. My own thinking about spiritual assessment and treatment is just in its infancy, but it is an area I feel stronger about, in terms of need, as I develop.

Spiritual aspects can be brought out in therapy or not, depending upon one's frame of reference. Take the example of physical exercise. One can look at the reason for exercising simply as being to keep in good condition, to feel good, physically fit and mentally alert. On the other hand, if one wants to, a spiritual significance can be placed on physical exercise. The body can be looked at as the "temple of the living God," one of the places where one communes with God. If the "temple" is not kept in balance by appropriate exercise, how can the God-force work to its full potential through the person?

The same logic can be applied to dietary considerations. If one has faulty eating patterns, it could be said that one is clouding up the full expression of one's spiritual self.

Assertiveness training may also be talked about along these lines. Assertion may be considered to have a spiritual base, in that one of the basic premises of assertion is to "treat others as you would have them treat you." Another religious precept which could be applied here is "what you sow you must reap." In this context, the more you manifest assertion to others the more you foster assertion toward yourself.

Much more could be said about analyzing the spiritual importance of these and other approaches, but at this point, it should be noted that all of these therapies work quite well without speaking of them in these terms. It is my feeling that therapy should be open to spiritual concerns. There will be clients who will need and want to deal with matters of this nature. Here again, referral to appropriate consultants is important. If a client has a strong leaning toward a particular religious denomination, the appropriate clergy will, of course, be a valuable referral source.

Holistic-Eclectic Treatment: The Case of Mary

I gather information about total functioning so that we—the client and I working together—can see where help is most needed. I am a little idealistic for some of my clients, but most don't like the complaints that they have whether they are psychological, physical or spiritual! Once they understand that a *total* treatment program may greatly improve or rid them of the complaints, they are ready to begin, even with some treatments which are not purely psychological in nature. I try to select a starting point or points in therapy appropriate to how complaints show themselves and what I think may help the fastest. For most of my clients I end up using an eclectic variety of approaches, rather than just one.

The case below demonstrates how I treated one client with multiple problems using a series of approaches. Her case was selected because Meditative Therapy was not the primary treatment and actually played a secondary role to the other approaches.

Although only 21 years old, this young woman revealed a history of instability which included two suicide attempts around age 16 and three "nervous breakdowns," the first at age 18, the second at age 19, and the third at age 20. Mary presently felt on the verge of, as she described it, "flipping out" again. Despite her difficulties, she had not been to any type of mental health professional before. She and her husband had one child who was three years old.

Pre-testing with the Fear Survey Schedule and Willoughby revealed that many items were marked at the highest or next highest point on the scale. She also reported that she became depressed easily, had low energy levels, became easily upset, and felt nervous and restless a good deal of the time. Her father caused her a great deal of difficulty because she felt intimidated around him and unable to express feelings to him. She felt that he never made a mistake and it was "horribly frightening" for her to make one. As one might guess, she was very non-assertive.

Questioning about her physical functioning revealed that she had developed bronchitis at age 3 and still had bouts of it at least twice per year. She also presently had acne, a problem of 10 years duration. Around the age of 18 she was involved in two auto accidents during which she experienced whiplash. She had received treatment, but reported having two vertebrae which were still quite painful. In addition, since the accident her kidneys caused her intermittent pain especially upon awakening in the morning. Other findings were that her bowel movements were irregular (taking place only once every two days or longer), her diet and exercise patterns were not satisfactory, and she felt tired a good deal of the time and fell asleep easily during the day even though she slept adequately each night.

Treatment Approach: Initially, I encouraged Mary to change her diet to high protein, low carbohydrate. This was suggested primarily because of low energy levels, nervousness, acne, depression and difficulty with her bowel movements. I also encouraged her to exercise regularly. I then taught her deep muscle relaxation and we constructed a thirteen-item hierarchy in order to employ systematic desensitization for her fear of making mistakes. (Many of the items centered around interactions with her father.) After successfully proceeding through the hierarchy, assertiveness was taught to her, using *Your Perfect Right* (Alberti & Emmons, 1974) as a basis. Mary was referred to an M.D. who specialized in back problems, for treatment of her painful vertebrae. After nine therapy sessions with me she was feeling quite well and wanted to have her husband come in with her for some marriage counseling. During the first joint session, I asked Mary and her husband to re-enact an argument concerning the handling of their 3-year-old. During the role playing, she became defensive, irrational, and started crying. As we explored this area of childhood she became excessively upset by events that reminded her of her own childhood. One example centered around her child's bike being stolen. When she found out about it she was shattered and started crying. Also she appeared to be excessively "soft" in disciplining her child. We decided to employ Meditative Therapy. Prior to her Meditative Therapy experience the results attained to that point (3 months of therapy) were evaluated. Those results, plus a final evaluation of results, are given below. First, let us see how she reacted to Meditative Therapy.

Meditative Therapy Themes and Experiences: Mary underwent five Meditative Therapy sessions and the main focus seemed to be on her childhood, primarily the pleasant times she had. Samples of Mary's childhood themes include playing with favorite toys, re-experiencing her old neighborhood, and enjoying a vivid fantasy life. Mary's only other consistent experiences were frequent feelings of coldness.

An analysis of Mary's transcripts revealed that there was *discharging, extended discharging,* and *reinforcement* in each of her five sessions. *Understanding* took place in three of the sessions and she experienced no *abreaction* or *new experience.*

Results: Mary's treatment totaled 17 sessions. Results were evaluated first after 11 sessions (3 months from the start of therapy), and second after 14 months from the start of therapy. After the 3-month evaluation of results Mary went through the 5 Meditative Therapy sessions. Changes in scores for the Fear Inventory and Willoughby are given in Table 9-1. It can be noted that she changed a great deal, as evidenced by the drops in her scores.

Table 9-1
THE CASE OF MARY
Fear Inventory and Willoughby Changes
At 3-Month and 14-Month Intervals

Inventory	Pre-Therapy Score	Post Score (3 months)	Post Score (14 months)
1. Fear Inventory	126	69	43
2. Willoughby Personality Schedule	53	17	8

Table 9-2 below gives her evaluation of specific complaints at the 3-month and 14-month points. The rating scale went from "no improvement" to "total improvement" on a 7-point scale.

Table 9-2 THE CASE OF MARY Degree of Improvement At 3-Month and 14-Month Intervals		
	Evaluation at:	
Presenting Complaint:	**3 Months:**	**14 Months:**
Bronchitis	No new "bouts" at this time	Average improvement
Kidney Pains	Total Improvement	Very Much Improved
Two Painful Vertebrae	Very Much Improved	Much Improved
Acne	Slight Improvement	Average Improvement
Nervousness	Total Improvement	Very Much Improved
Low Energy Levels	Total Improvement	Much Improved
Sleep Difficulties	Much Improved	Total Improvement
Bowel Movements	Much Improved	Average Improvement
Depressions	Total Improvement	Total Improvement
Fear of Making Mistakes	Much Improved	Very Much Improved

As can be seen by the tables, she noted a great deal of improvement in her complaints and this improvement was maintained nine months following completion of all therapies. The Fear Inventory and Willoughby scores confirm the same degree of improvement.

Evaluation of Therapy: Mary's View: Mary was very enthusiastic about her outcomes at 3 months from the start of therapy. She gave the following written comments at that point.

stages of Mary's individual counseling with me she and her husband were also going to a marriage counselor. Evidently they could not reconcile their differences.

As in the case of Kerrie, we have to wonder what caused the wonderful outcomes in this case. Mary felt that the dietary changes and the assertiveness training were the most important factors. I agree, but at the same time believe that systematic desensitization was crucial. Getting rid of a deep-seated fear of making mistakes sets the stage for learning to be more assertive and even for staying on a diet. I also feel that Meditative Therapy was important because it helped her feel better about her past.

What Happened to Meditative Therapy and the Inner Source? I realize that this example of Mary's therapeutic experiences will be highly disappointing or deflating to some readers. Up to this point I have touted the Inner Source experience and outcomes highly. In reading the example of Mary we find that she had excellent outcomes with minimal contribution from the Meditative Therapy process. Some will feel that this is an incongruent situation.

Let me backtrack as a first step in attempting an explanation for the seeming disparity. Why didn't I, as the therapist, decide to use Meditative Therapy with Mary when she first came to see me? My decision to begin with other therapies in lieu of Meditative Therapy was based on my judgement that Mary was not ready for it initially. This is where therapy becomes partly art rather than science, intuition instead of hard fact. I make a decision to apply a certain approach or not based on the individual's responses: feelings, thoughts, behaviors. Ideally I will have the person undergo a trial Meditative Therapy session in order to allow the person to make the choice, but in this instance I decided to employ other methods first. I felt that Mary needed to get to know me better, to learn to trust me, in order to respond optimally to the Inner Source process.

Once the client begins a method like systematic desensitization, assertion training, or Meditative Therapy, the client and I watch to see if the desired changes take place. If, after a reasonable period of time, the changes are not ensuing we switch to another approach. The basis of a dynamic, holistic-eclectic system is enlightened trial and error based on watching client response. The reason I eventually started Meditative Therapy with Mary was because the therapies used up until that time had not gotten to the problem area of her childhood. I made the guess that Mary was ready for Meditative Therapy by that time and that her Inner Source would deal with this problem.

Mary's Inner Source did not contain any dramatic abreactive or new experiences. It was not very "powerful" with her in terms of producing "heavy" material such as was true with Kerrie. Mary's Meditative Therapy was very gentle and straightforward. It appeared to have the single psychological purpose of helping her feel better about her childhood. From my knowledge about the full range of the workings of the Inner Source, or the full extent of possibilities of the Inner Source, I could have encouraged Mary to continue Meditative Therapy for more therapist-facilitated sessions. Unfortunately, that is a "frill" that I cannot justify in my work. My role is to help the person overcome the major portion of his or her presenting complaints. Once the bulk of one's life is apparently working well, as judged by reductions in complaints and client satisfaction, I must go on to other clients. I certainly wish that I could have taken the time to help facilitate Mary's Inner Source experience further. Perhaps at some point down the line she would have begun to experience "awakening" more completely. I make no judgements about why each person's Inner Source chooses not to be ready for the same level of experience that another's Inner Source is ready for. Some are ready for the stream to flow forcefully; others are ready only for a trickle.

This case and the other material in this chapter have been presented in order to illustrate some of the possibilities inherent in an holistic-eclectic treatment program. Such a program goes beyond the use of ony one method or series of methods of a psychological nature. For any given case it is difficult to predict what the key therapy will be leading to a successful outcome. For some, Meditative Therapy will be the crucial treatment; at times assertiveness training will be; at times dietary approaches; at times medical treatment. Despite the fact that certain therapies stand out

out for certain clients, it is still imperative that a *total treatment* approach be used. We are whole persons, psychophysiospiritu-logical persons, and should be treated as such.

The way I decide as a therapist which therapy to use with clients depends upon many factors. As I watch the person's response and listen to his or her Inner Source I may switch to another therapy after only one or two sessions. As a client you are my source of knowledge. If you are not responding well to Meditative Therapy or do not like it or believe in it I will usually switch to another approach. I try not to force my way upon you, but instead try to "go with" your feelings.

10

The Inner Source, Meditative Therapy and You

> *Thus, man is by no means merely a product of heredity and environment. There is a third element: decision. Man ultimately decides for himself! And, in the end, education must be education toward the ability to decide.*
>
> — *Viktor E. Frankl*

You may be trying to sort out and decide what to do with the material you have read to now. Perhaps one or more of these questions occurs to you: (1) Shall I go through some Meditative Therapy sessions? (2) Is Meditative Therapy dangerous? (3) Can I allow my Inner Source to work on my own without going to a therapist? (4) How should I select a therapist to help me with Meditative Therapy? (5) What are the Collective Characteristics of the Inner Source? (6) Does the Inner Source have a divine nature?

To help in your decision-making, and to bring this part of the book to a conclusion, I will comment on those questions.

1. Shall I go through some Meditative Therapy sessions?

I hope that you will engage in some type of inner experience. In my own life I began with hypnosis and actually practiced self-hypnosis for several years before I started concentrative meditation. I also went through systematic desensitization and the Standard Exercises of Autogenic Training prior to going through an initial series of 13 Meditative Therapy sessions with a friend as facilitator.

Of course, each person must decide for him or herself if or when to try an advanced method such as Meditative Therapy. If you have doubts about your readiness, but would like to become more ready, I suggest beginning with the more gentle procedures such as deep muscle relaxation, meditation or autogenic standard exercises. On the other hand, if you feel that any type of eyes-closed experience is not for you at this point, I respect that decision. I am not trying to push anyone into doing something which she or he is not ready to do.

2. Is Meditative Therapy dangerous?

You will recall that I have previously stated that one should have an average of 5 to 10 therapist-facilitated Meditative Therapy sessions prior to starting self-Meditative Therapy. These intensive experiences can be frightening and even dangerous for some people until their progress has reached a certain point, especially if a trained therapist is not present. There have been reports that simple concentrative meditation methods have produced disastrous results in some cases. Patricia Carrington, a clinical psychologist who wrote *Freedom in Meditation* (1977), reports on disturbing reactions she and other psychologists have observed with trainees in mantra meditation, especially Transcendental Meditation. One patient made a serious suicide attempt, another had a schizophrenic breakdown, apparently precipitated by meditation, and several persons experienced re-stimulation of symptoms of emotional illness. Meditative Therapy, attempted without therapist super-vision, could foster the same type of experiences.

I do not make the latter statement because either meditation or Meditative Therapy are *inherently* dangerous, but because both approaches are misunderstood. Anything that people have partial knowledge about is potentially very dangerous.

The individuals to whom Carrington referred who had negative reactions to meditation should have been carefully screened for prior physical and psychological problems before being allowed to go through meditation training. Meditation is *not* therapy and most meditation teachers are not professional therapists. Any person who has had a history of disturbing physical and/or psychological problems should not be taught to meditate unless he or she is carefully supervised by a professionally trained therapist. This therapist should be one who is knowledgeable about Meditative Therapy and, hopefully, holistic therapeutic concepts.

Evidently Carrington and the other psychologists whom she quoted were not familiar with the workings of the Inner Source. Had they been, they would have understood that the Inner Source will at times spontaneously begin to produce reactions once a state of altered consciousness begins. Properly understood, the curative workings of the Inner Source will be allowed to unfold in a supportive, therapeutic environment. They need not be overly frightening, cause the client to run off and try to commit suicide, or be misinterpreted as being schizophrenic. The Inner Source produces very logical, purposeful reactions, but if the person experiencing or observing these reactions is ignorant of this fact, it can be confusing and even dangerous.

One of the vital points I try to get across in the therapeutic section of this book (see Chapter 11) is that there is no danger if the therapist and client understand how the Inner Source works and trust it to decide what to do. The Inner Source may produce some powerful reactions, but these are natural and are not to be feared. I contend that it is best to let these reactions take place as fully as they wish. Carrington, following the standard exercises model of Autogenic Traning, urges the meditator either to stop meditation for a time or to reduce the meditation time in order to slow down the reaction taking place. "Undermeditating," as Carrington terms it, is an acceptable resolution in many cases, but the Inner Sources of some people are ready to release large amounts of disturbing material. Carefully supervised Meditative Therapy is the best alternative in these instances (see question 4 below).

I have included a therapist section in this book to provide professional therapists with vital background instruction in how to properly handle Meditative Therapy sessions. Most therapists have been taught to be too leery of "disturbing" reactions, such as have been reported in this book. Their reaction is often to try to shut off or drug down such reactions, to shock them away, or to look at the person as psychotic and recommend institutionalization. Some people having these type of reactions *are* psychotic, but most are simply trying to get well and, if allowed the natural way of the Inner Source, will come out whole. A sensitive and well-trained therapist is the best insurance that the difference will be recognized and treated properly.

Psychiatrist Lee Sannella, in the introduction to his book *Kundalini—Psychosis or Transcendence* (1976), beautifully states the point I am trying to make in terms of what he calls "the kundalini experience:"

> Tissues are torn, blood vessels severed, blood spilled, much fluid is lost; the heart races and the blood pressure soars. There is moaning, crying, and screaming. A severe injury? No, only a relatively normal human birth. The description sounds pathological because the symptoms were not understood in relation to the outcome: a new human being.

> In a darkened room a man sits alone. His body is swept by muscular spasms. Indescribable sensations and sharp pains run from his feet up his legs and over his back and neck. His skull feels as if it will burst. Inside his head he hears roaring sounds and highpitched whistling. Then suddenly a sunburst floods his inner being. His hands burn. He feels his body tearing within. Then he laughs and is overcome with bliss.

> A psychotic episode? No, this is a psycho-physiological transformation, a rebirth process as natural as physical birth. It seems pathological only because the symptoms are not understood in relation to the outcome: an enlightened human being.

> When allowed to progress to completion this process culminates in deep psychological balance, strength, and maturity. Its initial stages, however, often share the violence, helplessness, and imbalance that attend the start of human infancy.

3. *Can I allow my Inner Source to work on my own without going to a therapist?*

If you read this book in its entirety, *including the therapist's section*, and understand all of the requirements and cautions for undergoing Meditative Therapy and all the possible reactions that may take place during the therapy, you may wish to begin on your own. I urge you to proceed only with full consideration of the cautions noted in question 2 above, and following the guidelines listed below. The same applies to those who are willing to have a friend assist them, either by exchanging sessions or by having the friend serve as the "therapist" without taking a turn as the "client." If you choose either of these alternatives, there are a few suggestions I would like to give you about how to proceed.

The first suggestion is to *set up some way of judging whether or not you are making progress*. My approach would be to make a list of the things you are trying to overcome. This would be a list similar to those prepared for Jack, Kerrie, and Mary. This list will be composed of physical, mental, and spiritual components and may include both things you would like to see reduced and those you would like to see increased. You may derive help in constructing your list by analyzing the inventories in the Appendix. Remember that this list will not be exhaustive because your Inner Source knows more about you than you do consciously, and it will not be limited by your list, if you will always allow the Inner Source to do what it wishes to do. If you are having a friend help, you may decide to share your lists or not.

My next suggestion is to *treat yourself holistically-eclectically*, along the lines given in Chapter 9. I want to reemphasize that this is the ideal way to be treated, whether by a therapist or by yourself. Pay attention to your diet and exercise patterns, and make changes where you need to. Don't worry about what treatment is causing you to change and don't get upset if certain problems don't go away no matter what you seem to do. Your job is to be patient and to keep striving. If a problem doesn't go away and you know you are doing the best you can, don't lose faith or give up. Keep your eyes open for new ways to help yourself, and make sure that you keep up a basic program of help such as following a good diet, a good exercise program, regular relaxation-meditation and Meditative Therapy, and a system of keeping your daily life clear, such as more adequate assertive behavior.

Another suggestion for those who will be doing Meditative Therapy on their own or with a friend is to *seek the help of a knowledgeable therapist if you get bogged down* in some way or another, particularly with Meditative Therapy. Talking about what you are doing with an objective professional sometimes can get you started on the right track again if you have gotten to a point where you aren't quite sure what is needed. It would also be a good idea to re-read this book or pertinent sections of it as you proceed. The books by Luthe and Kitselman also contain valuable information. Check with a knowledgeable therapist when you feel you are having difficulty with Meditative Therapy.

A final caution needs to be mentioned: If you are going to exchange sessions with a friend, it is best to have each person begin with an uninterrupted series of at least five sessions before switching. After both have completed five sessions, you can begin alternating every other week or two weeks.

4. How should I select a therapist to help me with Meditative Therapy?

If you decide to follow my strong recommendation that you have some therapist-facilitated Meditative Therapy sessions first, then learn to do it on your own, what is the best way to proceed? Let us say that you are presently going to a therapist. In this case, I would ask him or her to read this book, explaining that you have an interest in trying the method. After reading the book, if your therapist does not wish to use Meditative Therapy, ask to be referred to a therapist who would be willing to do so. This does not necessarily mean you will end your relationship with your present therapist; it only means you will go to someone else who is willing to do Meditative Therapy as well.

It is worth mentioning that some therapists will resist the notion of trying a very new approach with which they are not familiar. Nevertheless a well trained and flexible professional will be open to your opinions about the direction of therapy. Don't hesitate to be assertive in asking for what you want.

If you are not going to a therapist presently, but do wish to go through Meditative Therapy, the first step is to find a therapist with a good reputation and who is willing to help you with Meditative Therapy. These two requirements may not always be found in one therapist. It is possible that an individual therapist with a good reputation will be unwilling to use Meditative Therapy, and some who are willing to use Meditative Therapy may not come highly recommended. One of the best ways to find an acceptable therapist is to find someone who knows the person and how he or she works. I suggest two methods: First, that you check with at least three mental health workers who are not in private practice to find out who they would recommend from the therapists who are in private practice. You could check with junior college or university counselors, high school counselors and psychologists, pastoral counselors, community mental health workers, psychology teachers, and so on. To find out who has a good reputation in any non-private practice setting you use a similar procedure. For example, to find a therapist in a community mental health clinic you should check with private practice, junior college or university counselors, and so on.

The second method is to find someone whose judgement you trust who has been to the therapist (as a client) and who feels that the person can be recommended. Perhaps you are willing to rely on one person's judgement, but it would be better if you could find several who have been to a particular therapist and feel good about him or her.

Whichever method you select, and perhaps you can use both methods, the ideal way to make your decision is to make an appointment and see how you feel about the therapist in terms of knowledge and in terms of personal qualities. Listen to what the therapist says about what methods are used to help others. See what types of questions you are asked and observe how the therapist responds when you ask questions. At some point, you should explain that you have this book and would like to have Meditative Therapy sessions. Be open to the fact that the person may wish to use other methods also. The therapist will want to know something about your background and the difficulties you are having, for example. Hopefully, the therapist will even use an holistic-eclectic approach as outlined in Chapter 9 (although he or she may not call it "holistic-eclectic," check for the therapist's awareness of physical and spiritual considerations, as well as psychological). Whatever the approach, make sure that at some point the therapist is willing to help you with Meditative Therapy.

If you find that you do not like the therapist or do not feel that he or she is helping you to your satisfaction, don't be afraid to switch therapists. I realize that this is an extra expense, but it is worth the money. There are usually several acceptable therapists in an area; therefore, there is no use staying with one whom you feel is less than satisfactory. If you find yourself switching therapists regularly, be mindful that you may have a physical rather than psychological problem or that you aren't willing to be helped yet.

In reading this section you may have noticed that I do not differentiate between various types of mental health workers when I use the term "therapist." Therapists come from a wide variety of disciplines within the field of mental health, such as social workers, psychiatrists, counselors, psychologists, and so on. It is always good to know what qualifications the therapist has, but this problem will usually be solved for you by using step one above. That is, if other professionals recommend the person, he/she will usually have acceptable credentials. You should be wary of those who advertise in the newspaper or in other unprofessional ways. (Although this type of advertising is presently deemed unethical by most professional societies, there is some indication that such standards may be changing.) For now, however, it is best to stick to those who are qualified through licensing to practice within their own field of mental health. I say this realizing some states do not yet license certain groups of mental health professionals. Check local mental health associations, community mental health centers, or university college counseling/psychology clinics for local licensing standards, so you may adequately assess who is qualified.

5. *What are the collective characteristics of the Inner Source?*

If we analyze numerous observations which have been made about the ways in which Inner Sources proceed and sift them down, what would be some of the enduring or collective qualities of the Inner Source? What are the resulting universal characteristics when a large amount of information about Inner Sources is synthesized? I believe that these qualities can be stated in terms of five major factors: *Constancy, Lovingness, Objectivity, Power, Wisdom.*

Constancy: Your Inner Source is always as close as closing your eyes. No matter how much you shut it down, are afraid of it, make fun of it, or fear it, your Inner Source is always ready to begin to help you, immediately, if you make the choice. If you allow it to help you, and then decide to give it up, it will always be ready to start again without any malice, without any condemnation.

Lovingness: The Inner Source is your advocate, it shows the ultimate amount of love for you. Your Inner Source wants you to be at your highest level of development and will do whatever is needed to help. When all others have forsaken you, when you are at the lowest point of your life, whether you are a criminal, a prostitute, a rapist, a cheat, a murderer, or whatever else is judged as lowly, your Inner Source loves you and will help you automatically, if you so choose. Your Inner Source is extremely patient with you. No matter how many times you fail, no matter how many resolutions to change you do not keep, no matter how many mistakes you make, no matter how much you do not love, you are loved by your Inner Source.

Objectivity: The Inner Source does not take choice away from you. You decide when to allow it to work or, if it starts on its own, you can choose to shut it down. If you want help making a certain life decision, your Inner Source may present the best way to deal with the situation, but you can always decide not to accept its wisdom. Isn't it intriguing that we have the power over something that is much more intelligent and loving than we are? Your Inner Source never takes your power to choose away from you, it never forces you to do anything, you are always in charge.

Power: In chapter 3 I summarized Kitselman's remarks concerning E-therapy. He gave the "ten powers of E" and also stated that we each could overcome fear, hatred, grief, that we can develop supernormal powers. These claims show the potential power of the Inner source. Kitselman is assuming, and I agree, that if one "E," or Inner Source, can do something, or possesses a certain trait or ability, then all "E's" can do so.

The Inner Source has access to realms of knowledge that go beyond our personal banks of knowledge. The Inner Source, when looked at collectively, has the power to take us to new levels of being beyond what is presently realized as our outside limit of development. At some point in time each can reach the height of perfection that the ultimate Inner Source has reached.

Wisdom: The Inner Source is very ingenious in the ways it helps. It takes a vast amount of data and presents it in unique and varied ways. The Inner Source also shows great wisdom in dealing with each person according to his or her personal maturational level. It is very careful to never go beyond what each person needs on all three tracks of response: psychological, physiological, spiritulogical.

6. *Does the Inner Source have a divine nature?*

Dr. Barbara Brown, one of the chief spokespersons for the biofeedback movement, in a speech at the 1977 International Conference on Meditation held in Chicago, Illinois, stated that mind goes beyond brain. Quoting several well-known brain researchers such as Sir John Eccles, Dr. Wilder Penfield, and Dr. Roger Sperry, to back up her contention, she reached the conclusion that "mind directs and brain mechanism executes."

Dr. Karl Pribram, noted brain theorist of Stanford University, is quoted in the June 21, 1976 issue (Vol. 1, No. 15) of *Brain/Mind Bulletin* as saying, "The brain we know now allows for the experiences reported from spiritual disciplines, whereas the brain I was raised on was a computer."

My presentation throughout this book of the magnificent workings, goals, outcomes and qualities of the Inner Source, combined with the comments of Drs. Brown and Pribram, have led me to characterize the nature of the Inner Source as divine.

In Chapter 1 I stated that the name chosen for the Inner Source makes little difference because it still works quite well no matter what label is affixed to it. I said that I do not know if we can call it a God-within or a superconscious or a biological wisdom, or, for that matter, an Inner Source. I would like to reiterate the truth of this important point, but to now depart from my stance of "neutrality" and speak in spiritual terms. If such discussions "turn you off" please feel free not to read on. All of the magnificent outcomes reported in this book have taken place without any mention of spiritual concepts to the clients involved. The clients who have experienced Meditative Therapy with me as guide have seldom, if ever, heard me discuss the Inner Source in spiritual terms and this has not prevented them from experiencing excellent outcomes. In short, *the Inner Source does not require that you "believe" in it, or accept any particular religious or spiritual orientation, only that you allow it to work for you.*

The Inner Source has been described as divine by authors writing both from an Eastern and Western viewpoint.

Paul Brunton, writing from the perspective of traditional Yoga, has thoroughly described for Westerners what he calls the Overself. Two of his most notable books on the subject are *The Quest Of The Overself* (1937) and *The Wisdom of The Overself* (1943). Brunton has the highest regard for what he terms the Overself. He calls it "the ray of God in man, the source of all enduring bliss, divine consciousness, man's essential being, fadeless, earthless, ageless, timeless, unlimited, and the innermost living core." All of his references to the Overself point directly to its divine nature.

In the book *The Three Pillars of Zen* we gain insight into the Zen Buddhist view. In addition to being called *Bodhi-mind* and *Buddha-nature*, there are over ten other names mentioned including "Essential-nature, Mind-essence, Original-nature, Real-self, and True-self." Kapleau (1967), the editor of *The Three Pillars of Zen*, states that the Bodhi-mind is "the innate dignity of man, the vibrant inner awareness of living Truth, intrinsic wisdom and the reverse of the mind of delusion and ignorance." Later in the book Bassui, a Zen master, indicates that everyone is perfectly endowed with the Buddha-nature.

Although these Buddhist descriptions do not refer directly to the divinity of our Inner Source I feel that the implication of such stands out.

Writings originating from Western teachings focus more directly on our Inner Source as a God-within.

In an essay on self-reliance, Ralph Waldo Emerson, the famed American author, stated that "God is here within." In a later essay, he elaborated on this belief speaking in terms of an *Over-soul:*

The Supreme Critic on the errors of the past and the present, and the only prophet of that which must be, is that great nature in which we rest as the earth lies in the soft arms of the atmosphere; that Unity, that Over-soul, within which every man's particular being is contained and made one with all other; that common heart of which all sincere conversation is the worship, to which all right action is submission; that overpowering reality which confutes our tricks and talents, and constrains everyone to pass for what he is, and to speak from his character and not from his tongue, and which evermore tends to pass into our thought and hand and become wisdom and virtue and power and beauty. We live in succession, in division, in parts, in particles. Meantime within man is the soul of the whole; the wise silence, the universal beauty, to which every part and particle is equally related; the eternal One. And this deep power in which we exist and whose beatitude is all accessible to us, is not only self-sufficing and perfect in every hour, but the act of seeing and the thing seen, the seer and the spectacle, the subject and the object are one. We see the world piece by piece, as the sun, the moon, the animal, the tree; but the whole, of which these are the shining parts, is the soul. Only by the vision of that Wisdom can the horoscope of the ages be read, and by falling back on our better thoughts, by yielding to the spirit of prophecy which is innate in every man, we can know what it saith. (p. 262-263)

Another statement by Emerson reveals more of the depth of the Oversoul:

All goes to show that the soul in man is not an organ, but animates and exercises all the organs; is not a function, like the power of memory, of calculation, of comparison, but uses these as hands and feet; is not a faculty, but a light; is not the intellect and the will; is the background of our being, in which they lie — an immensity not possessed and that cannot be possessed. From within or from behind, a light shines through us upon things and makes us aware that we are nothing, but the light is all. A man is the facade of a temple wherein all wisdom and all good abide. What we commonly call man, the eating, drinking, planting, counting man, does not, as we know him, represent himself, but misrepresents himself. Him we do not respect, but the soul, whose organ he is, would he let it appear through his action, would make our knees bend. (p. 263)

The Inner Source is our God-part, our direct link to God. Where else, but within our own person, does our divine nature commune with us? This position is not a new one. Our higher nature, whether called the Universal Mind, the Bodhi, the Over-self, the Oversoul, the God-within, has been spoken of for centuries.

University of Illinois psychologist, O.H. Mowrer, has noted that the church itself may have fostered a misconception of God as something outside of ourselves. In fact, suggests Mowrer, there is sufficient evidence to conclude that God is also within us, "a part of our own selves and innermost experience." Mowrer cites I Kings from the Bible:

And behold the Lord passed by, and a great and strong wind rent the mountains, and broke in pieces the rocks before the Lord, but the Lord was not in the wind; and after the wind an earthquake, but the Lord was not in the earthquake, and after the earthquake a fire, but the Lord was not in the fire; and after the fire—a still small voice (18:11-12).

The still small voice is perhaps the ultimate way that the God-within or Inner Source communicates with us, but as we have seen throughout the book, there are many, many ways the Inner Source signifies itself.

The Cayce material speaks of our internal link to God in the following manner:

Oft has it been said, as of old—not in the storm, not in the earthquake, not in that of anything outside of *self* may *God* be found by man; for to ascend into heaven or to descend into hell He is there—in thine own heart! The kingdom is within. When self closes the door to the heart, to the attributes of the Father, the Son, self *alone* separates self from that knowledge, that power of His love, His attributes, His faith, His knowledge and power in the earth;   for I am persuaded, neither powers without, nor trials, nor tribulations, may *separate* my soul from its

Maker. *Only* self—made one *with* His power—denying that He is existent within self *separates* self from the Maker.

Perhaps the vital factor in the ultimate importance of Meditative Therapy is that it leads us to an exploration of our spiritual nature, which to me is our highest calling. Although in this book I have stressed the therapeutic benefits of Meditative Therapy, I do recommend that once you contact your Inner Source that you then continue to do so regularly for the rest of your life. Developing our spiritual nature is a continual, eternal process.

The End

In closing this part of the book I would like to share some unique ways in which our Inner Source finishes its journeys. There are, of course, many ways for a Meditative Therapy session to end. Some individuals will simply feel nothing else coming in, others will feel their eyes just pop open, and others will begin noticing the sounds of the building more clearly, or will be thinking of what they need to do the rest of the day. Most endings follow these types of patterns, but once in a while there will be unique endings, some of which are now shared.

It's done, I can feel myself pushed up into full consciousness, like coming out of sleep.

Now it seems to be deciding whether or not to end it now. Kind of feels like I'm going into different states of consciousness, up and down, from one state into another. That's it, my eyes just popped open.

What time is it? (*9:15*) The word "love" just went through my mind several times, then it said, "Look at the time." And I'm done now.

Now I see a little man up in my forehead, and he's in the middle of a stage taking bows. And that's it, it's over.

I just saw myself curl up on my right side and go to sleep. Now I just saw the words "The End." I think it's the end.

Part II

FOR THE THERAPIST

"Perhaps in the coming generation of younger psychologists, hopefully unencumbered by university prohibitions and resistances, there may be a few who will dare to investigate the possibility that there is a lawful reality which is not open to our five senses; a reality in which present, past, and future are intermingled, in which space is not a barrier and time has disappeared; a reality which can be perceived and known only when we are passively receptive, rather than actively bent on knowing. It is one of the most exciting challenges posed to psychology."

—Carl Rogers

181

11

Facilitating
Meditative Therapy:
Procedures and Cautions

I have discussed throughout this book the power of the Inner Source to bring about changes in one's life. The support of a professional therapist is essential to "monitor" the initial stages of getting in touch with this power, and to help the individual to develop an independent capacity to allow the Inner Source to work. Thus, this chapter presents detailed instructions for the therapist to provide that solid foundation for the client's future work with his or her Inner Source.

Therapist Preparation

An adequate background in therapies which work with the Inner Source can be obtained by reading and studying the material in this book, including the Appendices, and the original sources given in Chapters 2, 3, and 12. In my own research I prefer to go to original sources whenever possible in order to be able to understand the complete story. The summaries provided in this book should serve only as a stimulus to delve further. The sources should be read, re-read and discussed with others. Further, one should check out (read) the references offered in these books. I believe the professional should become an "expert" on a therapy which he/she intends to use.

At some point it would be a good idea to have a series of Meditative Therapy sessions yourself. It is not clear whether you should have personal experience with the therapy *first* before using it with clients. In my own case I utilized Meditative Therapy with clients for over two years before I began having sessions myself. I then underwent 13 sessions with the assistance of a friend and presently try to do sessions on my own about once per week. Prior to using Meditative Therapy I put myself through the Autogenic Standard Exercises (Luthe, 1969 a) over a period of 3 or 4 months. The idea to be stressed here is that one should at some point undergo the Meditative Therapy experience in order to gain first hand knowledge about its workings. It is powerful, and can be frightening to the client. Reassurance from personal experience of the therapist is very supportive.

Learning through your own experience in facilitating others in Meditative Therapy is the next key step. The more sessions you listen to and, preferably, record, the more you learn about the great diversity and wisdom of the Inner Source. I have personally recorded over 400 individual sessions in my own handwritten notes. At first this was done because of the expense involved for audio recording. In time, however, I came to realize the irreplaceable knowledge I gained by handwritten recording. Writing down session content word for word is not necessarily easy and, of course, not always possible because of the speed with which some clients report, but it is worth the effort. Shorthand skills are useful, and if one can afford audio tapes these would be invaluable for "back up." (Luthe requires that all who undergo Autogenic Abreaction purchase or have access to a tape recorder.)

Personal Qualities of the Therapist

Professional use of any type of therapeutic approach requires certain qualities in the therapist. Not all are suited to use assertiveness training, hypnotherapy, bioenergetics, Rolfing, rational-emotive therapy, or client-centered therapy. The same is true of Meditative Therapy since certain characteristics seem to be helpful in order to be able to facilitate it successfully. The personal qualities most needed are patience, trust, tolerance and openness.

Patience is necessary in Meditative therapy because of the amount of time required for the therapy. Although we never know exactly how long a session will last, it is best to allow 1½ or 2 hours. Sitting quietly and recording for this period of time might prove to be boring for some professional therapists.

Trust means that one must be accepting of anything the Inner Source wishes to do, to have the faith that the Inner Source will never violate anyone or require anything that cannot be handled. There will be times of doubt, but if one can be patient and trusting the Inner Source always goes toward the positive in the end. It may appear to take backward steps at times before it is able to go forward, but growth often follows that pattern. A useful guide is to remember that usually ''all things come to those who wait.''

Because the Inner Source may go backward, or into ''darkness,'' before it goes forward, or into ''light,'' the therapist must have a great deal of *tolerance*. The facilitator must be able to tolerate a good deal of ''heavy'' or ''powerful'' material, such as the client's experiences with pain and upset, experiences of murderous aggression, ''violent'' bodily movements, reliving of traumatic events from the past, parapsychological experiences. Listening to this type of experience it is almost impossible not to ''feel'' with the person. Identifying with what the client is going through will at times elicit reactions in the therapist, such as sadness, exhaustion, exhilaration, anger, crying. There is also the possibility that the session content may trigger some of the therapist's own material that needs to be dealt with through therapy.

Openness is the final quality I would like to emphasize. There are times when the Inner Source appears to be very ambiguous and contradictory in what is being presented. The Inner Source is very difficult, if not impossible, to understand at times and even seems to produce nonsense at times. If one can simply be open and wait non-judgementally, the end result is worthwhile. No matter what happens it is best to trust and accept rather than to criticize what transpires. Even if some of the material presented goes against one's belief system or background of experiences, it is most therapeutic to be open and accepting if possible.

I do not claim to manifest all of these qualities to the optimum myself. I feel that I continue to improve from observing the Inner Source at work in myself and in my clients. It could be stated that the Inner Source possesses these qualities, and others such as love and forgiveness, to an infinite degree and thereby serves as a good model for others to follow.

One may, of course, have all of the qualities mentioned and still not have the desire to conduct Meditative Therapy. There are many paths to the same therapeutic goals. You may not like Meditative Therapy, or may think it's okay, but not for you. So be it.

Should you elect, as a professional therapist, to attempt Meditative Therapy with your clients, please study carefully the balance of this chapter.

Is the Meditative Therapist Really Non-Directive?

Throughout these discussions you will detect a certain ambivalence on my part regarding how "active" the meditative therapist's role should be. Perhaps I can clarify my position by restating that it is of *primary* importance to *trust the client's Inner Source.*

Because the client may be resistant, or fearful, or non-trusting, I will act in a "directive"—perhaps even "pushy"—manner, *to get the client to stay with the therapy and allow the Inner Source to work.*

I consider this directiveness to be facilitative in that my responses are given in order to help the Inner Source, to get the client to step aside consciously and allow it to carry out its therapeutic and creative journey. When one raises a garden or a child there is a need to be directive at times, but this direction should not be too harsh and overburdening. The natural ways of growth are best when facilitated to parallel those already inherent in the organism.

I must make a judgement in each case, of course, about the client's *capacity* to proceed, and in so doing I follow these general guidelines:

1. The ultimate decision in every case lies with the client;
2. I "push" only those clients who clearly have trust in me;

3. I try to remain sensitive to the client's strength and do not push beyond what I consider to be a "strong encouragement" to proceed;
4. I do not attempt to break the spirit of the client;
5. I do not push for any particular result or direction, only to allow the Inner Source to do its work;
6. I encourage the client to consider the alternatives, and point out again the potential of Meditative Therapy.

In short, the therapist must demonstrate his/her confidence in the therapy and encourage the client to trust the process as well. In that regard, all therapies are "directive." In Meditative Therapy, the therapist and client agree to trust the Inner Source. Once that commitment is made, both remain "non-directive," allowing the power of the Inner Source to work in *its* wisdom.

Role of the Therapist in Meditative Therapy

The therapist is very important in Meditative Therapy, despite the non-directive nature of the process, and the curative leadership of the Inner Source. Specifically, the therapist is responsible for: (1) selecting clients; (2) introducing and instructing clients in the process of Meditative Therapy; (3) answering questions which the client may have; (4) prompting the client to continuously describe what is taking place; (5) reminding the client to be patient and not to interfere with the process; (6) handling fears and resistances; (7) making sure that the individual allows the session to finish properly; (8) assigning homework; (9) being available between sessions as needed; (10) following up after Meditative Therapy is completed. Each of these areas will be dealt with in greater depth in the remainder of this chapter.

Selection of Clients

It is my belief that *each individual* should have the opportunity to observe the workings of his or her Inner Source. After contacting the Inner Source, the client may decide not to continue. There are certain clients who will choose not to participate in Meditative Therapy after hearing a basic explanation. I respect this decision and attempt to help the best I can with other approaches. There are also clients with whom I decide not to begin Meditative Therapy until other methods are employed. I recently analyzed my choice of therapeutic approach for my twenty-five most recent clients. The group included seventeen counseling center and eight private practice clients; there were sixteen females and nine males. Meditative Therapy was my choice for twenty clients; assertion training was chosen for three and client-centered for the remaining two. Of the five with whom I did not begin with Meditative Therapy, I subsequently utilized it with two.

Interestingly, Luthe elects to use Autogenic Abreaction in less than fifteen percent of his cases. It is my observation that the Inner Source begins its work with each person on his/her own level in a very wise, step-by-step manner. I feel that it is desirable for each person to be allowed to choose whether or not to get in touch with the Inner Source at some point in therapy based on actual experience if possible.

If I was just beginning to use Meditative Therapy with clients, my first step would be to select a few for a type of "pilot study," using some combination of the following categories: (1) those who have been interested in or involved in some form of altered state of consciousness such as meditation, hypnosis, relaxation, or psychedelic drugs; (2) individuals who have been deeply involved in spiritual or mystical movements; (3) those who are deeply involved in and moved by religion, no matter what faith; (4) those who have shown an interest in parapsychological phenomena through personal experiences, reading, contact with others; (5) those who are under tension which manifests itself in observable signs (involuntary jerks, twitches, tics); (6) persons with whom I have very good rapport or mutual trust and understanding.

The reason for the first four choices is that these individuals tend to be more open to the altered state of consciousness type of experience. The fifth choice is given because these individuals have overt signs that their Inner Sources are under stress and pressing to release it. Usually, if they will undergo an initial session, the results will be reinforcing enough in the form or relaxation to the system to encourage continuing. The sixth choice is included because established rapport is a very good basis to enter a new venture. Because of the need to establish rapport I usually will not start Meditative Therapy with a new client until the second session, and often not until the third or fourth.

It should be noted that Meditative Therapy, like all powerful techniques, should be utilized with appropriate regard for contraindications (see Chapters 1 and 13, and Appendix G) as well as material later in this chapter).

Introducing the Client to Meditative Therapy

Clients who agree to participate in Meditative Therapy should be given a general introduction to the therapy. An example of the form such an introduction might take is given below:

"Today I would like to explain about a new approach which I feel might be helpful to you. It works on the assumption that each of us has inside a source or intelligence that knows everything about us and knows what to do to help. This Inner Source seems to be very wise and capable of doing anything to set you free, so to speak, or to get you going toward your full potential."

At this point I will usually say, "How does that sound?" or "Do you have any questions?" Individual clients will either say that it sounds okay and want to know what to do to start, or they will have questions. Questions should be answered honestly, but in a general manner because of the individual differences in response each person has to the therapy. For example, to the question, "How does it work?" I might answer as follows: "Well, it works by having you visualize with your eyes closed such things as colors or patterns or events from the past that have bothered you. The human system seems to store pain that hasn't been completely dealt with from bad experiences. If it gets a chance to release the pain it will. Sometimes your Inner Source will do this by recreating pain or by having your body jerk or twitch or cry. So the therapy can be upsetting at times." At this point I may offer some examples of what other clients have gone through, but I am always quick to point out that each case is different and there is no way to predict precisely what will happen to them.

It is my preference to give the explanation about Meditative Therapy near the end of the session just prior to the one in which I would like to start the therapy. In this way the person will have at least a week to think about the therapy and to come up with further questions to be answered before beginning. Some questions about what will take place during the therapy can only be answered by saying, "We will have to wait and see because each person's Inner Source operates differently, depending on that person's needs." Although the therapist will want to try and answer as many questions as possible, it is not possible to prepare one for all of the eventualities of Meditative Therapy. Most clients ask only a few questions and are willing to try the therapy after a basic explanation similar to the one given above.

Explaining about Meditative Therapy a week before you plan to start permits arrangement of an appointment time of at least 1½ hours for the first session. You never know how long a particular client's sessions will last until you become used to how that particular Inner Source functions. Sessions may last anywhere from 20 minutes to over 2 hours, so it is best to have extra time if it is needed.

If the client has no questions at the initial MT session, the therapist should explain how to proceed. It is helpful to give an additional statement about ending the session by saying something like: "As you proceed in the session today be sure that you pay attention to when your Inner Source wants to finish. It will usually let you know when it is done for the day." By sensitizing the client to this fact you will lessen the chances of missing when the Inner Source is finished. With more experience, you will usually be able to tell when the session is finished, but it is, of course, best that the client learn to figure it out. Sometimes I forget to mention this factor before the session begins and so will interject it at an opportune time during the session.

The essential things for the client to do are: (1) lie back, close the eyes; (2) watch patiently; (3) describe continuously what is being experienced; and (4) allow the Inner Source to do what it wants to do to help. I usually remind the client not to interfere with the Inner Source, but simply to trust in what it wants to do. It seems to be very wise: more so than the client or the therapist.

One other factor to be mentioned to the client at the end of the first session concerns a possible build-up of anxiety or pressure just prior to the next session. The Inner Source will often begin preparing in advance material to be released. Remember that Kerrie (Chapter 8) could hardly climb the stairs at times in order to get to the office and would have tears appear "automatically" once in the office. Some will simply feel edgy or depressed. The build-up can take many forms, including dislike of the therapist, so it is vital that the therapist mention the possibility of the pre-session build-up.

I have not kept track of the frequency of this phenomenon, but some report it and others do not seem to experience it. Therefore, mentioning it to the client only as a possibility is important, because clients who do experience it may misinterpret it and stop coming unless they have been warned. A recent example concerns a client of mine who actually came for the second Meditative Therapy appointment, but as he was sitting in the waiting area, kept getting more and more depressed and upset. The build-up had started earlier that day and had gotten progressively worse. Unfortunately, I was five minutes late for the appointment, so he simply decided to leave. Several weeks later we did get back together and he told me, why he had left unexpectedly. During the evening of that same day, he had a "heavy" time. The message from the Inner Source was, as interpreted by the client, "I wanted to stay and go through with it and you blew it by leaving." Fortunately, if the person can realize what is taking place and go through with the session, the Inner Source will clear the feelings and the client will feel much better. Build-ups will usually become less and less of a factor after several additional sessions have been completed, as the Inner Source eliminates problems which have produced them.

Answering Client Questions

Most client questions come during the initial minutes of the first, and possibly the second, session. These questions relate primarily to whether or not the client is doing the therapy "correctly." Below

are several actual questions, followed by my responses, taken from
Meditative Therapy transcripts.

Questions	Responses
"Am I just supposed to exper-ience it or what?"	"Yes, and just describe what is happening."
"Whatever I feel, I say?"	"Yes."
"Should I just start telling you?"	"Yes."
"Should I report what I am thinking about?"	"Yes, anything you think or see or feel."
"I'm not sure where to start, right now I'm aware of my body functioning."	"Just describe it."

It is a good idea to reassure and reinforce client questions to
encourage continued description of what is happening. The
following examples from actual sessions suggest how the therapist
might respond in the early stages of Meditative Therapy.

Client Description	Therapist Response
"My stomach's becoming tight."	"Okay."
"My face doesn't feel so hot, it's cooled off, but I get this blue. It comes and goes."	'Mhm. How does the rest of your body feel?"
"I feel like waiting, waiting, waiting in the fog."	"Mhm."
"Just noises, tense, colors, different patterns."	"Just describe those."
"Not really much in the way of colors, just flows, no set pattern."	"Keep watching and describing."

Once the therapist feels confident that the person is proceeding well, this minimal amount of direction may be dropped. Knowing what types of process events to watch for, the therapist can determine whether or not the therapy is progressing as it should. While there are wide variations in client response, there are certain types of events which indicate that the therapy is proceeding in the direction planned by the Inner Source. These signs along the way may be of either a physical or psychological nature. When the client experiences bodily reactions, such as feelings of falling, tingling, heaviness or lightness, pain or discomfort, there is a good chance that the therapy is working correctly. If one reports seeing lights, colors, patterns, or objects such as clouds or houses, or events from the past, these mental or visual signs usually indicate that the therapy is going as it should. Inner directed thought patterns are also a good sign to watch for, but it should be determined that the person is not consciously deciding to think of certain areas, but simply allowing the Inner Source to prompt one's thinking. The therapist needs to listen carefully in connection with thoughts in the Meditative Therapy process because there seem to be two types: everyday, waking, purposeful thought; and inner-directed thought which is being presented by the Inner Source. Because thought patterns are a crucial indicator of the correct working of the Inner Source, examples of outer-directed and inner-directed thought are given below. The outer example is from a man's first session; the inner example is from a woman's first session.

An Example of Outer-Directed Thought:

I don't know, I've been dreaming all day, daydreaming, about what this teacher was telling me to put out effort to understand. I tried to force things out of my mind, but it didn't work—like hang gliding, skiing, backpacking. Those were all I could think about. I just can't concentrate; my mind wanders. Last night I went to a concert, then worked on my senior project until about 10 p.m. I understand the process well. And I read about Lindberg and I bought "Centennial," something important to read when I go on vacation.

An Example of Inner-Directed Thought:

I feel bored very often (*shakes head*). I see my living room for some reason, I don't know why, and I think about energy. My living room is my trap because I feel so comfortable there. Hmm, I can hear the noises outside very clearly. (*shakes head*) I see nothing now. I'm saying some Lord have mercy on us. That makes me want to cry. Oh dear, I don't even really believe I don't think and yet I revert to all my prayers. Oh dear, (*wipes tears*). I went jogging this weekend and when I smelled the fresh dew of early morning it felt so good, but I wanted to cry then, too (*takes a deep breath, fidgets*). I'm not too comfortable, I say what ever comes will come. I thought of mother, father and some sexual image, very vague. And I cut it off before it's even actually there. I don't, know, I'm feeling all kinds of fragments or sentences. Then, well, I'm alright. I'm kind of battling inside I think. Off to battle on a horse — Don Quixote — he was fighting fantasies. A (*voice cracks*) my horse is dead (*starts sobbing, covers mouth*). I think I'm nuts (*stops sobbing, wipes tears, shakes head*). It's alright, it's alright now (*shakes head*). I really feel dumb. Oh, I don't understand that about the horse, I've never had a horse.

I tell the difference between inner- and outer-directed thinking by listening to the content, the voice qualities, and the bodily reactions. In the first case above, the content was "here and now" and seemed to jump around. Also, the voice quality was light and airy and there were no significant body reactions, like feelings of heaviness, spinning, crying, pain. In the second case, the content was "here and now" at times, but evolved into something "heavy." Also, the voice quality was more serious or studied, and even cracked or became a whisper at times. Finally, her body reaction was to cry as she got further into the content.

The content in the first example above stayed the same for about 15 minutes, so I finally intervened and asked the client to try restricting himself to only visual reactions and body reactions. This move will usually get the client on the right track. It is important not to be too quick about intervening, however, because the Inner

Source may be working with something which can only be discovered as time progresses. As the client gains in ability to do the sessions alone, he or she will come to know when thoughts are inner- or outer-directed.

In order to further clarify whether or not the therapeutic process is on the right track, the initial several minutes of two different clients first sessions are presented below. These are both examples in which the process was working correctly according to physical and mental events taking place. (Observable client physical reactions and therapist comments to the client are placed in brackets.)

Starting time 8:15 a.m. — (moves her left arm — lowers arms to sides) (8:18) my head and forehead feel really hot and dark, like there is a big cloud hanging over my head [Mhm] — my face doesn't feel so hot, it's cooled off, but I get this blue, it comes and goes. [Mhm] — [How does your body feel?] feels kind of tense, I'm trying to relax [don't try to relax, let it be tense if it wants to be] mostly tense in my upper arms — I feel that most of my vision is out of my right eye and my left eye is all black — Am I supposed to tell you all my passing thoughts type thing? [mhm] — (moves left arm) — my arms still feel tense, maybe I should shake them or rub them (do what you feel prompted to do] (lifts left and rubs it with right hand) — (left index finger twitches) (deep breath) my stomach's becoming tight [mhm] — (moves arm, deep breath) my stomach, seems like someone is stirring it or something, hard to explain (laughs) Just that there is movement in there or something. I'm wondering why. When things bother me they tend to go to my stomach. Seems like there are other places it could bother me. — my left leg is very tense (moves it slightly) — I'm getting these really bright orange impressions. (8:35).

Starting time 6:15 p.m.: — should I go ahead and relax? [not purposefully] Freda comes to mind; group setting; she's sitting next to me — now I'm flying really fast in a superwoman outfit, looking down on everybody. It's cold, kind of trying to land, but can't — can't get my feet down — really strange — I see Bishop's

Peak, foggy, cold, but pleasant. Smell it. Very relaxing and soothing. On top sitting there—cold, legs are getting tingly. Strange, really very strange. Left foot especially, like the foot is waking up. Now light is coming through and webbing and weird fluctuating and some blue spots and lines and things are moving. Uncomfortable, like I want to open my eyes. Chin and neck are tight, really strange. Eyes are going crazy.—Flying over Bishop's Peak again and something very hot is in front of me. Cold to very hot, I really don't like it, I'm going to move away. Very hot, very strange. I'm going back to the mountain, I don't like it. I see my dog, she wants to come inside, drinking water out of the toilet—Now on the beach and she is chasing birds—grabs me by the sleeve pulling my jacket off—cold—foot in the water and cold—Eyes are doing weird things again. Duck pond. Feeding ducks. And at Freda's apartment and she has a cat, sits on my lap. Now going outside, neat house. Very cloudy. Out in her garden, really nice. Looking at my lamp. Feel my left arm, especially, getting numb, really strange. Eyes feel funny too, big weights on them. Head too. Pushing it to the mat. Lot of wavy lines in front of my eyes. Harold is at the door and he is naked. Okay! (*deep breath*) I would really like to shut the door, but I can't do that.—I'm flying, I got away. I still see him, very difficult to get away from. Also having hostile thoughts. (*rubs eyes, deep breath*). (6:25)

As can be observed, the first case was a 20-minute segment whereas the second was only a 10-minute segment. There were wide variations between these two sessions. The first was relatively slow-paced with more therapist support, while the second was very fast moving and changing and required almost no therapist interjection. Both, however, were working properly according to the content described.

It would be good at this point for the reader to review the *Process of Therapy* sections for each of the three non-directive approaches to the Inner Source (Chapters 3 and 12). By becoming familiar with what possibilities exist concerning process you will become more comfortable, relaxed, and able to recognize when a session is going along in the right direction. I have only dealt with one case where the Meditative Therapy process could not seem to work in the right way. I am quite certain in retrospect that this was due to fear on the individual's part. She had been hospitalized several times in mental hospitals, had received shock therapy and drug treatments, and had reacted with bad side effects to both treatments. Unfortunately, the thought of Meditative Therapy triggered off some of these bad memories and she was not able to trust. In addition, because her experience came up early in my own Meditative Therapy career I didn't have enough confidence and knowledge to encourage her to trust sufficiently.

Prompting the Client to Describe What is Taking Place

Another duty of the therapist is to keep the client verbalizing. This doesn't mean that one must describe continuously, but if there are long pauses and the individual does not appear to be asleep, it is useful to ask what is taking place. If there are events taking place and the person is not describing—emphasize continual description. Also, the effort to verbally describe the experience may sensitize the client to the importance of seemingly "trivial" occurrences (body feelings, random thoughts).

Emphasis on Patience and Non-Interference

The therapist is to remind the client to be patient and not to interfere with the therapeutic process. It is best for both to trust what the Inner Source wishes to do. Examples of how the therapist might handle this are given below.

Client Statement	Therapist Response
"Now I feel shaky inside, I feel like crying."	"Yes, just let it happen."
"Now I have a feeling of wanting things to happen, though I know I shouldn't want to force it."	"Right, just be patient. It works very subtly at times, so let it do what it wants to do."

"What if I don't see   "That's okay, there may be
anything?"   periods where you won't, just let
                                        it do anything it wants."

"I feel real small, but puffy   "Just try to let it happen
sometimes. — I don't like the   anyway."
way I feel."

Handling Fears and Resistances

The therapist must be able to handle the fears and resistances of the client, which are often related to the examples in the preceding section, because the client at times will have a tendency to fear or resist the therapeutic process when it gets to be uncomfortable.

Of the natural and synthetic approaches to the Inner Source discussed in Chapters 2, 3, and 12, only Luthe (Vol. 6), in writing about Autogenic Abreaction, presents a thorough and systematic analysis of resistance. He devotes 87 pages to this very important subject and his treatment of the topic goes beyond any, including those found in psychoanalytic sources. The material is essential reading for anyone planning to do Meditative Therapy. Luthe divides resistance into five broad categories. (1) Antagonizing Forms of Resistance, (2) Facilitating Forms of Resistance, (3) Essential Forms of Resistance, (4) Indirect Psychophysiologic Resistance, and (5) Resistance and Autogenic Abreaction at Home.

I feel that most resistances in Meditative Therapy are based on fears of various kinds. For most people, when they think about the topic of resistance in psychotherapy, it seems to be characterized as an underhanded way of "beating the therapist at his own game," or an unconscious desire to destroy one's chances of getting well, and so on. It has been my observation that the reason clients don't "cooperate" is that they are afraid. They have some very real reason why they are unwilling to proceed.

There are five readily apparent fears which may come up before, during, or after Meditative Therapy: (1) Fears of Self-Disclosure; (2) Fears of "Deep Mental Illness; (3) Fears of Pain and Discomfort; (4) Fears of Losing Control; (5) Fears that the Therapy is not working properly.

Fears of Self-Disclosure: This fear relates to the idea that the person does not wish to share with the therapist what is taking place during Meditative Therapy. Although most are willing to discuss the problem with the therapist, some will just not return for further sessions. If the individual is willing, very often the fear can be "talked out" so that therapy can continue. On at least one occasion I have allowed an individual to be in therapy without any verbal description. This alternative is not very good, however, because the therapist has no way of knowing if the person is allowing the Inner Source to do what it wants to do. There are no check points provided in order to see if the therapy is going correctly. The fear of self-disclosure can also be closely related to the other fears discussed below.

Fears of "Deep" Mental Illness: The very setting of Meditative Therapy will provoke fears in a certain percent of the clients. Requesting that the client lie down on a pad, couch, or the carpet seems to automatically reinforce all of the stories they have seen or heard about "deep" analysis or probing of the inner recesses of the mind. Closing the eyes appears to bring up fears related to the idea that one may uncover some deep dark secret from the unconscious mind which could not be faced. Once again, through sharing these fears with the therapist, reassuring discussions will often free the client to proceed. Usually these fears are quite evident from the observable reactions of the client to the description of the therapy. The therapist should invite the individual to explore the fear further.

At times during the therapy one will be presented with material which will trigger some of these fears. The person may have a parapsychological experience of some type or start feeling "weird" feelings or seeing unusual things. The therapist can generally handle these fears by simply reminding the person to accept what the Inner Source wishes to do and to describe, not interpret, what is taking place.

Fears of Pain and Discomfort: Even though the therapist doesn't want to unduly alarm the client, it is a good idea to explain at some point during the initial stages of therapy that *both* positive and negative events take place during Meditative Therapy. There will be certain individuals in whom this will set up a block because they know from past experience that certain subjects or events bother them. They seem to reflexively brace in anticipation of upcoming pain or discomfort.

During the actual process of Meditative Thearpy there are bound to occur what Luthe calls "side-effects" to the therapy. Such things as crying, various aches and pains, psychological discomfort, very likely will take place. Because these are not pleasant and are sometimes a little scary, some clients decide to "shut off" the unwanted reaction. That is, they decide that they will not cry anymore, they will refuse to feel dizzy any longer, they won't deal with the topic of sex because it is disgusting.

My approach in these cases is again to encourage trust in the client's Inner Source. It has a very good reason for each experience, no matter how painful, and so it is best to follow what it presents. Chances are that the very thing the person is afraid of going through is exactly what will be of most therapeutic value. Once it has been experienced, the outcomes are usually worth the pain, upset, and discomfort.

As a therapist, this is probably the place that I personally become the most directive. If the client attempts to open his or her eyes, sit up, or start to leave the room, I am likely to give a lecture about trusting the Inner Source. I will state that there is a very good reason why this is happening and that one may as well get it over with instead of trying to run away. I may say something like, "How many years have you been holding onto this junk anyway? Look what it's doing to you, wouldn't it be better to get rid of it? Now lie down and let it do what it wants to do."

Fears of Losing Control: This fear relates to most of the fears mentioned above. The client fears "letting go" and trusting, because of the feeling of losing control. Giving up the known and familiar, however inadequate, in favor of the unknown can shake one's very foundations and be very frightening.

In all cases of fear or resistance to Meditative Therapy, I reaffirm that the individual is to trust the Inner Source, to let go and to not interfere with what needs to take place. The Inner Source is very wise, and in the final analysis it always works toward the good, toward the positive. There are, of course, times when the client must experience pain and discomfort in order to be set free from some undesirable difficulty.

Within this context it is appropriate to discuss the word *choice*. The individual who is facing the pain and discomfort ultimately needs to decide whether or not to continue with the therapy. For most of my clients there is very little difficulty in choosing to stay with the therapy because most aren't beset with what might be called overwhelming circumstances. There are some, however, who come to a distinct point where a choice must be made. I perceive my role in these instances to be that of pushing a little, but not forcing the client to proceed against his or her will. Each person has his or her own degree of readiness and alone must judge whether or not to go ahead.

Two specific cases come to mind which will help to deal with fears and resistances to following the Inner Source. The first involves a woman who had trouble allowing herself to cry. The following quote comes from the first 30 minutes of her initial session. (Therapist remarks and client observable reactions are in brackets [ ]):

Start: 12:55 p.m. My head feels heavy. Now the weight is more on my stomach—a blue line across—tension in the small of my back—colors changing to red, one center spot. I'm feeling tired. Things moving to my eyes and to the back of my neck. I felt like taking a deeper breath. My vision gets some light from the lamps. My stomach is moving back and forth. Tension again in shoulders and neck, my eyes seem to feel some kind of a repetitive movement, like tensing and letting go. My body is relaxed, hands are, right shoulder is getting tense. It is almost as if there is stuff going across, but it is so fast I can't catch it. [*That's okay.*] I'm just feeling tired, my right shoulder is still tense. A little tense on left, but not the same. I don't really feel anything in my legs, my arms feel heavy; they are warm. Color is light blue, seems to move back and deeper, back further into my head. I feel like I want to cry. [*Let it come if it wants to come.*] I fight it. [*Don't, let it do what it wants to do.*] (*She starts sobbing*) (*1:00*) (*She moves her left hand over her eyes.*) I don't want to cry. Everything seems to be concentrated and my head feels heavy. My neck is tensing again, I'm relaxed and tingly. Now it is like light radiating from concentric circles. My head still hurts, comes from neck and reaches up and grabs it. Not a strong force, just holding it. Now a blue spot with a black border. Green now, then blue. Dark center, small, moves in and out. Changes really fast, now all blue. Oval shaped—now gone. Shoulder still tight (*stomach growled*) My leg's tight again; my back a little bit. Tenseness has moved to left shoulder. I still feel tired. I'm starting, I guess, to feel hungry (*stomach growled*) Color and circle came back. Right arm feels really heavy; shoulder hurts (*coughs*)—stomach's gurgling. (*starts crying again*) (*1:10*) I want to cry, but I'm angry too. I don't know what to do. I want to let it go. I want to let it go. [*Let it do what it wants to do.*] (*She sits up crying.*) I'm all tense, neck hurts. (*She lies down, still crying*) I'm mad, so mad. (*stops crying*) My stomach muscles are all tense, I just hurt inside somewhere, in my chest, it feels funny. I always thought pain comes in colors and it's kind of purple. I just noticed that when I cry my stomach hurts. (*starts crying*) I don't want to cry, I don't want to cry, I don't want to cry anymore. [*Let it happen.*] (*Sits up and cries*) oh, (*sobbing*) my head hurts. (*lowers her head*) Feels good to stretch my back muscles. (*still sitting*) I feel like I could cry forever. I'm tired of crying. [*Don't block your Inner Source. If it wants to cry, let it do what it wants to do.*] Crying makes my head hurt. I'm mad, I'm so mad! (*starts beating the pad*) oh, oh. (*sobbing*) I want to swear. [*Go ahead.*] Shit, shit! My head hurts. (*lies down*) My back hurts. I want to rest, to sleep. I want to sleep when I feel like it (*stops crying*) (*1:20*) My head feels almost apart from my body. I don't feel my neck. My stomach's tensing up and letting go again. I don't feel good. It's hard to feel like crying and not cry. I've cried a lot and it doesn't do any good. My shoulder is tight and tense, upper part of my body feels heavy. My head doesn't hurt now. Now it does. (*starts crying*) It makes me mad to cry. [*I told you to let it cry.*] It makes me mad. (*stops crying—starts crying*) My mind said that I hated Lloyd (*husband*). I don't feel that. I've felt it, but I don't feel it now. I just, I just—my neck's tight, twitching. My mind is all black and blue spots; pretty blue. Right side of my head hurts, and my neck. (*1:25*)

This first session lasted a total of 90 minutes and followed throughout much the same pattern as in the segment given here. She had a total of 7 sessions of Meditative Therapy, during which she was finally able to allow herself to cry when her Inner Source prompted it.

The next case also illustrates the idea of having to make a choice about whether or not to go ahead with the therapy despite the prospect of some negative material. This was a young woman's first session, and she found herself having to deal with situations centering around bad memories about her mother's mental illness and her own fear of mental illness.

Starting time: 1:25. (*laughs*) All I see is black and usually when I try to see that I can't. I feel like I am floating out of my body. I felt it before, but as soon as I thought it, it went away. I feel like I'm starting to get a pain in my throat, really heavy. And I had to go to the health center after being here last week because of an upset stomach. And I am on a liquid diet and I know its mostly emotional, besides, I ate chili beans that night. (*begins crying*) I want to stop, I don't want to do this. [*Stay with it.*] I feel, I feel so terribly alone (*still crying*) I keep trying to explain to my emotions why I should be grown up and not cry and I always cry. [*Just let it do what it wants to do.*] I feel like you're watching me and I shouldn't cry. I keep saying that I want to die, like I could turn off all emotions and I keep analyzing why I shouldn't feel that. [*Don't intellectualize.*] I feel real hot. I feel like I want to run away, like it's too scary. Like you're always holding back and really don't want to know. Like I'm falling into a tunnel, like just in my forehead, but in a tunnel and I'm falling and falling. But I hear the typewriters and I know I'm not. I feel like my head is 3 feet lower than my feet and I'm just tilted. (*1:40*) (*whispering*) I keep falling like I'm going real far away. Like a telescope or a tunnel, but I keep falling back and it gets bigger and bigger or I get farther in it. (*opens her eyes*) [*How do you feel?*] Awful, I don't want to do this. (*closes her eyes*)

I've heard too many crazy people and I don't want to sound like that. Like all my life I've worked and worked to be okay.

At this point we continued discussing her fears about letting go, insanity, crying and so on. I tried to encourage her to continue the session. After a short period of time she said, "What should I do?" My reply was that I thought she should close her eyes and allow it to finish. At 1:52 she closed her eyes and immediately began sobbing:

I feel like I can't go back there. (*sobbing*) Like I keep seeing my mother screaming and screaming and I have to swallow it, just swallow it. I always wanted a mother I could hold. I feel like I have to be my own mother (*sobbing*). I feel like I have to be her mother. We were at X, my mother just screamed and screamed, like for 24 hours. She screamed and screamed and we were sent to the beach. (*opens eyes*) I don't feel any better. [*Let it finish.*] (*closes eyes*) It just hurt and everybody was staring at us. My sister said promise you won't do that anymore. She did, but then she did it again and again and father said it wasn't her fault. She's the poor kid. I kept wanting someone to understand how I felt. He only cared about how it looked to all the neighbors and we were so scared. And she would do all of those awful things and it didn't matter, but it did and I kept feeling I shouldn't be grown up and I don't feel any better. [*Don't stop it, let it finish. You always stop it too soon.*] Like everybody lied, everybody tried to cover it up (*1:58*) —

This session lasted another twenty-five minutes. She continued to be reluctant until about the last 15 minutes when she finally allowed it to flow uninterrupted. In subsequent sessions she was able to allow her Inner Source to function without any of her interruptions.

Allowing the Meditative Therapy Session to Finish Properly

Remember that the Inner Source is able to start a session on its own without any "inducements," such as special breathing techniques or drugs. The Inner Source is also quite capable of finishing a session on its own without any special emphasis by the therapist or the client. It is a good idea for the therapist to point out to the client just prior to the first session that the Inner Source starts and stops on its own, and to watch closely and follow its prompting. We can never predict precisely when a session will end, but the Inner Source usually makes it quite clear that the session is done for the day. Examples of endings appear under the section *The End* in Chapter 10.

It is crucial that the Inner Source be allowed to finish on its own without interruption by the therapist or the client. Most of the dangers of Meditative Therapy center around not allowing the Inner Source to do what it wants to do. Not allowing a proper finish is probably the most vital concern in this regard. I have had to learn this the hard way by having made mistakes, and hopefully can spare you the same mistakes by sharing mine. The most prominent example occurred in my early use of the therapy when I failed to allow the Inner Source to adequately finish a young woman's first session. Shortly after the session she fainted and in falling suffered a hairline fracture of the jaw. (Subsequently, it was also discovered that she had a very low blood sugar condition.) I as the therapist should not have allowed her to leave the office until I was absolutely certain she was okay. I have also had other cases where the individual, after leaving the office, has had to sit down to regain their balance due to feeling dizzy or faint. In one instance the person was driving on the freeway and had to pull over. In another case the individual slightly bumped another car in the parking lot. Needless to say, I am *extremely* cautious now and make very sure that each client is finished, clear-headed, and can walk straight before I allow him or her to leave the office.

In cases where the client feels finished and then feels groggy, heavy, or sad, I wait several minutes to see if that clears. If such feelings seem to persist, I will have the client lie down and allow the Inner Source to finish. A good rule of thumb is to make sure that the person feels at least as good as when the session began.

In instances where the session must be interrupted due to special circumstances or where the individual insists on stopping before completion, I warn about the possible consequences and give instructions to take it very easy.

Another concern related to the end of the first Meditative Therapy session involves the scheduling of appointments. I have found it best to have the person come back once a week, and to make a series of two-hour appointments in advance to ensure weekly appointments without interruption. Especially during the early stages of Meditative Therapy there should not be long lapses between sessions. Interruptions are acceptable after the individual has a good working knowledge of the process, (usually after four or five sessions or more, depending on the person).

Because most of my work is conducted in a university setting, I watch that no one is started in the therapy too closely to a long vacation break. As with any powerful therapeutic procedure, the therapist must be sensitive to the limits of his or her own setting.

After the first session is completed, be very careful to check with the client to find out his or her reaction to the therapy, to provide appropriate encouragement or reassurance if the process is working correctly, or to find out what needs to be changed to help it work correctly. Typically, the client will either know that the process is working and accept it or will ask a question such as, "How is this going to help me?" At this point it is good to point out some of the signs which indicate that the therapy is working properly or to explain some of the theory relating to how the therapy works. I usually give my impression of how the therapy appears to be working and ask for patience for a few sessions in order to see what the results will be in relationship to feelings and to the presenting complaints. If I get the feeling that the individual *really* does not wish to proceed, I shift to another therapy.

Assigning Homework in Meditative Therapy

Over the years, I have assumed that it would be unreasonable to pile extra work on university students who are typically loaded down with homework already. Lately, however, I have encountered several more severe cases which have made me realize the need for more stringent emphasis on therapeutic homework for Meditative Therapy. I am now stressing that clients undergoing the therapy engage in some form of extra session work. The source of these tasks once again is W. Luthe's work in Autogenic Abreaction. Luthe feels, and I have come to agree, that homework exercises can greatly facilitate one's understanding of therapy and therapeutic progress and that they also serve as a necessary safety valve when one is experiencing between-session side effects.

Luthe describes six basic homework exercises. The first centers around his requirement that the client undergoing Autogenic Therapy audio-tape-record his or her sessions. His suggestion is that as soon as possible after returning home from a session one should transcribe word for word the entire session. In cases where a complete transcription is impossible, one should at least make out a summary of the material. The second homework task is to reread the transcription of the session *out loud* twice per day. This is vital, according to Luthe, in cases where the individual is experiencing a great many between-session reactions, such as crying easily, various aches and pains, sleep disturbances. By reading the session content over and over out loud, one is able to further facilitate overcoming disturbing material.

My experience with having clients reread session material out loud over and over again is that it produces variable emotional reactions depending upon what took place in the actual session. Some will feel little emotional reaction during the session and later when rereading, whereas others find high initial emotions being triggered quite easily once again. Some will gain little insight into their material, whereas others feel that they have gained new understandings by reading the material out loud several times.

The third suggestion deriving from Autogenic Abreaction research is that one should write out what is termed a *thematic commentary*. By analyzing and writing about what the Inner Source is trying to do to help, and what the presented material has to do with the past and the present, the individual greatly facilitates progress. Luthe indicates that this particular procedure is needed more when the session content is less clear-cut. There are times when the content is rather abstract or symbolic so that more time is needed in order to figure out the meaning. When the content meaning is very obvious, little analytic commentary is required.

Drawings of pertinent Autogenic Abreaction session material is Luthe's fourth assignment. His main interest is for the individual to prepare sketches which represent details or the patterns of images which have been presented in therapy. Although I have not required this exercise as such, I have had clients spontaneously draw things. One of my clients recently was confronted with "the devil" in one of his sessions and it so intrigued him that he drew a picture of the image. Others have drawn patterns of light, machines, or flying saucers. Certain individuals with artistic abilities may come up with new ideas on how to initiate or complete a project.

Luthe believes that the four suggestions given above most closely follow what the brain is attempting to do in order to heal the person. In addition to these tasks, Luthe recommends that one keep practicing the Autogenic Standard Exercises, making sure to keep progress notes, and that one make notes on dreams. Luthe indicates that the brain may repeat dreams or parts of dreams in order to facilitate its journey in Autogenic Abreaction. Also, dreams may bring up new material which has not been dealt with in one's sessions. Moreover, Luthe is quick to point out that there is no time spent in Autogenic Therapy on interpreting dreams as such.

Luthe may suggest that a client seek out more information about a past event, such as an accident or childhood event. In my work I have found clients doing this spontaneously out of curiosity. For example, after one session in which a young woman spent a great deal of time re-experiencing an old house she used to live in, she made a special trip in order to check out some specific details given in the inner journey. Another client who had relived a birth experience in therapy checked out the details of the birth with his mother the next time he saw her. The two experiences matched up quite closely even though he claimed to have not previously known the details.

Although not homework exercises as such, the next two suggestions from Autogenic Therapy research are very important for other reasons. First is the indication that one should avoid further overloading of an already overloaded or disturbed brain. For example, if an individual is inordinately frightened by horror or scary movies, these movies should be avoided until the brain has a chance to be rid of the difficulty. Other examples might be to avoid amusement rides, funerals, driving an auto, flying, or swimming.

Luthe states that we even have a tendency to be attracted to things that disturb us because the brain attempts to neutralize events which bother it. Of course, the desired result cannot be achieved because it would take many repetitions with the right variables controlled instead of being an unsophisticated random attempt as appears to be the usual case. The brain, left to its own internal devices, is very precise, whereas when dealing with outside events, it cannot control the situation fully, according to Luthe.

Keeping a day-to-day journal of reactions to the Meditative Therapy experience, in addition to rereading session transcripts out loud, is the primary homework assignment I employ. The content of the journal has many possibilities:

1. Summarizing the session in one's own words.
2. Writing down the central topics dealt with.
3. Noting bodily reactions, psychological-emotional reactions, spiritual reactions.
4. Recording experiences or feelings that occur while rereading the transcript aloud.
5. Attempting to figure out what the Inner Source is trying to do to help.
6. Noting changes during the week that seem to be a result of the session.
7. Keeping questions or comments one would like to discuss with the therapist.
8. Recording dreams one has experienced that seem related to the therapy.
9. Keeping drawings one has made of the session content.
10. Writing down overall thoughts and feelings about what is taking place.

The idea is for the individual to keep an account of the total reaction to Meditative Therapy. Obviously, one will need to gear the intensity of such recording to the amount of time available and to one's interest in helping oneself.

The journal for the week should be read by the therapist prior to the beginning of the next session and necessary points discussed. Discussions, however, should not use up session time needed by the

Inner Source to do its work, and should avoid unnecessary interpretation of material.

Bibliotherapy is another possible homework suggestion to help enhance Meditative Therapy results. One may wish to read about subjects that keep recurring in the sessions. And such suggestion by the therapist should be stated in such a way as to not present undue pressure or direction to the individual. I usually indicate that if the client feels prompted to investigate a certain topic further, there are books I could recommend as starters. Thus if one keeps being reminded of dreams, or of extra sensory perception, or of certain symbols, perhaps one will wish to investigate these topics further. Similarly, one may be moved to re-acquaint oneself with music being presented by the Inner Source, or perhaps with art work. Certain individuals working or studying in specialized fields may need to reread some of those categories of books. One client, for example, gained some information about Einstein's writings and felt prompted to reread the material.

Despite these suggestions for homework, one should be reminded to be careful about interpreting Meditative Therapy material within any one system, such as Freudian, Jungian, or behavioral. One ought not place any limits on the Inner Source by burdening it with one particular view of what it is trying to do to help. The major changes in Meditative Therapy take place *without* any interpretation, and often without any insight into causes by the individual *or* by the therapist.

Availability Between Meditative Therapy Sessions

Between Meditative Therapy sessions the therapist should be available to answer any questions which the client may have and to handle any needed emergency treatment. It is helpful to give the client the therapist's office and home telephone numbers, and, in instances where the therapist will be out of town, the phone number of another therapist who is knowledgeable about Meditative Therapy. At the completion of the first session the therapist should explain to the client that there is a possibility that reactions of various kinds may occur between sessions. The therapist may say,

"Let me give you my phone numbers now in case you need to call me during the week. Call me if *anything* happens. Perhaps nothing will happen, but if something bothers or upsets you, make sure you call me. Once the Inner Source begins helping you, it will often continue to do so during the week between sessions. If you should happen to get physically sick call me. Or if something else concerns you, just call me and we can talk about it."

Only a small percentage of clients actually call the therapist between sessions. The calls I have personally received usually center around psychologically upsetting feelings and/or reactions. Reactions which clients have reported include these:

I was watching *The Waltons* and started crying, sad to hysterical, back and forth. I felt like I was crying for a lot of things.

I've been getting flashes of things I hadn't realized before and also crying spells. I haven't cried for years, even after my auto accident where I had my brain injury.

Two peculiar things have occurred that have never happened to me before. Just the tip of my penis has been itching all day and also itching on my behind. And a big red welt there, on my behind, which has been there since the last session.

I've been feeling depressed and my stomach has been upset. I've not been myself.

My thumb was really painful, I couldn't concentrate because of it. Also, my lower back hurt a lot for two days. I've had kidney problems several times in the past. I've also noticed that my legs have not hurt for the first time, for as long as I can remember, when there are severe weather changes.

When I receive a call from a client who is concerned about a between-sessions reaction, I first check out how serious the reaction is in order to decide whether or not the person should come in for an emergency session. If the person is feeling out of control or overwhelmed, I invite him or her to come in as soon as possible.

Whatever else that I do when someone calls I do make sure that he or she understands that there is no reason to become unduly alarmed because the Inner Source is simply trying to help. The reactions are normal and natural and, as during the therapy, it is best to simply be patient and allow the reactions to work themselves out. My purpose is to offer reassurance that these reactions are understandable, acceptable, and helpful. Generally a discussion of this type is enough to hold the person over until the next regular session, but it is good to be cautious if there are any doubts and to schedule an immediate appointment when needed.

Not only "negative" reactions take place between Meditative Therapy sessions. Good, positive feelings and reactions take place also. One woman, after her first session reported that she "felt a peaceful feeling, at one with myself, almost with roots again. I feel steady and able to just be easy, at home with myself." Another said that after her first session she visited with people more during the week than ever before. She stated that she was no longer afraid of rejection, or that people would not be friendly. She added later that "I don't feel nearly as unsure of myself as I did before. I feel now all the time like I used to feel once in a while." Others will report that they had great amounts of energy between sessions, or that sex was better than ever before, or that they "felt like a kid" all week, or that they had beautiful dreams or memories. The point is that the client should endeavor to accept what happens, whether positive or negative feelings are produced.

Follow-Up After Meditative Therapy

At some point it becomes apparent that the client is ready to discontinue Meditative Therapy with the therapist. Although this decision should be made jointly, I try to encourage the individual to undergo a minimum of five therapist-facilitated sessions. Whenever the decision is made to discontinue, the individual should be encouraged to continue Meditative Therapy on his or her own, or to at least practice some form of relaxation or meditation once formal sessions with the therapist are terminated. I also encourage clients to keep up other skills gained from therapy, such as following an adequate diet, exercising regularly, or being assertive.

Ideally, the therapist should also conduct a follow-up of the outcomes of all Meditative Therapy clients. Invaluable information about the workings of the Inner Source and the effectiveness of Meditative Therapy can be gained with appropriate follow-up measures. Moreover, such follow-up is consistent with the therapist's ethical responsibility to assess client progress in some systematic way. If the follow-up process becomes too time-consuming or expensive, at a minimum a random sample follow-up could be conducted to assess the effectiveness of therapy.

In any event, the therapist should be available for clients who wish to initiate follow-up contacts at some time after therapy is complete.

Self-Administered Meditative Therapy

I have stated the opinion that one should begin Meditative Therapy with at least five therapist-facilitated sessions, because of the potential powerfulness of the process. Sessions can at times be filled with great upset, pain, crying, and unusual events and feelings. Unless there is someone present, preferably a therapist, who knows how the therapy works and can answer questions and provide reassurance, an individual may have a tendency to become scared and shut off the process or not let the process work fully.

I would like to once again give a strong caution that those who have had traumatic histories should definitely have therapist facilitated-Meditative Therapy sessions first. I refer primarily to painful and upsetting experiences with auto accidents, major injuries, major surgery, painful and upsetting experiences with parents or significant others, deaths in the family, divorce, or other strong emotional upsets. A similar caution applies to those who have undergone heavily negative religious or sexual conditioning. I am especially concerned about those who have had a *series* of these type of experiences. For example, I recently worked with a woman who had experienced an alcoholic mother, parent's divorce, deaths of several close friends and relatives, two near-death major injuries auto accidents, a traumatic marriage and subsequent divorce, and *other* painful and upsetting experiences. There is no way that I would recommend that a person with this type of history commence Meditative Therapy without the assistance of a qualified therapist.

Each person needs to make his or her own decision in this regard, but considerable caution and forethought is advised.

Another reason to have a therapist present is that other methods are often needed to treat the problems detected by the therapist before Meditative Therapy or those discovered as a result of material arising during Meditative Therapy. I prefer methods which take into account the whole person.

Kitselman (1950) indicates that one can trade back and forth with a friend in order to have sessions without a therapist. Nevertheless, I consider it best to go to a therapist first before using this alternative, in part because the friend is probably not knowledgeable and/or competent enough. In addition, there may be material arising during Meditative Therapy which one might not wish to disclose to a friend, for fear the friend would think badly of him or her, be embarrassed by the content, or not keep it confidential. Therapists are trained to deal with matters of this kind. Once there have been a series of sessions with a professional therapist, having a friend help can be a useful alternative.

Luthe indicates that with Autogenic Therapy the advisability of sessions without a therapist depends upon the individual client, but that only 35 percent can eventually complete the sessions on their own at home. Remember that he considers Autogenic Abreaction to be the "big gun" of therapy and, as such, is only reserved for the most difficult cases. So it is safe to assume that his sample is heavily loaded with difficult cases.

I am much more lenient regarding with whom Meditative Therapy should be used initially, or who should be encouraged to undego Meditative Therapy alone. At this time I place almost no restrictions on either of the two questions. I utilize the therapy with most of my clients, and encourage them all to do it on their own once they have completed a basic series of therapist facilitated sessions.

Over the years, even though I have encouraged self-administered Meditative Therapy, I basically leave the decision up to each individual client. I had no planned program to help them begin on their own other than what they had learned during the therapist-facilitated sessions. This type of philosophy produced a variety of responses. Some would feel able to do the therapy alone almost immediately whereas others would be fearful of trying at all. These latter reactions finally encouraged me to set up the following systematic plan for self-administered Meditative Therapy: (1) The first step is to recommend suitable reading materials. If the client has not already been reading about Meditative Therapy and related topics, I recommend readings on the non-directive approaches in Chapters 2 and 12. When this book is completed it also will be recommended reading. These sources can be being read as one continues self-administered Meditative Therapy sessions.

(2) The first self-administered Meditative Therapy session should be in the therapist's office during the same time period as the previous sessions. The therapist should not be present during the session, but be available immediately after in order to check how the session went and to answer any questions or concerns. The session should also be audio-recorded so that the therapist can listen to it later and determine if the client adhered to the Meditative Therapy requirements.

(3) If everything was acceptable in step 2, the client should be encouraged to go through three additional once-per-week sessions alone or with the assistance of a friend. During these three sessions one is reminded to continue describing the content out loud and to tape record the sessions.

(4) An appointment should be set up to discuss the progress made during these three sessions and to iron out any difficulties that may have arisen .At this point it may even be good to conduct one more therapist-facilitated session if the client feels it would help in the effort toward successful self-administered Meditative Therapy.

(5) Thereafter, I recommend a once-a-week Meditative Therapy session alone, depending upon the needs and desires of the individual client.

(6) A follow-up session with the therapist is desirable after 3-6 months, or sooner if needed by the client.

Difficulties one might encounter when undergoing Meditative Therapy alone are basically the same as have been discussed earlier for therapist-facilitated Meditative Therapy. One should avoid efforts to control, direct, or interfere with the path of the Inner Source. One must patiently accept what the Inner Source wishes to do and trust that it will always know best how to help. If fears or resistances come up these should be dealt with or fought through in order to continue. Each person's Inner Source always has his or her unique best interests at heart, and in the final analysis may be trusted not to violate or hurt the person. It possesses an infinite amount of wisdom and love, and always strives to help the person grow toward his or her highest potential.

I personally look at Meditative Therapy as both curative and preventative. Events that cause us pain or upset are continually taking place in our lives, and of course there is a good amount of past material that needs to be handled. The Inner Source is always as close as closing our eyes when we wish to be helped.

12

Background Material on the "Inner Therapies"

In Chapters 2 and 3, a brief introduction to "synthetic" and "natural" therapies was presented as a background for understanding Meditative Therapy. This chapter examines those approaches in greater depth for lay and professional readers who wish more material. Although I strongly recommend that therapists in particular consult the original sources cited here, this summary will provide a helpful overview of relevant information.

Synthetic Inner Therapies

This section begins with historical background of synthetic approaches to the inner life. Next, a short analysis of the difference between Meditative Therapy and Free Association will be given. Third, additional information concerning LSD-assisted therapy and Primal Therapy will be presented. Fourth, several other synthetically-oriented inner therapies will be briefly summarized.

The task of analyzing the synthetic inner way is not an easy one because of the wide range of approaches falling into this category. To remedy the problem, several well known approaches are summarized in order to give a general flavor for all synthetic approaches. In addition, I have briefly noted as many additional related approaches as I could locate.

Hypnosis, Hypnocatharsis, and Free Association

MacHovec (1975) in his article "Hypnosis Before Mesmer," has stated that there were methods in ancient times similar to hypnosis. Therefore, it is safe to assume that synthetic methods have been in existence for a long period of time. As far as a so-called "scientific" beginning for methods of this type is concerned, Mesmer's work has been mentioned. Lisette Moser (1967) tells us that one of Mesmer's contributions was that he was the first writer to try to explain this phenomenon by the scientific method.

Mesmer first wrote about animal magnetism in 1772. By working with individuals in an altered state of consciousness, he was able to effect cures of psychological and physical illnesses of substantial magnitude. His theoretical explanation is limited, as is much of that put forth by other directive theorists. Mesmer also had a forerunner, a Jesuit Fr. Gassner who, according to Moser, had similar methods and results to those of Mesmer.

Joseph Breuer and Sigmund Freud's work, *Studies in Hysteria*, is the earliest of the modern "scientific" methods among the synthetic approaches. In proposing their hypnotic method in 1895, they recognized that the method was in actuality not new. They credited Janet in 1889, Delboeuf in 1889, and Binet in 1892 with utilizing processes similar to their own.

I have selected two quotes from *Studies In Hysteria* which provide a background for the other synthetic methods in this chapter.

We found, at first to our great surprise, that the *individual hysterical symptoms immediately disappeared without returning if we succeeded in thoroughly awakening the memories of the causal process with its accompanying affect, and if the patient circumstantially discussed the process in the most detailed manner and gave verbal expression to the affect.* (Italics theirs)

We can now understand in what manner the psychotherapeutic method propounded by us exerts its curative effect. It abrogates the efficacy of the original non-abreacted ideas by affording an outlet to their strangulated affects through speech. It brings them to associative correction by drawing them into normal consciousness (in mild hypnosis) or by eliminating them through medical suggestion in the same way as in somnambulism with amnesia.

Freud eventually dropped the hypnocathartic method because he felt that not all patients could be hypnotized. He invented the eyes-open method of *free association* to uncover subconscious material.

Table 12-1
A Comparison of Meditative Therapy and Free Association

Comparison Point	Free Association	Meditative Therapy
Recognition of an Inner Source conducting the process	No recognition of an Inner Source	Recognition and trust in an Inner Source
Aspect of mind emphasized	Negative, infantile, repressed, subconscious aspects emphasized	Positive and negative aspects allowed: conscious, subconscious, superconscious
Vision	Eyes open, allows for less depth	Eyes closed, allows for more depth
Client attitude	Active searching	Passive, allowing
Physiological Reactions	De-emphasized	Equal emphasis on the full realm
Psychological reactions	Primarily emphasized	of Psychophysio- spiritulogical
Spiritulogical reactions	De-emphasized	response
Therapist interpretation	A crucial factor in the therapy	Of little importance in the therapy
Amount of time	One hour per day	Variable time period (1½ to 2 hours), once per week

Recently, a psychiatrist friend of mine who knew a little bit about my work with Meditative Therapy decided that he and his staff should know more about the approach. He came up to me and said, "I wonder if you could come over soon and tell us about your free association method?" As soon as he saw my face reflexively contort, he quickly added, "I know you don't call it that, but anyway . . ." He went on to set up a time for me to give the presentation. What I explained in that session, and what Table 12-1 speaks to, is that indeed free association and Meditative Therapy are not the same.

In the table free association and Meditative Therapy are compared on 10 factors. The information included on free association comes from three books: *A General Introduction to Psychoanalysis* (1924), and *Therapy And Technique* (1963) by Sigmund Freud, and *Theory of Psychoanalytic Technique* (1958) by Karl Menninger. The table is self-explanatory.

LSD-Assisted Therapy

Additional material on LSD is presented in three categories: (1) spiritual outcomes; (2) psychotherapeutic uses; and (3) a re-statement and expansion of criticisms.

Spiritual Outcomes: LSD produces a wide variety of religious content plus alterations in religious attitudes, often quite dramatically. Masters and Houston (1966) present a table which I have reproduced below on the religious imagery present in a group of LSD participants, including educators, clergymen, attorneys and other professionals.

Downing and Wygant (1964) indicate that 60% of a sample of 42 participants, after a single dose LSD session, felt that their religious attitudes were changed. Also 60% felt that their feelings about life after death had changed and 60% trusted God or life more than before taking LSD. (The 60% figure may not have always represented the same people for all three statements.) Leary (1965) reporting on the use of psychedelic drugs with 69 full-time religious professionals, one-half Christian or Jewish and one-half from Eastern religious, indicated that 75% felt they had intense

Table 12-2
Religious Imagery [1]

	N = 206 subjects Percent
Religious imagery of some kind:	96*
Religious architecture, temples and churches:	91
Religious sculpture, painting, stained glass windows:	43
Religious symbols: cross, yin yang, Star of David, etc.:	34
Mandalas:	26
Religious figures: Christ, Buddha, saints, godly figures, William Blake-type figures:	58
Devils, demons:	49
Angels:	7
Miraculous and numinous visions, pillars of light, burning bushes, God in the whirlwind:	60

Cosmological imagery: galaxies, heavenly bodies,
    creation of the universe, of the solar system,
    of the earth (experienced as religious):
	14

Religious Rituals	
Scenes of contemporary Christian, Jewish or Muslim Rites:	8
Contemporary Oriental rites:	10
Ancient Greek, Roman, Egyptian, Mesopotamian and similar rites:	67
Primitive rites:	31

"mystico-religious" responses. Also, over one-half felt that they had the deepest spiritual experience of their life. Leary also presents summary data from several questionnaire studies concerning psychedelic experiences of 1,000 subjects. He concludes that if the setting is supportive, but not designed to provoke a spiritual response, 40% to 75% still report intense religious experiences. If, on the other hand, the setting is spiritually stimulating plus supportive, 40% to 90% report intense revelations and mystico-religious experiences.

---

1. From R.E.L. Masters and J. Houston, **The Varieties of Psychedelic Experience.** New York: Holt, Rinehart and Winston, 1966. Reproduced by permission of the publisher.

Pahnke (1967) narrows down the exact factors involved in psychedelic religious experiences, including 9 characteristics of "psychedelic peak or mystical" experience:

(1) Unity.
(2) Transcendence of time and space.
(3) Deeply felt positive mood.
(4) Sense of sacredness.
(5) The neotic quality.
(6) Paradoxicality.
(7) Alleged ineffability.
(8) Transiency.
(9) Persisting positive changes in attitudes and behavior.

He states that, depending on how complete the experience must be regarding these 9 criteria, 20% to 40% of his psychedelic subjects had a peak experience. So it can be observed, that even with stringent criteria, at least 20% undergo a dynamic life change along religious lines when involved in properly conducted LSD sessions.

There has been some question concerning the validity of drug induced religious experiences versus those which are termed naturally occuring. R.C. Zaehner's book *Mysticism: Sacred and Profane* (1961) is the main source arguing against psychedelic drug induced religious experiences. An excellent article by Huston Smith (1964) attempts to offer rebuttal to Zaehner. Personally, I like Leary, Alpert and Metzner's (1964) notion that it is relatively easy to produce an illumination experience with LSD, but that it only had lasting effects on those who have had years of prior preparation with some form of religious/spiritual training, whether traditional or non-traditional.

Psychotherapeutic Uses: LSD and other psychedelics have shown great potential in effectively, and at times dramatically, treating a wide variety of disorders including alcoholism, homosexuality, frigidity, and other psychiatric disorders. Therapy outcome, of course, depends on the set and setting variables mentioned in Chapter 2. Interpretation of the content of the LSD sessions will depend a great deal upon the therapist's particular framework whether it be Freudian, Jungian, or other theoretical approaches. Going beyond this factor one is still able to document impressive results which derive from the drug experience in and of itself. Unger (1964 a) has documented the profound changes one may experience when LSD is used psychotherapeutically and provides an excellent bibliography concerning the subject up to 1963 (1964 b). Caldwell's (1968) bibliography is more up to date and is an excellent job of presenting LSD sources. Grof (1975) also demonstrates the therapeutic powerfulness of the drug. LSD treatment is not a cure all by any means, but used with the right set in a good setting, under proper supervision, LSD therapy has been demonstrated to be very helpful for many people.

Critique: My main objection to the use of LSD is that I feel that by taking LSD, one's Inner Source is limited in some manner. There may be certain activities the Inner Source wishes to engage in, but the person will be unable to proceed, being suppressed by the drug's effect. On the other hand, there may be areas which the Inner source does not wish to present to the individual immediately, but because of the drug's effect the Inner Source gets "locked in" to responding before it is ready to do so. A third difficulty is that, because the Inner Source is controlled by the drug's effects, it cannot terminate a session when it wants to do so. The Inner Source may be forced to cover a great deal of ground when in actuality it would be better to go much more slowly in order that the material could be integrated at the client's own unique pace. All of these points add up to the fact that the system is not allowed to unfold in its natural way.

Huxley and Grof offer viewpoints which are contrary to mine. Huxley (1972) suggests that through ingesting a psychedelic drug, one's "deeper self" is allowed to work and to choose the most advantageous experiences for the individual. He felt that the deeper self only made use of the mind changing powers of the drug to produce what experiences it needed in order to grow. If one is supposed to uncover deeply buried memories that would happen, but if that wasn't necessary maybe another response such as seeing the beauty of the world would be presented. Grof (1975) holds a similar view, indicating that there are no specific, unalterable pharmacological effects resulting from taking LSD. He feels that this is true regardless of what type of phenomena is selected to be analyzed: changes in the pupillary response; muscular tone; or psychological response. He states that phenomena arising from LSD session are amazingly diverse and never the same for any two people, or even the same for one person when comparing various sessions.

The arguments of Grof and Huxley *seem* to make sense and appear to answer my concern over the use of LSD, however there still is considerable uncertainty about effects of the drug.

Can the Inner Source still choose its own way if it is being primed to respond in other directions? Grof says that the Freudian psychodynamic theories are "largely" supported by the outcome data of psycholytic LSD therapy. The data from Meditative Therapy offer minimal support for a statement of this type. I am suspicious about to what degree therapeutic directiveness is guiding the appearance of some of these "unalterable" materials, especially the psychodynamic response, in LSD.

Another objection of mine to LSD use centers around the issue of side effects. Most psychotropic drugs such as tranquilizers and antidepressants either suppress symptoms or cause bad side effects. LSD does not appear to suppress symptoms, but there is still not enough data available to determine whether or not LSD depletes the system in order to produce its results. Dosages are often high even in the psycholytic approach and may tend to be abrasive or to drain or exhaust the system. There is some question about whether or not the drug may cause a hang-over effect similar to what alcohol produces. Of course, the range of response in alcohol use is highly individual, and one may assume the same is true of LSD.

The point is, who should decide what dosage one shall receive and on what criteria is this judgement made? The *natural* way of Meditative Therapy is, to me, much more valid because the Inner Source is capable of deciding what "dose" of altered consciousness it needs during any given session to accomplish its goals.

It is my belief that the natural, drugless methods of Meditative Therapy and other therapies should always be given a fair chance to work with the Inner Source before attempting to use any synthetic methods, such as LSD. It may seem naive of me to not be overly concerned about the "dangers" of LSD administration, but with our current state of knowledge, it appears that if the drug use is supervised by well-informed and responsible experimenters, there is little chance of great danger (See Clark, et. al., 1975) The U.S. Army most likely was not handling their experiments correctly, if the newspaper accounts are correct, because the Army experimenters did not always tell the subjects that they had taken LSD and did not provide adequate supervision. The essential requirements of LSD administration are that the subject *must* know the possible outcomes of taking LSD, that he or she *must* be properly supervised during and usually after the subsequent drug experience, and finally, that the individual should be instructed about possible reactions which might occur after leaving the experimental setting. The last requirement refers to "flashback" phenomena which may occur even after the drug effects have "worn off," a recurrence of some phenomena previously experienced in or stimulated by the LSD sessions.

While I reiterate that if the individual is properly instructed, there appears to be little need to worry about danger, my preference is to use the natural mind-manifesting methods such as Meditative Therapy. I personally would never administer LSD.

Primal Therapy

Further explanation of the Primal method of Janov will be presented in terms of several areas: (1) background (2) therapeutic approach (3) results and (4) critique.

Background: Although Janov focuses primarily on the parents as the cause of mental illness, in the *Primal Scream* it is stated that not every Primal Scene directly involves the parents. Some of the major scenes are due to physical traumas of various kinds. However, he does feel that if parents could be totally loving and kind no mental illness would develop.

Over the years, Janov's writings appear to report more and more on physical pains, especially centering around the birth process. Such traumas as the cord strangling the baby, harsh handling with forceps or hands, and being unduly isolated from the mother can be so painful as to cause repression. An excellent example includes a photograph of bruises which appeared on a 48-year-old female primal patient during a birth primal. She was re-experiencing being roughly held upside down by the delivering doctor. Janov goes on to say that until a pain (physical or psychological) is fully integrated one will suffer symbolically. He indicates that prototypic pain is a necessary but not complete reason for one to want to commit suicide. To make it complete the individual must also have a very repressive early life, or an overly religious home atmosphere, or attend a harsh military or parochial school, or experience similar repressive environments.

In *The Anatomy of Mental Illness* (1971) and later in various *Journal of Primal Therapy* articles, Janov postulates that certain brain components and systems are involved in "splitting off" the client from his or her real feelings. He mentions the reticular activating system, the hypothalamus, and especially the limbic system, with the latter termed the key inhibiting agent of feelings, the repressor of pain. The hippocampus and amygdala are parts of the limbic system which are pointedly involved in repression. The brain is said to naturally protect one from pain and that Primal Pains are no exception. These two components have direct connection to the frontal cortex which Janov feels acts as a "gate to consciousness." Shutdown because of too much physical and/or psychological pain is one of the brain's vital functions.

Therapeutic Approach: The way to alleviate neurotic suffering is to overthrow one's defense system. By breaking open the patient's memory bank the repressed pain can be experienced fully and become integrated into the system. The first three weeks of therapy are very intensive: one is not allowed to work or go to school. The patient is seen each day for sessions of two to three-and-a-half hours. The therapist is available to this particular patient only and is on call at anytime of the day or night. Initially the therapist uses isolation, sleeplessness and elimination of alcohol, smoking and other external stimuli for neurotic patients. At times one may be required to stay awake all night.

Psychological harassment is used as a device to trigger deeply repressed feelings. Because one protects him or herself so completely against feeling primal pain it takes considerable effort to break down these resistances. The therapist may use force or violence to crush the defense system thoroughly and expose the underlying causes of pain. One who talks softly is forced to talk louder; one who is being intellectual about problems is pressed to an awareness of feelings. The homosexual may be called a "fag" to produce tension and get him close to real feelings. Janov describes one case in which a patient left the room to go to the bathroom and was locked out when he tried to return. He was eventually let back in to proceed with the strong feelings which had been brought up by the incident.

Despite this use of force and use of the language of force (crush, break open, violence, overthrow) the therapy does not give the appearance of being brutal. For example, Janov states in "The Dangers in the Misuse of Primal Therapy:"

A premature bust means that defenses are assaulted too quickly leaving the patient open to too much pain. The result is an overload and shutdown, rather than an opening up. A bust doesn't mean that the therapist says to the patient, "I hate you, you're disgusting; your nose is too big and you are the kind of person I could never like." That is merely cruelty masquerading as therapy. A bust is simply telling the patient the truth about himself—"you talk too much. You're always talking about yourself," for example. If the patient has been rattling on to flee a feeling, he might stop and start to get underneath his defense. As the defense is stopped and as he starts to feel he may say, "I always talked to hold their attention because I always felt they wanted to get away from me." From there he will soon be into his Pain; something underlying his defense. The bust will have aided integration. (1974 b) p. 284

The therapist appears to serve as a catalyst to stimulate the process of "primaling." In order to help one "get into" feelings, props may be utilized in the therapy. At certain times items like teddy bears, baby bottles, and sad or nostalgic movies are presented in order to start the chain reaction primal process of contact with old, painful feelings.

Once the process begins it seems to go on its own for periods of time. The therapist does remain silent at times since a primal may be mainly physical, with jerking, convulsing, or shaking. In addition, the client learns through becoming familiar with the process how to initiate his or her own primals. Evidently the therapist takes a more secondary role after the first three weeks of intensive therapy.

Analyzing Janov's writings in sequence, from the *Primal Scream* through his more recent articles in the *Journal of Primal Therapy*, it appears that he has become more open in his therapeutic approach. He even states that his is not a static but a dynamic, changing system which incorporates new knowledge gained from working with patients. Two examples will make this point more clear. In the *Anatomy of Mental Illness* he talks about using a strobe light to evoke feeling in difficult cases. In a later journal article he seems to revoke the use of the strobe light as dangerous. Also, he has now altered his initial approach with the prepsychotic patient, who typically has had a history of hospitalization for mental difficulties. Instead of using isolation or not allowing smoking, great care is taken to handle this patient slowly. Discussion is used along the way to help strengthen intellectual defenses as therapy progresses. Indeed, preparatioin of the pre-psychotic is quite the opposite to that of the neurotic.

Results: Janov feels that the only way to truly evaluate therapy is on the merits of each individual case. Each patient is a result of his or her own unique set of circumstances. All mental illness is the result of repressed pain but, as Janov believes, it is folly to group specific disorders and try to isolate causes.

The Anatomy of Mental Illness is the first thorough analysis of· changes taking place in Primal Therapy. The report is a follow-up of 25 patients who had an average stay in therapy of 8 months.

General post-treatment results showed that all felt mostly tension free. Most didn't smoke, none drank, most were completely off pills. All claimed excellent marital adjustment and felt relaxed as parents.

Specific symptoms eliminated included high blood pressure, high pulse rate, arthritis, hypothyroidism, constipation, headaches, allergies, and backaches. Although two homosexuals said they were no longer gay, Janov does not state if any homosexuals remained homosexual. He did say that four patients still overeat, three still smoke a little, and four still use marijuana on occasion.

There was no exception to the feeling that therapy was of great benefit, so much so that all would recommend it to others. Also not one reported a willingness to ever enter another kind of therapy.

In another study reported in *The Anatomy of Mental Illness*, neurophysiological measurements of patients undergoing Primal Therapy were made on experimental (Primal Therapy) and control groups. Blood pressure, pulse, and rectal temperature were monitored before and after each session.

Results showed significant changes in pulse and rectal temperature for both the Primal Group and the control. No explanation is given why the control group had significant changes in their variables. Some brain wave data was collected, but was incomplete. Throughout Janov's writings he refers to the fact that brain waves are lower in frequency and amplitude and that rectal temperature is permanently lowered by Primal Therapy. However, I have been unable to find a definitive scientific study released to back up the claims for brain wave changes. Janov also stresses that dreaming is less symbolic, sexual activity is often less in frequency but more satisfying in quality, and that post primal people become less aggressive and more moral in the true sense of the word.

Present physiological measurements taken on each patient are EEG, pulse, blood pressure, and core temperature at the following intervals: pre-primal, three weeks, three months, six months and one year. For certain selected clients there are additional tests of blood cell count, urinalysis, a variety of serum chemical indices and twenty-four hour urine hormones.

Results of one study (McInerny, 1974) showed that pulse rate changed significantly from an average of 74 to an average of 66 over the 6-month period. 68.18% showed pulse reduction, 18.18% showed an increase and 13.63% showed no change. Body temperature dropped a significant 0.54° after 6 months: 81.81% had a decrease, 13.63% had an increase, while 4.66% showed no change.

Taking both the pulse and temperature scores together, it was found that after 6 months 63.8% of the group of 22 showed declines in both readings. Results at the one year reading for the selected group of 8 were seen as following the same general trend.

Critique: Janov has many excellent ideas and has produced a good number of therapeutic successes. In many ways his method is far ahead of most psychotherapies, however his strong claims about Primal Therapy and his criticism of all other therapies make it difficult to remain objective. Indeed, Janov does not appear to thoroughly understand some bf the methods he criticizes.

Another criticism centers around Janov's lack of instruction or openness to others who might wish to conduct the therapy. He does invite one to enroll in his Institute for Therapy and Training, but that alternative is quite time consuming and expensive. Also, it appears that even therapists who have been trained by Janov, but later decide to leave and practice on their own, are suspect by Janov's criteria. Considerable doubt is placed in one's mind about their abilities to be free from "neurotic hang-ups" in administering Primal Therapy. We are led to believe that the only "authentic" and "safe" version of Primal Therapy can be found at the Institute. By not thoroughly explaining his techniques and approach to therapy, Janov is isolating the method from true scientific research. The cornerstone of scientific method has always been replication of results in different laboratories and clinics with objective, neutral experimenters.

Janov does appear to be flexible in his methods within his theory, but by focusing almost exclusively on the parents as the cause of mental illness Janov is not allowing the natural process to unfold as completely as it is capable of doing. It is extremely narrow, perhaps even harmful or dangerous, to infringe upon the workings of the psychophysiospiritulogical wisdom when it is underway. Once it begins its work it needs to be allowed to do anything it chooses to do to free its own system of hinderances.

My response to Janov's approach is that by reacting as he does, the brain or Inner Source will be blocked from it's full response potential. My feelings are embodied in the following short quote from Janov himself (1974 b):

When Primal Therapy is done slowly and methodically there is no reason why *any* feeling the patient arrives at on his own has to be disintegrating. But we must remember that we cannot integrate feelings we are deprived of; so to arbitrarily decide that there are certain feelings a patient must avoid is to seriously rob him of crucial experiences. (p. 290)

It is my impression that Janov is arbitrarily limiting the Inner Source.

Other Synthetically Oriented Approaches

Free Imagery-Emergent Uncovering: Joseph Reyher, with the Department of Psychology at Michigan State University, first wrote of his method in the *Journal of Clinical Psychology* (1963). At that time he called the method "free imagery." In a recent unpublished paper, written sometime after 1972, he refers to the method as "emergent uncovering." He sees the method as an "eyes-closed free association." The client is instructed, while seated, to close the eyes and report everything that comes into the mind: images, feelings or physical sensations. "Thoughts" are not to be reported. One is to focus on the internal images that arise, which Reyher links mainly to primary process.

Although free imagery-emergent uncovering often leads to "intense abreactions and regressive behavior," the method is utilized as an uncovering technique rather than a therapy technique in and of itself. Reyher states that the method should not be used when it interferes with regular therapy. The uncovered material is used as the work for the conventional face-to-face "interactive methods of psychotherapy." What is uncovered, according to Reyher, is repressed material or the pathogenic process within.

Spontaneous Introspection: Albert Steinkirchner, M.D. has written a book called *Self Psychotherapy* in which he presents what he calls a new technique, "spontaneous introspection" (1974). The book presents case material dating back to 1964, the starting point of the therapy. Instructions which are given to one beginning the therapy are to close the eyes and watch the spontaneous images that arise. These images come without any conscious planning and are thought to come from the activation of natural forces, one's inherent psychological forces. Before starting, the client is to clear his or her mind of thinking and daydreaming because one is to focus exclusively on the mental images. These will in turn produce thoughts and ideas and insights. After about 3 hours of introspection, unresolved childhood events start appearing and this is supposed to be when real emotion is felt. This childhood material is called "maturational conflict" and is unconscious emotional conflict.

Games, Art, Music, Kundalini, Biofeedback, Imagery . . . : Researchers seeking alternatives to LSD-assisted therapy have discovered interesting approaches. Jean Houston and Robert Masters in an article called, "The Experimental Induction of Religious-Type Experiences" (1972), and in their book, *Mind Games* (1972), discuss other methods in lieu of LSD. They focus on two devices, an "Altered States of Consciousness Induction Device" and the "Audio-Visual Environment Device." Helen Bonny, who had previously worked at the Maryland Psychiatric Research Center helping to facilitate LSD sessions through the use of music, found that music alone could accomplish the same state of consciousness. Bonny and Louis Savary in their book, *Music and Your Mind* (1973), speak of the therapeutically catalytic quality of music listened to in an altered state of consciousness.

Akhter Ahsen has written extensively about the therapeutic value of the eidetic image. Two of his basic works are *Basic Concepts in Eidetic Psychotherapy* (1973), and his most recent work, *Psycheye* (1977).

The ancient concept of Kundalini has been explored for its therapeutic implications by Lee Sannela in his book, *Kundalini — Psychosis or Transcendence?* (1976). He was partially inspired by the work of Gopi Krishna, who has written *Kundalini, the Evolutionary Energy in Man* (1967) and *The Awakening of Kundalini* (1975).

Biofeedback research has produced approaches which have implications for inner therapeutic experience. Thomas Budzynski has written two articles which are pertinent to inner experiencing:

"Some Applications of Biofeedback-Produced Twilight States" (1972) and "Tuning in on the Twilight Zone" (1977). Alyce Green, Elmer Green, and E. Walters in an article called, "Psychophysiological Training for Creativity" (1971), mentioned conducting research with "alphatheta brainwave feedback, reverie, and imagery" and with "theta reverie." Green and Green also have a new book out which deals with their research. It is called *Beyond Biofeedback* (1977).

Therapeutic approaches which stress mental imagery are numerous. These are most thoroughly explored in the excellent book, *Waking Dreams*, by Mary Watkins (1976). The book includes a good chapter on imagery approaches in European countries where methods of this type have been thoroughly explored. Many of the techniques given in Watkins' book were important contributors to Roberto Assagioli's Psychosynthesis method. One method Watkins mentions deserves special recognition because she feels it is the most successful attempt to synthesize European therapeutic imagery work. It is the work of Roger Fretigny and Andre Virel on what they have termed "Onirotherapies." In their book, *L'Imagerie Mentale: Introduction a l'onirotherapie* (1968), they discuss their own and others' work.

In the United States, where there is a great upsurge of interest in imagery-related therapeutic approaches, there is a new journal devoted to the subject. The *Journal of Mental Imagery*, first published in Spring, 1977, is under the editorship of Anees A. Sheikh of the Department of Psychology, Marquette University.

Other synthetic methods of interest are John Lilly's book, *The Deep Self: Profound Relaxation by the Isolation Tank* (1977), the book by J. Hart, et. al., *Going Sane: An Introduction to Feeling Therapy* (1975) (an offshoot of Primal Therapy), and the Pecci-Hoffman Process (a psychic approach to psychiatry) described in an article by B. Pixa (1975).

Natural Inner Therapies

The purpose of this section is to augment for the professional the brief discussion of natural therapies given in Chapter 3. Included

are an analysis of Frederking's "Deep Relaxation with Free
Ideation," and more detailed material on "E-Therapy" and
"Autogenic Abreaction."

Deep Relaxation with Free Ideation

My first knowledge of Walter Frederking's therapy came from
reading an article by Wolfgang Kretschmer, "Meditative Techniques in Psychotherapy" (1972). Intrigued by Kretschmer's short
summary, I secured a copy of the Frederking article which was
originally published in the journal *Psyche* (1949). I had the material
translated from the German and, while Kretschmer had indicated
that the work should be called "Deep Relaxation and Symbolism,"
my translator disagreed. She felt quite strongly that the therapy was
more appropriately translated as "Deep Relaxation and the
Creation of Images." After studying the translated work I agreed
with her fully since "the creation of images" appeared to more
closely "fit" the essential nature of the therapy than the word
"symbolism." Later I discovered an article by Frederking (1955),
written in English, where he used the term "Deep Relaxation with
Free Ideation."

Background: Deep relaxation with free ideation is a therapy which
Frederking derived over a 12-year period. Even though the article in
Psyche appeared in 1949, evidently the original research began in
1936. The method itself was distilled from three different sources:
psychoanalysis, psychocatharsis (credited to Frank, 1913) and
certain relaxation exercises. His main reason for the establishment
of a new method was because of his increasing objections to the
conceptual constructs of psychoanalysis and the related dream
interpretations.

The development of the therapy was also guided to a large degree
by the results of mescaline intoxications. Frederking personally
underwent mescaline drug experiences as did many of his patients.
Several different approaches were utilized. For some, mescaline
was used prior to deep relaxation and free ideation; for others the
procedure was reversed. Another approach was to alternate using
the drug and non-drug therapy, switching back and forth. On the

whole, it appears that Frederking employed mescaline intoxications only when he felt that deep relaxation with free ideation was not able to work for the individual.

Frederking's basic idea was that the patient's experience is the key factor in the therapeutic process rather than the analytical and interpretive capabilities of the therapist or the patient. There are curative abilities inherent in the visual and physical aspects of the deep relaxation with free ideation process. There is a natural ability of the organism to heal itself once the deep relaxation is induced and the free ideation begins. Frederking likens the free ideation to the true dream in that neither can be "arbitrarily influenced," that is, consciously determined.

Concerning the role of interpretation in free ideation and deep relaxation, Frederking takes a dim view. He feels that much of the material is obvious and not difficult to understand by the patient. Certain phenomena, however, are not easy to interpret. Despite this fact Frederking is hesitant to involve any special system of interpretation. He states (1949):

Of course one can interpret the phenomena in the vein of and with the method of Freudian or Jungian analysis. But these lead one to assume, as the two examples show, a different behavior. The experiences of our female patient are poetry-like, or like a lyric drama that is being created and represented by her at the same time. This entity that is closed within itself does not need to be transposed into a different domain or supplemented by it, just like a work of art doesn't need this if it contains no foreign elements. It could very well be that what happened to this patient in this sequence of scenes may have been the deepest and richest insight and experience of her life. To break something like this into pieces, would be equivalent to taking away its essence.

Therapeutic Approach: Even though the therapy is essentially non-directive in nature, during the initial two or three sessions one is guided to some extent. First, the person is guided step by step into a deeply relaxed state. He or she is told that the body gradually becomes heavy and vague and that visual images of various types will be appearing in the inner visual field. One is told to focus on these images shutting out all other thoughts. The person is also told to focus on different parts of the body and describe what is taking place. Frederking feels that by narrowing one's attention down to these visual and physical phenomena and describing them that they will start to flow freely. Once the free flowing, uninfluenced, process starts coming, the therapist drops his minimal influence. Concerning the role of the therapist, Frederking (1949) explains it as follows:

> In the case of not a few patients, even with the patient who had shown such talent in free ideation, the experience stopped abruptly or became rather vague, as soon as I left the room, and began immediately when I opened the door. Several (patients) succeeded in having intensive experiences at home, but they almost always felt tuned in to me. It is further remarkable, that not a single patient, not even a creative artist showed any urge to draw, something that Jung and others were able to elicit. Never did I witness a convincing Mandala—or similar experience of individuation with my patients, as Jung came to know. On the other hand I was able to observe the various symbols of transformation, similar to those that develop in mystical unions, i.e., death and rebirth, rejuvenation, purification, expiation, chastening, transfiguration, exhortation of evil spirits and similar things.

In the early stages of the first session one may notice physical changes such as eyelid flutters, heart beating quickly or a reaction similar to some current physical problem such as a backache, headache and so on. As time progresses one begins to experience other reactions which are less typical of the relaxed state such as consciously felt changes in body size, shape and position. Limbs may seem longer or shorter, or as being swollen or shrunken. The left limb may seem different from the right. The body may bend to one side, bow or turn, or even seem unevenly heavy. The person might feel a rising or sinking sensation.

During a second stage one may begin seeing colors, then single objects (a horse, a tree, a profile), at first rather dimly. This stage soon proceeds into a third stage where one experiences physical and visual sensations that may have more meaning.

Frederking presents two case histories to illustrate this third stage. Some of the physical sensations which occurred were as follows: the body seeming to float, hands feeling as if clenched when visibly they were relaxed, dizziness, headaches, compulsive thoughts, a roaring inside the head, visual experiences partially centered around reliving fearful memories in a cathartic manner, seeing colors, patterns, squares, a tunnel which gradually increased in size, a boat rocking on the waves.

Much of the material follows themes which present themselves in varous symbolic direct ways. If these themes are not readily understood they will typically become clearer as sessions unfold. However, Frederking holds that *all* of the material will never be fully understood; some events seem beyond our interpretation.

Frederking gained his experience with deep relaxation with free ideation from a sample of "several hundred" people, most of whom were not actual patients. He states that only a small percentage were significantly neurotic. He does present two relatively detailed case histories. The first, age 40, is described as having increasing apprehension after experiencing a number of frightful events in childhood and adolescence, compulsive thoughts and continual light, cramplike headaches. The second was a 34-year-old woman who was unable to consummate her marriage of two months due to violent vaginal cramps. She also suffered from migraine headaches.

In addition to these two cases, he does refer to treating an asthmatic, a moderate stutterer, cases of epilepsy, one with a nervous circulatory disorder, one with spasm of the large colon, cases of impotence, cases of frigidity, one who had a strained relationship with his father during childhood and adolescence and one who was slightly brain damaged.

The only hint concerning the number of sessions one undergoes in deep relaxation with free ideation again refers to the two case histories. Case one underwent 30 one-half hour sessions and case two lasted 5 sessions. The amount of time for each of the 5 sessions was not given.

Results: Specific outcome data is provided only in reference to the two cases noted. The 40-year-old man's symptoms disappeared and he was described as "considerably calmer" after therapy. The 34-year-old woman was able to consummate her marriage at the end of the treatment period, and reported that her stay in therapy and the first few days of her return home were the "high points of her life." No mention is made of any progress in her migraine problem, nor of any other systematic evaluation of results.

Critique: Frederking is directive to a minimal extent in two areas: he "leads" the client into deep relaxation; and he tells the person in therapy to shut out thoughts. Neither of these steps are needed in order for Meditative Therapy to proceed. Both steps actually interfere with the inner workings. Thought patterns are just as vital as physical and visual phenomena.

A second criticism relates to the implication that Frederking's three stages of the therapeutic process hold true for all cases. I have never been able to narrow down the occurring phenomena into specific stages that hold true across the board for all people. Perhaps in general such stages hold up, but in my experience no two people respond the same in Meditative Therapy.

A third criticism focuses around the inadequate presentation of treatment outcome. And, of course, the lack of systematic follow-up data to determine if the results were lasting for the two cases reported.

Fourth, he does not place the therapy into total treatment perspective. We have no idea if this is the only therapeutic approach employed or not.

Finally, Frederking does not speak to the possible problems or dangers which may arise when one employs a therapy of this type. He does hint in one section that the therapy may not work as well when one does it alone without the therapist's presence. Otherwise, there is no mention made of potential rough spots or of necessary cautions.

There are many exciting ideas Frederking presents. One is his statement that a typical form of the creation of images is the "magic theatre" described by Hermann Hesse in his famous novel *Steppenwolf*. Hesse was also referred to as the "poet of the interior" by some of the experimenters working with LSD.

It is also of interest to note that Frederking ("Like all good Germans," says my translator), completes his article in *Psyche* with a quote from Goethe: "One should not try to find anything behind phenomena. They themselves constitute the moral (teaching)."

E-Therapy

The only material to be added to our discussion of E-Therapy centers around results of treatment, and criticisms.

Results: Only one case is reported in Kitselman's book *E-Therapy*. A 35-year-old woman became depressed and irritable when attempting college again after many years lapse. She was in the B-C-D range in her school work. Other symptoms were a deathly fear of water, frequent yelling at her children, and slow reading speed accompanied by low comprehension.

The client underwent a total of six E-Therapy sessions. After her first session she had a feeling of extreme physical and mental well being, "lost five or ten years of age," according to friends, lost her depressions, and significantly lowered her irritability. After completion of treatment her grades improved to A's and B's, her reading speed and comprehension were greatly improved, and she no longer had her fear of swimming. Kitselman even states that on exams she would simply "ask E for help" and she would instantly get the answer if she had read it at any time.

Critique: The most obvious criticism of Kitselman's work is that only one case is presented. Also, claims are made which are not verified by sample cases. No mention is made of other therapeutic methods, implying that the therapy is a cure-all, if only "E" is working properly. Finally, no discussion is given concerning possible dangers involved in the therapy.

Autogenic Abreaction

There is a great amount of material available on Autogenic Therapy. The work has been summarized into six volumes:

Vol. I   *Autogenic Methods,* Schultz and Luthe, 1969
Vol. II   *Medical Applications*, Luthe and Schultz, 1969

Vol. III *Applications in Psychotherapy*, Luthe and Schultz, 1969
Vol. IV *Research and Theory*, Luthe, 1970
Vol. V *Dynamics of Autogenic Neutralization*, Luthe, 1970
Vol. VI *Treatment with Autogenic Neutralization*, Luthe, 1973

The material summarized in these works comes from nearly 3,000 technical references, including many experimental studies, written by scientists from all over the world.

The following discussion of autogenic abreaction focuses on these dimensions: (1) background-theory, (2) therapeutic approach, (3) results of treatment, and (4) criticisms.

Background-Theory: Luthe presents impressive evidence for the role of the brain in human psychological, as well as physical, functioning. He indicates that the entire neurohumoral axis of the brain is directly involved in the self-normalizing activities of the autogenic state. The cortex, thalamus, reticular (centrencephalic) system, hypothalamus, pituitary, and adrenal are all intricately associated. He describes a brain mechanism which consists of a ganglionic system with connections to the cerebral cortex of each hemisphere and other subcortical structures. This mechanism is called a "brain-directed safety discharge system" and is considered to be involved with the reticular formation and thalamic structures and the limbic system.

Therapeutic Approach: Autogenic therapists must emphasize the requirements of *passive acceptance, non-interference, an unrestricted verbal description,* and *brain-directed termination.* In addition, the therapist must also learn to *correctly handle the various types of brain-antagonizing forms of resistance.* In order to comply with this step, one must become well acquainted with normal patterns of brain response and with various dynamics of brain-antagonism. In Part I of Volume Six, Luthe provides a lengthy and thorough discussion of various kinds of resistance. "Resistance" in this instance goes well beyond the generally accepted psychotherapeutic definition of the term.

Another device which the therapist needs to utilize in Autogenic Therapy is homework assignments. Although there are wide variations in the amount and type of homework assigned, dependir upon the unique features of each case, most patients need four to six hours per week, according to Luthe. Therapeutic homework may involve transcribing the autogenic abreaction session, making only a summary of a session, rereading the session content several times, writing an analysis of the content, keeping notes on dreams, or making drawings.

Figure 12-3 illustrates the relationship of the various elements of autogenic treatment. Table 12-4 presents a detailed description of phenomena experienced during Autogenic Standard Exercises.

The range of cases treated by autogenic methods is quite varied, and includes, as may be seen from the volume titles listed above, almost any mental or physical disorder that comes to mind. Medical cases are categorized into problems of the gastrointestinal tract, of the cardiovascular system, of the respiratory tract, and vasomotor disturbances of endocrine and metabolic functions. Psychotherapeutic cases are placed in categories such as neurologic disorders, brain injury and epilepsy, psychotic disorders, psychoneurotic disorders, personality disorders.

In the presentation of autogenic abreaction case material, Luthe describes each one in multiple terms. Most individuals are listed as suffering from anxiety reactions, varying degrees of depression, multiple psychophysiologic and phobic reactions, what is termed "ecclesiogenic syndrome" (which relates to problems based on faulty religious conditioning), personality disorders, and similar problems. Dr. Luthe is extremely thorough in his analysis of each individual case. At a San Francisco workshop in 1975, he stated that the longest list of symptoms he had figured out for one individual was over 100!

The amount of time needed for treatment is highly variable depending upon the individual. Most cases treated take from 2 to 8 months. Individual autogenic abreaction sessions last 60 to 90 minutes and are from 7 to 14 days apart. In rare instances an individual may need to be seen twice in one week. The reader must remember that the client spends much of the treatment time alone at home, without the presence of the therapist, for both autogenic abreaction and the standard exercises. For autogenic abreaction the therapist must be more cautious in allowing self-administration.

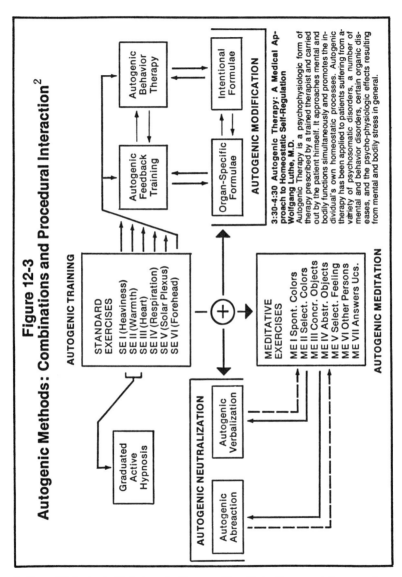

Figure 12-3
Autogenic Methods: Combinations and Procedural Interaction[2]

2. From W. Luthe (ed.) **Autogenic Therapy.** New York: Grune and Stratton, Inc., 1969. Reproduced with permission of the author and publisher (see also Appendix G.)

Table 12-4
Training Phenomena During
Autogenic Standard Exercises[3]

Categories	Modalities of Training Phenomena
1. Motor	
(a) Somatomotor	Twitching, jerking, trembling, involuntary movements, muscular tension
(b) Reflexmotor	Coughing, laughing, twitching of eyelids, sneezing, crying, swallowing, yawning, sucking, vomiting
(c) Visceromotor	Changes in respiration, heart action (e.g., palpitations, tachycardia, cramplike sensations), gastrointestinal motor activity (e.g., cramp-like sensations, borborygmus), salivation, perspiration, urogenital functions (e.g., erection, ejaculation, orgasm, vaginal contractions, micturition)
2. Sensory	
(a) Somatosensory	Heaviness, warmth, coolness, burning, tingling, numbness, pain, pressure, circulatory sensations (e.g., pulsations, bloodflow), tension, electrical sensations, feeling of stiffness, lameness as if paralyzed, swelling, itching, restlessness, disagreeable feelings (nonspecific) Changes of body image: detachment of parts of body, disappearance of specific deformation of parts of body
(b) Viscersensory	Pain and disagreeable sensations in throat, feeling of suffocation or strangulation, oppressed respiration, pain or other disagreeable feelings in the abdominal area, feeling of pressure or cramp-like sensations in the stomach, circulatory sensations in abdomen, nausea, feeling of hunger, urge to urinate, sensations in chest and cardiac area (e.g., pressure, tension, circulatory disturbance, pain, warmth)
(c) Other	Sleep, drowsiness

3. (Same footnote as Figure 12-3)

(Table 12-4 continued)	
Categories	**Modalities of Training Phenomena**
3. **Vestibular**	Dizziness, vertiginous sensations, turning, spinning, floating, sinking, flying, lopsidedness, displacement, falling, rocking, swinging
4. **Auditory**	Simple tones, noise, buzzing, music, voices
5. **Olfactory**	Agreeable, disagreeable sensations
6. **Gustatory**	Related to food, others (e.g., varnish, wood, sperm)
7. **Visual**	Uniform colors, cloud-like formations, shadows, simple forms, objects (static, dynamic), faces, differentiated images, filmstrips, cinerama-strips
8. **Affective**	Anxiety, fear, depression, euphoria, longing for love and affection, feeling of loneliness, insecurity
9. **Ideational**	Intruding thoughts (difficulty of concentration), memories, planning

Luthe indicates that for a group of 100 patients, 39% could undergo autogenic abreaction at home after less than 15 therapist-supported sessions.

Results: Analyzing the results of autogenic abreaction treatment is a very difficult task. Luthe essentially never applies autogenic abreaction without first having one undergo at least some portion of the standard exercises. It is thus impossible to evaluate the results of autogenic abreaction in isolation. Luthe does indicate that there are instances where minimal amounts of time are spent on the standard exercises prior to starting autogenic abreaction. For one group of 100 patients he reports that 13% had only one or two weeks prior to starting and an additional 23% had only three or four weeks before autogenic abreaction was initiated. No results of treatment are given for this group of 36, however.

A great deal of research has been conducted on the outcomes of treatment for the standard exercises. The medical and psychological benefits of these mental exercises are thoroughly documented. Volume IV, *Research and Theory*, is almost completely devoted to an analysis of the physiological changes that accompany completion of the standard exercises. Volume II and Volume III contain analyses of the results obtained for a variety of medical and psychological disorders, but basically only evaluating the standard exercises as the therapeutic agent. As a basic summary, Luthe has given the following analysis of the results of Autogenic Therapy:

Clinical results demonstrate that many patients suffering from a variety of long-standing psychosomatic disorders like chronic constipation, bronchial asthma, cardiospasm, and sleep disorders have been cured or have improved considerably in periods ranging from two to eight months.

It has been observed that behavior disorders and motor disturbances like stuttering, writer's cramp, nocturnal enuresis, certain states of anxiety and phobia and other neurotic disorders can be treated effectively. Over periods ranging from a few weeks to several months, depending on the particular case, patients have reported that their anxiety, insecurity and neurotic reactions have smoothed out or have gradually lost their significance. Generally, an increase in emotional and physiologic tolerance, with a considerable decrease in the previous need for reactive affective discharge, is reported. Social contact becomes less inhibited and more natural. Interpersonal relations are reported as warmer and more intimate with certain persons and less emotionally involved with others.

It has been noted that autogenic therapy improves self-regulatory functions and thus not only enhances a person's overall capacity for psychophysiologic adaptation but also increases bodily resistance to all kinds of stress.

Furthermore, it has been observed that with the help of autogenic training, unconscious material becomes more readily available. Dream material and memories can be more easily reproduced by trainees than by other patients, and free association also appears to be enhanced. (p. 3, Volume I)

Critique: My main criticism of Autogenic Abreaction Therapy is that there is no analysis of therapeutic outcomes for autogenic abreaction in and of itself, and no follow-up data are presented. The reader is left to observe how powerful the results of standard exercises administration are and can only assume that autogenic abreaction is substantially more powerful.

It is clear that Autogenic Therapy is a well-researched approach, and its extensive and successful application are impressive evidence of the value of the natural inner therapies.

13

A Final Word
to the Therapist

Within the Meditative Therapy process the Inner Source does not restrict itself to only one method. Using this fact as a springboard, I would like to reiterate my strong recommendation that the therapist employ an holistic-eclectic approach to complete health. My personal goal for clients is to help them overcome as many of their presenting complaints as possible *and* to leave them with *tools* which can be self-applied. Meditative Therapy is only one tool which will be of ongoing value to a life-long growth process. Physical exercise, dietary measures, spiritual concepts, assertiveness training, are also invaluable tools to practice throughout life to carry one to higher and higher levels of personal development. I suggest that therapists expand their treatment package to include the whole, psychophysiospiritulogical, person.

Perhaps a review of the "Psychophysiospiritulogical Chart of Inner Space" in Chapter 4 will help to stimulate your thinking in developing assessment and treatment programs.

Critique and Limitations of Meditative Therapy and of this Book

This book has been written to show the potential of Meditative Therapy. It is not an exhaustive treatment of the subject, mainly because no experimental studies with appropriate follow-up have been conducted. This is a most serious criticism. One of the purposes of this book is to stimulate further research. I have presented case histories showing the value of Meditative Therapy, but there must be more sophisticated analyses than have been given here. There must be comparisons made between Meditative Therapy clients and no-treatment controls. Also needed are comparisons with synthetic approaches such as those described in Chapter 12, and with approaches from other areas such as Behavior Therapy, Gestalt Therapy, Jungian Analysis and Psychoanalysis.

A related criticism deals with inadequate physiological testing of Meditative Therapy participants. Hopefully, others will be more thorough along these lines and provide complete analyses of client functioning before and after each session and before and after therapy. From observation it is clear that some stomachs will gurgle and gurgle; breathing is dramatically altered in certain cases; back disorders change for the better in some; migraine headaches improve in certain instances. Hearts, lungs, heads, stomachs, legs, arms, backs are affected during Meditative Therapy, but are there *measurable* physiological changes that accompany the treatment? We are only in our infancy along these lines of analysis.

One important limitation of this book is the lack of a thorough analysis of foreign language references. Frederking's article (1949) refers to some excellent-sounding titles, and Luthe's works reference many articles from the professional literature which are in German, French, or Spanish. I am certain that some of these materials contain valuable information about the functioning of the Inner Source, to which I have been unable to gain access at this time.

Another limitation of this book is the inadequate delineation of appropriate treatment recipients. At what ages should children be allowed to participate? Would Meditative Therapy be valuable in treating severe medical disorders such as diabetes, high blood pressure, heart disease, cancer, and so on? Should Meditative Therapy be used with the mentally retarded? Will the therapy work with schizophrenics and other psychotics? There has not been adequate experimentation to answer these and similar questions of this nature. A major step forward in this area is the recent development of a statement of "Precautions for Autogenic Therapy" by members of the International Committee on Autogenic Therapy (see Appendix G). For the moment, this statement, *although somewhat more limiting than my own views*, must be considered the most adequate reference in answering the question, "For whom is Meditative Therapy inappropriate?" Professionals are urged to exercise appropriate caution in applying this or *any* powerful therapy.

Are there differences in response between men and women in Meditative Therapy? Do Blacks, Chicanos, Germans, Asians, react differently than the sample given in this book? Does one's religious background help or hinder response in Meditative Therapy? Does Meditative Therapy foster creativity or extra sensory perception? Should Meditative Therapy be conducted in groups? These are all questions only hinted at in this book and which need to be studied systematically.

A limitation which has been stated throughout the book deserves mention one more time. Meditative Therapy is not a panacea, not a cure-all. Some are ready to believe that getting in touch with one's Inner Source will clear up such problems as faulty eating habits, poor physical exercise patterns, lack of assertiveness, difficulties in dealing with one's marital partner. Although these problems are indeed solved in some cases through Meditative Therapy, I have found that in many instances they are not and need further work with other methods. One may be led to the answer for a particular problem in certain instances, but it seems to me clearly better to take an holistic-eclectic approach, and to deal directly with these difficulties by using more appropriate methods.

Time alone, and life experience are critically important contributors to healing. Therapy does not exist in a vacuum and there are life events which are often more crucial in helping one grow than any formal therapeutic method will ever be.

Appendix A

SAMPLE FEAR INVENTORY ITEMS [1]

The Fear Inventory or Fear Survey Schedule (FSS) is a self-report test wherein one can rate the degree to which various things and experiences cause a fearful or unpleasant reaction. Four sample items are given below:

	Not At All	A Little	A Fair Amount	Much	Very Much
1. Enclosed places					
2. Failure					
3. Being Teased					
4. Feeling Disapproved of					

The particular FSS which I administered to my clients contained 76 items. There is a much more thorough FSS which contain 122 items, and is available to professionals through the Educational and Industrial Testing Service. (EDITS), P. O. Box 7234, San Diego, Ca. 92107.

The scoring system which I utilized on the 76 item FSS was to give a 1 for Not at All; 2 for A Little; 2 for A Fair Amount; 4 for Much; 5 for Very Much. The total possible score was 380.

Appendix B
WILLOUGHBY PERSONALITY SCHEDULE [1]

Instructions: The questions in this schedule are intended to indicate various emotional personality traits. It is not a test in any sense because there are no right and wrong answers to any of the questions in this schedule.

After each question you will find a row of numbers whose meaning is given below. All you have to do is to draw a circle around the number that describes you best.

0 means "no", "never", "not at all", etc.
1 means "somewhat", "sometimes", "a little", etc.
2 means "about as often as not", "an average amount", etc.
3 means "usually", "a good deal", "rather often", etc.
4 means "practically always", "entirely", etc.

1. Do you get stage fright? 0 1 2 3 4
2. Do you worry over humiliating experiences? 0 1 2 3 4
3. Are you afraid of falling when you are on a high place? 0 1 2 3 4
4. Are your feelings easily hurt? 0 1 2 3 4
5. Do you keep in the background on social occasions? 0 1 2 3 4
6. Are you happy and sad by turns without knowing why? 0 1 2 3 4
7. Are you shy? 0 1 2 3 4
8. Do you day-dream frequently? 0 1 2 3 4
9. Do you get discouraged easily? 0 1 2 3 4
10. Do you say things on the spur of the moment and then regret them?
    0 1 2 3 4
11. Do you like to be alone? 0 1 2 3 4
12. Do you cry easily? 0 1 2 3 4
13. Does it bother you to have people watch you work even when you do it well?
    0 1 2 3 4
14. Does criticism hurt you badly? 0 1 2 3 4
15. Do you cross the street to avoid meeting someone? 0 1 2 3 4
16. At a reception or tea do you avoid meeting the important person present?
    0 1 2 3 4
17. Do you often feel just miserable? 0 1 2 3 4
18. Do you hesitate to volunteer in a class discussion or debate? 0 1 2 3 4
19. Are you often lonely? 0 1 2 3 4
20. Are you self-conscious before superiors? 0 1 2 3 4
21. Do you lack self-confidence? 0 1 2 3 4
22. Are you self-conscious about your appearance? 0 1 2 3 4
23. If you see an accident does something keep you from giving help?
    0 1 2 3 4
24. Do you feel inferior? 0 1 2 3 4
25. Is it hard to make up your mind until the time for action is past?
    0 1 2 3 4

---

1. From Wolpe, J. **The Practice of Behavior Therapy** (Second Edition). Elmsford, N. Y.: Pergamon Press, 1973. A short form of the Clark-Thurstone Inventory, known as "Willoughby's Neuroticism Schedule." See Willoughby, R. R., "Norms for the Clark-Thurstone Inventory," **Journal of Social Psychology,** 5: 91, 1934. Reproduced by permission of Joseph Wolpe.

Appendix C

FOLLOW-UP OF COUNSELING FORM

Please complete the following individualized evaluation of counseling form. Your feelings about your experience are extremely important to me. I need the feedback in order to have information concerning the usefulness of the various approaches which I employ. Also, I feel it would be good for you to evaluate your own progress.

After completing the form, place it in the envelope provided, seal it, and then return it to the secretary who will make sure I receive the material.

Sincerely,

Michael L. Emmons, Ph.D.
Counseling Psychologist

When you came to us for counseling in   19   you indicated that your difficulties were as follows:

A.	I.
B.	J.
C.	K.
D.	L.
E.	M.
F.	N.
G.	N.
H.	O.

1. Please rate the degree to which these difficulties changed on the following scales. Use the A. scale for the A. difficulty listed above, the B. scale for the B difficulty listed above and so on.

A.

Total Improvement	Very Much Improved	Much Improved	Average Improvement	Somewhat Improved	Slight Improvement	No Improvement

B.

Total Improvement	Very Much Improved	Much Improved	Average Improvement	Somewhat Improved	Slight Improvement	No Improvement

C.

Total Improvement	Very Much Improved	Much Improved	Average Improvement	Somewhat Improved	Slight Improvement	No Improvement

D.

Total Improvement	Very Much Improved	Much Improved	Average Improvement	Somewhat Improved	Slight Improvement	No Improvement

E.

Total Improvement	Very Much Improved	Much Improved	Average Improvement	Somewhat Improved	Slight Improvement	No Improvement

F.

Total Improvement	Very Much Improved	Much Improved	Average Improvement	Somewhat Improved	Slight Improvement	No Improvement

G.

Total Improvement	Very Much Improved	Much Improved	Average Improvement	Somewhat Improved	Slight Improvement	No Improvement

H.

Total Improvement	Very Much Improved	Much Improved	Average Improvement	Somewhat Improved	Slight Improvement	No Improvement

I.

Total Improvement	Very Much Improved	Much Improved	Average Improvement	Somewhat Improved	Slight Improvement	No Improvement

J.

Total Improvement	Very Much Improved	Much Improved	Average Improvement	Somewhat Improved	Slight Improvement	No Improvement

K.

Total Improvement	Very Much Improved	Much Improved	Average Improvement	Somewhat Improved	Slight Improvement	No Improvement

L.

Total Improvement	Very Much Improved	Much Improved	Average Improvement	Somewhat Improved	Slight Improvement	No Improvement

M.

Total Improvement	Very Much Improved	Much Improved	Average Improvement	Somewhat Improved	Slight Improvement	No Improvement

O.

Total Improvement	Very Much Improved	Much Improved	Average Improvement	Somewhat Improved	Slight Improvement	No Improvement

No.

Total Improvement	Very Much Improved	Much Improved	Average Improvement	Somewhat Improved	Slight Improvement	No Improvement

2. Please indicate in the space provided other changes, positive and negative, you've observed since beginning your counseling experience.

3. Answer the questions listed below only if they are check-marked with red.

 A. Do you feel you benefited from **Assertiveness Training?** Yes, No (circle one).

 B. Do you feel you benefited from **Dietary Suggestions and changes in your diet?** Yes, No (circle one). Please give specific reasons for your answer.

 C. Do you feel you benefited from **Meditative Therapy?** Yes, No (circle one). Please give specific reasons for your answer.

 D. Do you feel you benefited from **Regular Talk Therapy?** Yes, No (circle one). Please give specific reasons for your answer.

 E. Do you feel you benefited from **Systematic Desensitization?** Yes, No (circle Please give specific reasons for your answer.

 F. Do you feel you benefited from the use of the **Video Tape Recorder?** Yes, No (circle). Please give specific reasons for your answer.

 G. Do you feel you benefited from **Marital Counseling** sessions with your spouse? Yes, No (circle one). Please give specific reasons for your answer.

4. Which of the above therapies do you feel was the most beneficial to you?

5. What was the most outstanding factor in your counseling experience?

6. How might I improve my approach so as to be more helpful to future clients?

7. Have any other events taken place in your life during the counseling period that might account for the changes you have noted?

MEDITATIVE THERAPY FOLLOW-UP QUESTIONNAIRE

Please complete the following questionnaire concerning your feelings about your experiences with Meditative Therapy (closing your eyes and allowing an inner intelligence or higher self to help you). Keep in mind that you are not expected to answer in one way or another, that there are no right or wrong answers. I am only interested in hearing your honest evaluation of your experiences.

Sincerely,

Michael Emmons

Rate the following remarks on the scale provided:

0 means "not at all"	2 means "quite a bit"
1 means "a little"	3 means "very much"

1. **Looking back on your Meditative Therapy experiences, how would you rate the experience as a whole?**

A very pleasant experience	0	1	2	3
Something I want to try again	0	1	2	3
An experience of great beauty	0	1	2	3
Greater awareness of reality	0	1	2	3
Feel it was of lasting benefit to me	0	1	2	3
The greatest thing that ever happened to me	0	1	2	3
A religious experience	0	1	2	3
A very unpleasant uxperience	0	1	2	3
A disappointing experience	0	1	2	3
An experience of insanity	0	1	2	3
Did me harm mentally	0	1	2	3
Like traveling to a far-off land	0	1	2	3
Very much like being drunk	0	1	2	3
Return to feelings of childhood	0	1	2	3
Physical discomfort and illness	0	1	2	3

2. **How were you, or what were you left with, after your Meditative Therapy experiences?**

A new way of looking at the world	0	1	2	3
A greater understanding of the importance and meaning of human relationships	0	1	2	3
A new understanding of beauty and art	0	1	2	3
A greater awareness of God, or a Higher Power, or an Ultimate Reality	0	1	2	3
A sense of greater regard for the welfare and comfort of other human beings	0	1	2	3
More ability to relax and by myself	0	1	2	3

Improvement noted by people closest to me	0	1	2	3
Greater tolerance of others	0	1	2	3
A sense of futility and emptiness	0	1	2	3
A frightening feeling that I might go crazy or lose control of myself	0	1	2	3
Sense of relaxation and freedom from anxiety and tension	0	1	2	3
A better understanding of the cause and source of my troubles	0	1	2	3
A set of new decisions and new directions for my life	0	1	2	3
A new sense of fun and enjoyment	0	1	2	3
A sense of now knowing what life is all about	0	1	2	3
Colors have been brighter	0	1	2	3

3. Had you taken psychedelic drugs of any kind prior to your Meditative Therapy experiences?
   Circle
   Yes, No If yes, please list them and explain under what conditions you took them.

4. How would you compare the two experiences? Any similarities, etc?

5. What was your involvement in religion as you were growing up? Please explain.

6. How would you describe your involvement with religious or spiritual mattes as an adult prior to your Meditative Therapy experiences?

7. Have your feelings on religion and what it means changed any as a result of your Meditative Therapy experiences?
   Circle
   Yes, No If yes, in what way?

8. Have your experiences with Meditative Therapy changed your feelings about death in any way?
   Circle
   Yes, No If yes, explain.

9. Do you trust God or a supreme being or concept more than you did? How?
   Circle
   Yes, No

10. Have your ideas concerning parapsychological experiences such as ESP, out of body experiences, etc, changed as a result of your Meditative Therapy expeiences?
    Circle
    Yes, No If yes, explain.

11. Please explain what role I, as the therapist, played in your Meditative Therapy experiences.

12. Is there anything else you can tell of your experiences that was particularly exciting, disturbing, unusual, etc? Please share it with me.

Appendix D-2

MEDITATIVE THERAPY FOLLOW-UP DATA

The follow-up questionnaire was given to everyone who had gone through at least four Meditative Therapy sessions. Of the total group of 42 clients, 18 males and 18 females responded to the questions. Although most of these individuals received more than one type of treatment, when answering the questionnaire they were asked to restrict themselves to an evaluation of Meditative Therapy alone.

In order to help summarize the results, 0 and 1 will be counted as a "no" response and 2 and 3 as a "yes" response. The analysis below will be presented in terms of the percent responding either favorably or unfavorably to each statement.

Let us first look at whether or not participants on the whole felt good about their experience. When asked if the experience was a very unpleasant one (question 1, statement 8) 91% felt that it was not unpleasant. When asked it if was a disappointing experience (question 1, statement 9) 100% felt that it was not disappointing. In judging whether or not their experience was one of insanity (1,10) or did them harm mentally (1,11) 97% replied no. Most (97%), did not feel that the experience was like being drunk (1,13) or that it caused them physical discomfort or illness (84%, 1,15). The majority, (94%), did not feel that the sessions caused a sense of futility and emptiness (2,9) or that the session caused a frightening feeling which made them feel that they would go crazy or lose control of themselves (2,10).

The positively oriented questions tended to follow the same trend. Sixty-six percent felt that the experience was a very pleasant one (1,1) and 88% said it was something that they want to try again (1,2). When asked if the experience was of lasting benefit to them (1,5), 81% replied yes. Eighty percent believed that they had more ability to relax and be themselves (2,6) and 69% gained a sense of relaxation and freedom from anxiety and tension (2,11).

Summarizing these results, we can see that the Meditative experience is essentially a good one rather than a bad one for most people. For 40% of the group we can even make a much stronger statement because they indicated that the experience was the greatest thing that ever happened to them (1,6).

Two other questions which were descriptive of the Meditative Therapy experience showed the following results: 36% indicated that it felt like traveling to a far-off land (1,12) and 42% felt that they had a return to feelings of childhood (1,14).

The next grouping of questions relate to one's understanding of life and God. Although 66% gained a greater awareness of reality (1,14), only 31% felt that they now had a sense of knowing what life is all about (2,15) and 39% thought they now had a new way of looking at the world (2,1). Twenty-five percent believed that the therapy was a religious experience for them (1,7) and 31% felt that they had a greater awareness of God, or a Higher Power, or an Ultimate Reality (2,4).finally 36% thought that the experience was one of great beauty (1,3).

In the area of the effect Meditative Therapy has upon one's interactions with other people there were four questions. Fifty percent reported that they had gained a greater understanding of the importance and meaning of human relationships (2,2), that they had acquired a greater tolerance of others (2,8), and that those closest to them had noted improvement in their behavior (2,7). Thirty six percent thought that they now had a sense of greater regard for the welfare and comfort of other human beings (2,5).

Concerning how they felt about their own functioning after Meditative Therapy 58% indicated that they had gained a better understanding of the cause and source of their troubles (2,12). Forty-two percent believed that they had gained a set of new decisions and directions for their lives (2,13) and 34% felt a new sense of fun and enjoyment (2,14) after their Meditative Therapy experiences.

Two other statements dealt with esthetic outcomes of the therapy. Twenty-five percent thought that colors were brighter (2,16) and 28% gained a new understanding of beauty and art.

Presented below are the remaining items from the follow-up questionnaire. First, the question will be given, then a short paragraph explaining the response.

3. **Had you taken psychedelic drugs of any kind prior to your Meditative Therapy experience?** Thirteen individuals or 36% said that they had taken some type of psychedelic drug prior to Meditative Therapy. Of the 13 the frequency for each drug is as follows:

1. LSD, 2
2. Marijuana, 4
3. Combination of Drugs, 7

The third category would be where the individual took more than one drug such as Peyote, Mescaline, LSD or Marijauna in various combinations during the same experience.

4. **How would you compare the two experiences?** Originally this question was included in order to provide a comparison between the effects of drug access to the Inner Source versus the natural access. Clearly, this cannot be a just comparison because of the wide diffeences in set and setting factors and because of the minimal amount of users of psychedelic drugs in my sample. This finding about prior drug use did suprise me because of all the reports I've read in the popular literature about the frequency of drug use on the college campus. Instead of 36% I was expecting a much higher percentage.

5. **What was your involvement in religion as you were growing up?**
The responses were as follows:

1. A variety of religions, 1
2. Very little involvement,1
3. Presbyterian, 1
4. Lutheran, 2
5. No involvement, 3
6. Methodist, 4
7. Catholic, 19

Of the 53% designating that they were raised as Catholics, most fit the "cradle Catholic" description. That is, they felt that they had been very much involved in the church since birth. This high percentage responding Catholic is a surprising finding also because there is no particular reason to guess that the percentage would be this high, since the University draws from all parts of the state for its student body.

6. **How would you describe your involvement with religious or spiritual matters as an adult prior to your Meditative Therapy experiences?**
The group responded as follows:

1. Erratic involvement, 1
2. Interested in, read books about religion, 1

3. Fearful of Satan, 1
4. Hostile toward religion, 1
5. Agnostic, 3
6. No involvement, but searching to figure it out, 3
7. Still attend church, 3
8. No involvement, 6
9. No involvement, but believe in God, or a Natural Order or a Supreme Being, 6
10. Involvement in spiritual rather than religious matters, 10

By indicating that they were involved in spiritual rather than religious matters most seemed to be saying that they had personal, but nonstructured, non-church attending involvement. Several were practicing meditation and studying various systems of meditation.

7. Have your feelings on religion and what it means changed any as a result of your Meditative Therapy experience? Thirteen or 36% answered yes to this question. Below are representative responses:

1. "Closer to God. Traveling, but not knowing where. Frightened at times."
2. "I am more aware of a spiritual need and belief."
3. "I seem to have more faith in a Supreme Being. No longer the concept of heaven or hell or punishment for sins, but a good feeling and faith in a spiritual world."
4. "Reaffirmed and made stronger (my beliefs). Belief in the existence of a higher order or general purpose, God. Established the belief that God exists inside everyone."
5. "I found the source of spiritual power to come, paradoxically, rather than by trying to search out or find somewhere."

8. Have your experiences with Meditative Therapy changed your feelings about death in any way? Twelve or 33% felt that they were less afraid, more at ease, more positive about death now.

9. Do you trust God or a supreme being or concept more than you did? Eleven or 31% answered yes to this question. Most spoke about a positive experiencing now and felt that much of it came as a direct experience through them.

10. Have your ideas concerning parapsychological experiences such as ESP, out of body experiences, etc. changed as a result of your Meditative Therapy experiences? Fifteen or 42% replied yes to this question. Examples were:

1. "Before, I thought these things could possibly happen. Now I know they can. And feel too they are not weird or freaky."
2. "Curiosity has been aroused. Prior to Meditative Therapy I wsas sure it didn't exist, now I'm not so sure."
3. "Always thought it was 'kooky' and 'way out', but now I can accept it."
4. "Quite profoundly. Immediately increased ESP type experiences."
5. Definitely. There is much more to life than just the 'old 5 senses trip'."

11. Please explain what role I, as the therapist, played in your Meditative Therapy experience. The responses here ranged from a few being upset because they felt I was too passive and wouldn't tell them what to do or interpret what had happened, to praise because I helped them discover their Inner Source. Almost all of the responses were positive and used phrases like "doorman to my mind," "a key unlocking a door," "a middleman," "a guide," and "a facilitator" to describe my function. Many commented about the help they felt because I would encourage them to "let go" during the therapy. Another common response related to my helping encourage and reassure them when things got confusing or upsetting.

12. **Is there anything else you can tell of your experience that was particularly exciting, disturbing, unusual, etc?** This question produced a wide range of responses. Most were positively oriented and described increased trust in themselves and in their minds and bodies working together. These responses are difficult to summarize, therefore all but the two samples given in Chapter 4 are given below:

3. My out of body experience was very thrilling and exciting, especially because I had feared it so, but wanted to do it. It was very natural, like dreaming, only with a vividness not found in dreaming. I could feel the warmth of the sun, the pavement beneath my feet, even the cracks in the sidewalk. I could look down and see what I was wearing, feel the weight of my body, etc. as I walked along in Santa Rosa Park. My last Meditative Therapy session was a real bonus, a gift of joy. I saw the Babe of Bethlehem in a manger, the Holy Family, Mary and Joseph, and even the Wisemen and their camels in rich trappings. It was like a T.V. special in vivid color, and I was overjoyed, a real Christmas present. Since then the feelings of joy have carried over into my life which has been usually hectic - finishing up school, graduating, sending out applications and resumes, plus moving back to_____ . Before Meditative Therapy all the stress and strain would have been very trying on me, but I feel unusually calm and peaceful under the circumstances, where before I would have been in a frantic state - unable to eat, sleep, filled with anxiety. I feel in control, and little annoyances don't bother me, even the Post Office, waiting in line to send packages, shopping in stores, traffic, and packing up and shipping all my belongings by Greyhound. This is the supreme test of Meditative Therapy, and I went through it all without the usual nerves and tension I have experienced in the past. This Christmas will probably by my happiest one, as has been this past six months, and I credit most of this to Meditative Therapy, which has changed me, my attitudes toward life, toward myself, and toward my fellow man. I can truly say it is one of the most wonderful things that has ever happened to me, and I thank you for giving me the opportunity to experience it.

4. Not really; actually, I'm quite glad I'm through with it. I enjoy direct conversation and role playing much more and find it more effective.

5. I really enjoyed the experience and I believe in it. It helped me to understand unpleasant experiences in the past much better, therefore enabling me to handle those and other experiences much better. I feel that the experience has given me more confidence and a good inner feeling. I thought that it was really interesting the way my body would "take over" and do its own thing. It seemed that I always got a headache while I was in the therapy (sometimes even days before I would come in!) but it would always disappear when I was done. I think that my head (or mind) really got a good workout, which I feel is very healthy and important. I feel that the therapy is a great way of getting things out that have been stored or hidden in your mind for a long time. It is so healthy not to bottle things up inside. You have to let them out, and the therapy is a very constructive and successful way of doing it. It was really great!

6. I feel as though there is indeed a potential here to help me, but perhaps due due to the short period I was into it, I never realized the full potential. I'm considering (planning) on doing it on my own, but we'll see. I would like to get into it in the fall.

7. After my first M-T, I had a very interesting experience. I had always had trouble relaxing when my husband and I had sex. The evening after my first M-T, when I had sex with my husband, I was very relaxed and was able to get the maximum out of our intercourse that evening.The next time we had sex I was not as relaxed as the evening described above, but I have more and more sexual experiences that I feel I get the maximum from.

8. Three things that I recall as outstanding: (1) An experience with various forms of light throughout the session. The light filled my head and body. It left my eyes puffy, though, to the next day. (2) At some point, the images seemed to change from a dreamlike quality to extreme vividness in depth and detail. Color was more vivid; there was just more realistic life in the images. (3) An experience in which I saw my mind like a computer and all the tubes and etc. were being taken out and thrown away. Then my head was filled with water and seeds. Flowers grew, then people came by and picked them. This really left me with an uplifted feeling.

9. I wouldn't know "unusual" if it bit me.

10. During therapy, and since, I feel more aware of the variety of sensory experiences. Instead of one overall "sense of being," I gained a sense of how I felt in body, spirit, consciousness, etc. What I mean is that feelings were differentiated - what I saw, how my body felt, what I thought, were all separate parts of a composite sense of being. I find this very helpful now. If I'm feeling "down," I can use this understanding of the various things that effect my overall sense of being to help me find what's making me feel "down" and change it. I enjoyed and was surprised by re-living things from childhood, like running with a pinwheel in hand. I was also surprised by old hurts, ones I thought were gone, that still hurt. I feel better able to think about these now, especially about my miscarriage. I used to put it out of my mind and, though some hurt is there, I can think about it now. The ability to "let things go," to "let go" I would like to develop more. I still fight myself to "let go" and feel I'd like to learn to do the therapy myself. It really helped me get in touch with myself, and I found it exciting, although I often felt drained after a session. I learned a lot about myself and my relationship to my past, and also was intrigued by the variety of the experiences and the power which so paradoxically came from within, yet outside of myself. I guess I learned what I really **felt** about things, not just what I thought or felt I should feel.

11. Two things: (1) This is a most outstanding and beneficial device, because it leads to self-discovery and inner peace. While these are not objectives that can be attained fully in a few months, or grasped and retained as you do a concrete object, this therapy put me on the right road toward those objectives. (2) As I think about this, I have a strong desire to return to the therapy. I would like one or two more sessions. Having discontinued for awhile has not made me regress, but I wish to work harder on several aspects of my personality that are weak.

12. Went through birth experience - amazing; Tied it into present physical feelings - amazing.

13. As the sessions went on, I found more complete relaxation and freedom from uneasiness. My fears about getting hyperanxious were dispelled and I came to enjoy the positive, constructive, and "upbeat" sensations which I had on the floor in the office. Thanks very much.

14. Lots of things. A great rebirth occurred. The world was one. Everything was beautiful. Everything was so perfect. Like I was in the back seat with a driver. I was very relaxed and happy. My soul guided me to what I needed and still does. What disturbs me is the confusion now - I fight. I am not sure if what I am experiencing now is partially caused by it or if I am fighting an emotional problem as well as a spiritual upheaval, consequently going nuts. The experience was enlightening and beautiful. I learned a lot. I learned how to take care of myself and to listen to myself and not to run from my feelings - to relax and let things be. It taught me not to worry. It released me from a lot of past burdens; however, when it led me to the main problem in my life, man, I started running scared and I didn't want anyone to touch me. I started trying to control. I started weirding out. Everything frightened me. I didn't want anyone to touch me or help me, not even me. I started going crazy, so to speak. I've gone through a lot of physical pain and still do. Anyway, this is upsetting to me, yet I still run.

15. The Meditative Therapy at first was scary and I was scared of it and reality. My viewpoints on you, Doctor, changed from time to time, and I thought for awhile that I was insane; however, through your help and guidance I learned that this was just part of my learning process. Thank you, Mike, and God bless you. You have been a real friend, and I am so glad we knew each other.

16. Things pop into my head and I listen to them. I am beginning to tap a resource I was never even aware of. I accept and understand (in a new sense) information which is provided from within me. It casually comes in symbols. Through patience and allowance the symbols make sense. It is weird. I trust the Inner Source or these symbols more than a lot of "facts." The symbols are in the form of "visions."

17. Major thing, I learned to trust my feelings and not just to trust apparent facts and relationships as I had been taught was the only way. I finally felt like all the parts were a whole.

18. I really dreaded coming to some of the Meditative sessions.

19. Felt more relaxed than I can ever remember feeling without using alcohol or drugs - a real treat for me. Felt emotionally stronger afterwards.

20. I feel that there was no conclusion. If there was meant to be none, O.K., but I expected a summation of some kind. Thanks for all your time and effort.

21. Through the experience, I gained an awareness of the strong connection of mind and body. One helps the other for benefit or both.

22. The experience was enlightening. I saw images I wasn't aware existed and still don't understand their meaning. But afterwards, even after a series of seemingly senseless episodes, I felt freshened and rather renewed.

23. More memories of early life - liked that. Enjoy having some visual images being really clear. Much more aware of my physical reaction to emotional feelings.

24. It's so simple - all truths usually are. I feel that each time I am more open and receptive in my "regular" life. I am more aware of what my body is telling me. What was written here came through me and out onto the paper.

25. There have been some changes which I have noticed in myself which I think might have been contributed in part through Meditative Therapy. I have just finished reading **Open Marriage** which contained many things which I value and now find myself being able to accept. A few months ago this would have been very difficult - three months ago. I have become more aware of myself and my uniqueness and have really come to like myself. This in part could be due to Meditative Therapy and also the assertive training I have been having. I can feel my changes in my ways, but I am not sure exactly where the seeds of change came from. My changes and greater understanding of myself and other people has really helped me. Thank you for your **guidance!**

26. The neatest thing is that, even before the sessions were over, I did the Meditative Therapy on my own (see your notes). The best thing is that I can lie down and get rid of my anger (or whatever) when I need to - if I can be alone in my home. This is most "healing" and I find that I can rid myself of these negative feelings. I have continued to "grow" and now can look past my own personal needs to the needs of my husband and kids. (It was very disturbing to me during the time I felt so resentful of others and had so much self-pity. I was miserable and probably made others miserable.) I was (before) preoccupied with what I **should** be doing, but now feel satisfied with what I am already doing. I feel that a husband and wife **both** should have this and during the same period. Both should be allowed to work all the way through. This seems to be negative for a person if he is still unfinished.

27. First of all, my back had been bothering me quite a bit. After several sessions, it quit bothering me for about six months and hasn't bothered me near as much since therapy. Also I had a vision in one of my first sessions which seemed to keep occurring periodically. It was that of someone (an old woman) looking at me through a door. The room I was in was dark and there was light behind the woman, so all I could see was the outline of her, no features. After several months, I figured out it was out of my childhood and the woman was my grandmother. It was in a bedroom at her house I used to sleep in when small. That scared me because at one time a prowler had slit the screen and she had just sewn it back up. Prior to this vision, I had always been a little freaked out by noises at night which used to keep me awake. I was paranoid someone was breaking in and I would get up and check out strange noises. After my "vision" and until this day, I don't even listen to noises and never get up or lay awake. I just go right to sleep and never worry about it, which is great.

Appendix E

THE CASE OF JOHN

John, age 23, married, came in because he had great difficulty in staying in all of the classes he signed up for at the start of a term. During certain periods of time he would not even attend classes or do assignments for four or more weeks of a ten week quarter. He explained that part of the problem was that if he once missed a class or an assignment he would then have trouble going back because he felt embarrassed. Many, many times he had considered dropping out of school, but he hated to admit defeat, and wanted to live up to his own and others' high expectations. His family, his teachers, his friends had always said he had so much potential. In high school he had graduated 3rd in a class of 126, and always scored close to the top in achievement tests, so all expected greatness to continue. He experienced difficulties in college immediately, and during his fourth term ended up completing no courses. His father and a school dean had to persuade him not to drop out. After two more terms, he did better, and decided to transfer to his present school. By this time all who knew of his academic problems were wondering what had happened to him because he used to be such a "red hot." (the term is not an editorial technique to spice up the book, but an actual statement John often heard applied to him.)

His two and one-half year record since transferring showed the following split in performance: A's - 21, B's - 5, C's - 2, D's - 0, F's - 3, Incomplete - 5, and Withdrawals - 7. Also it is important to note that he completed only seven courses during his most recent year in school. This case was all the more complex because John would either do extremely well or extremely poorly. If he was able to stay in a class he would receive and A or B, but if he was headed for a C or worse he typically couldn't face it and would bail out. As can be seen from the two C's and three F's, he did get caught a few times before escaping.

Psychological Data: I did not administer the fear inventory or Willoughby to John. His initial interviews revealed that he was very perfectionistic, and feared not living up to his own or others' highest expectations. Moreover, he felt that he lacked self-discipline in school, and was overly sensitive to criticism.

Physical Data: John had been overweight in the past and still had a tendency to gain weight easily. Also in the past he had bronchial asthma and presently he had "smoker's lungs," and hayfever during the spring. His main physical difficulty was with his energy levels, which would fluctuate up and down drastically. At times he would absolutely not want to do a thing, and he often fould it difficult to get up in the morning. He would skip school, using "tiredness" as an excuse, and would often sleep in.

Treatment Approach: The initial treatment for John consisted of Meditative Therapy and dietary changes. The main dietary change I suggested was that he begin eating breakfast. Toward the end of his Meditative Therapy we decided to use assertiveness training to deal with situations centering around pressure from teachers when he wanted to return to class, and how to request time off at work when talking to his boss. Treatment consisted of two initial interviews, five Meditative Therapy sessions and three sessions dealing with assertive situations; a total of ten sessions.

Meditative Therapy Themes and Experiences: John's Meditative Therapy experience had many interesting facets. His sessions started out in a fairly straightforward manner centering around his ambivalence about life and himself. Below are sample segments from throughout his first session which point to this theme:

(a) God, it's weird when you want to have people think you're real cool, but you've got to be yourself - got to be satisfied, got to be satisfied.

(b) God, this ambivalence. It's not knowing - it's knowing everything.

(c) You talk like you're right and you are, unless you get too forceful, then you turn them off.

(d) I want to see everything, be everything. That's why I read everything.

(e) I'll fall asleep and when I awake you'll have men here with white nets to take me away. God, I don't have any problems. If i make them, I have them. If I get too wrapped up, I can't live. I have as many problems as I want.

(f) I'm dumb and smart at the same time.

(g) What am I running from? Why do I run? Ambivalence.

Physically, John gave the impression of being deeply relaxed during his sessions. I make this judgment based on his comments and reactions. Some of these are given below:

(a) God, my legs are dead, so good to relax.

(b) God, my body is dead, feels so good.

(c) Ever felt like you're asleep and you feel tense?

(d) Kind of go deeper and deeper, like sliding back into a mudhole, oozing back.

(e) Mind is resting. Separates mind and body, makes both feel better.

(f) My head is sinking right through my forehead.

(g) God, my arms are dead. Jesus, they're heavy, at first I thought they were strapped down.

(h) My cheeks are really heavy; eyelids are really locked.

He had seldom yawned during his fifth session, but he yawned 33 times in one hour. Many of these were deep yawns. In addition, he took eight deep breaths during the same time period.

Music dominated John's five Meditative Therapy experiences. He was continually either singing or listening to internally generated music during his sessions. Evidently music was an important facet of his life. Here are some quotes from his sessions which point in that direction:

Music is something that always has real meaning. (#1)

The thing about music is that you can lose yourself in it. (#2)

Got to think about every single note. That's how you concentrate and get into it. Like being healed. Almost doesn't matter what kind of music. It must be the listening and not the music. I know the words to almost every record. (#2)

As I mentioned, the content of John's first session was understandable in terms of his complaints. His next four sessions present no particular pattern. Examples:

(a) Looks like a defraction pattern. I get theta, get "n," get "d," got the wave length. (Yawns) A ring in my nose, double ring.

(b) (Opens eyes) I see radio waves coming off the end of my nose, just the interference pattern, where my nose is hitting the plastic mat. My arm is rippling - very fluid - I can see the flow of plastic in my arm.

(c) I can see a star - star - star, strange ones. Look like four lines. Around them is an aura, now changing, now spinning. White line, then yellow, then blue and purple.

(d) You know my eyelashes are smiles, from the inside I can see the smile. I feel my pulse in my hand. I see my skull, I see my hands on my skull. (Laughs) (Laughs) Shit! (Keeps laughing) Jesus! I'm too embarrassed, I don't know. (keeps laughing) Oh God! Wow! Oh God! (Laughs) I can't believe I'm doing this. I can feel how hot I am. How stupid. (keeps laughing) Oh God, Jesus, oh man! God, how dumb, let me open my eyes. (Keeps laughing)

(e) My head does feel hot. (Places hands on head) I'm aware of the sound of my hands. Weird sounds on my hair, almost snap, crackle, pop. And I know what it is and what color, white and black, like fire on sky. No it wasn't, it was my white hair being pulled out of my black scalp. My head feels very hot, like full of blood when running.

(f) I'm aware of the fact that without any strain my eyelids are completely relaxed, but closed tighter than they could ever be. I see a lot of flashes of light, arrowheads, light hitting each other. Pencil points, cosmic sections revolving at 100,000 rpm.

(g) I don't know, that was Judas. (stomach gurgles) (Yawns) Oh please, what was that wise old witch doctor, he was a sage, black, shrunken head. Full-grown shrunken head. (Yawns deeply) (Singing) I want to be a spaceman. Oh God, I just forgot, I was really deep into it, but I forgot. I was going to tell you about it.

(h) I was standing there watching Neanderthal man and Java man and modern man all chasing something. I couldn't figure out which one was the savage beast. I mean did we regress or progress? Now I know what I was, I was the one in the middle.

Results: Nine months after the completion of treatment, a follow-up of counseling form was completed by John. The outcome is given in Table E-1 below. Remember that the rating scale goes from 1 (no improvement) up to 7 (total improvement.)

Table E-1
THE CASE OF JOHN:
Nine-Month Follow-up Rating Degree of Improvement for Seven Complaints

Complaint	Degree of Improvement
1. Cutting out of school (won't attend classes or complete the homework 4-5 weeks of a quarter)	Total Improvement
2. Receiving incompletes and withdrawals in courses (procrastination)	Very Much Improved
3. Perfectionistic (not living up to own or others' expectations)	Very Much Improved
4. Sensitive to criticism	Much Improved
5. Energy level fluctuations	Much Improved
6. Tendency to gain weight	Much Improved
7. "Smoker's Lungs"	Much Improved

In addition to this outcome data it was possible to check his official student records of course performance. He completed eleven courses for 39 units and had eleven A's and one withdrawal and one incomplete, each in a different quarter. Even though the pattern was largely broken, there was still some difficulty remaining in classes as shown by the withdrawal and incomplete he received. As noted by the chart above, John had indicated that this aspect of his problem was not "totally improved," but rather "very much improved."

One other item on the follow-up questionnaire is of interest. John's reply to the request to indicate other changes, positive and negative, which they've observed since begining therapy:

"Positive - better able to manage my time - when I mis-manage my time I am able to realize my mistake and correct it

- have had, in general, a more positive outlook on life.

- in some areas, have better self-control (e.g. smoking)

Negative - in the past few weeks, have very strong urges to be violently agressive - want to hit, scream, curse, at objects or people - the rage is short, sudden, passionate and irrational - often takes little or no provocation.''

Several days later John wrote me the following letter:

Help! I was living a smug and self-satisfied life until a few weeks ago. Suddenly I feel as if I've regressed (in several areas) to a state below that when I first came to you. My problems are: .

1) Lack of assertiveness - my tendency to let others arrange my activities has crept up on me. It seems all my time is taken - promised to activities on someone else's behalf - and yet I tend to volunteer whenever anyone needs a lackey to step 'n' fetchet (both at work, school, etc.)

2) Temper - until I was about 14 or 15, I had a violent temper - I learned to master this problem (I thought). Perhaps I only masked it, because I have suddenly lost all control. My violent irrational rages in which I kick, hit and scream curses at inanimate objects are becoming frequent. This is definitely counterproductive. Since I indulge in these activities both alone and in the presence of others, my self-respect and respect from others are rapidly diminishing.

I could write (or talk) forever - but the question is, do I need help in getting started in the right direction to correct these faults? Or is the gradual awareness of them enough to get me going in the right way? I don't know what to do.
Thank you for reading this.''

We set up an appointment and he came in to describe problems being non-assertive in several areas of his life, but particularly at work. He allowed his boss to pile work on and John would become more and more upset, but would hold his feelings inside. One of the basic principles of assertion training is that it is best to keep one's life ''clear'' by handling situations as they come up. If feelings are held inside they build and often come out later against oneself and/or others. We agreed that he needed to get into more systematic training for assertion, and he enrolled in one of our ten-week groups which meet for one hour twice a week.

Seven months later, during which time he had also completed the assertive training, John wrote the following follow-up report:

My improvement in the seven areas has been maintained in general. There have been some deviations in certain areas:

1. Attending school -- total improvement maintained.

2. Procrastination -- have made slight regression since last report.

3. Perfectionism -- slight regression since last report.

4. Sensitivity to criticism -- improved beyond previous level almost to total improvement.

5. Energy level fluctuations -- completely stabilized.
6. Tendency to gain weight -- my weight has stabilized at my ideal even though I quit smoking.
7. Smoker's lungs -- I no longer smoke at all; am exercising to improve lung capacity, etc.

As far as my comments about positive and negative effects of therapy, I feel that these have changed somewhat. I can recognize when I mismanage my time, but still have problems correcting this mismanagement. My outlook on life fluctuates with my behavior (positive behavior --positive outlook; negative behavior--negative outlook.) My self-control is very good in some areas, but not so good in others (putting off homework.) I personally feel that my lack of self-control in certain areas is due to my failure to attempt to practice it.

My negative behavior -- strong violent agression -- was a very short run phenomenon caused by three factors: 1. failure to be assertive; 2. failure to use Meditative Therapy; and 3. the effects of withdrawing completely from a two-pack-a-day cigarette habit -- this lowered my violence threshold.

I feel that my regressive behavior in certain areas is due to my failure to continue the therapy as a mechanism for keeping my life clear. When I continue the therapy, combined with assertive behavior, I experience complete improvement in all areas.

Evaluation of Therapy: Therapist's View: The overall follow-up, 16 months after the completion of the original therapy, indicates that John's major problems are over and he now has the tools to keep his life in good shape and to help him continue his personal progress. Shortly after this follow-up was completed, John graduated from college and later entered a Ph.D. program at another university. From all appearances, he regained his status as a "red-hot," but this time it is a result of genuine inner self-confidence and concrete behavior changes.

John had dietary and physical exercise changes as part of his treatment, and also three sessions of assertion training in conjunction with Meditative Therapy. Although he had group assertion training, it was after his major changes had already taken place. Despite the other treatments, I feel, and John verifies, that Meditative Therapy was the key treatment. John stated in his first follow-up form that, "It (Meditative Therapy) provided a release mechanism for my major problems."

The case of John illustrates several key points. First, Meditative Therapy content does not always "make sense." Some of John's Inner Source experiences, taken out of context, would be seen as psychotic by some people. Although I do not personally understand why the Inner Source does things as it does at times, I have learned to be patient and wait for the outcomes. As we can see in John's case, they were excellent. Getting well, within the context of the Inner Source, means that we must be willing to undergo some "crazy" types of experiences.

A second important point in regard to John's case is that, once again, we are shown that several therapies are often needed to complete a thorough result. Meditative Therapy was the primary treatment method, but all methods used were important. In addition, we can see that follow-ups are a good practice. I will never know if John's urges to be violent would have passed without additional assertive training once his withdrawal from smoking was complete, but it appears that both factors were important.

Appendix F

THE CASE OF MARJORIE

Marjorie: "Things that used to control me no longer do; I am much more inner directed now."

A client of mine two years before who dropped out, Marjorie was now returning to school. She had been to other therapists over the years and returned to see me because a friend had told her about Meditative Therapy. My previous approach had been almost entirely based on a behavior therapy model and focused on using systematic desensitization and assertiveness training. Although she felt that she had gained something from the previous treatment, she still had major complaints.

Because of her previous experience with me and with other therapists, I decided not to repeat my administration of the fear inventory or the personality schedule. I also decided to focus mainly on Meditative Therapy. After two beginning sessions, Meditative Therapy was initiated with the third session.

Presenting Complaints: The initial interviews indicated that Marjorie had the following complaint pattern:

A. Depression
B. Exhaustion (really tired, lack of energy, don't want to arise in the mornings)
C. Major hostility toward self (have suicidal thoughts)
D. Dwelling on thoughts (on death of family members)
E. Hyperactive (drives self at a high pace, difficult to slow down)
F. Upset stomach (just lately)
G. Weight problem (gain weight easily, difficult to lose)
H. Sexual Problem (after intercourse experiences hostility, anger, fear, withdraws and wants to be left alone. Highly emotional.
I. Homosexuality
J. Menstrual periods (experience depression, headaches, chills, is emotional)
K. Sleep patterns (toss and turn a great deal)
L. Migraines (about one per year)

Physical Data: An analysis of Marjorie's eating patterns revealed that she would eat very little breakfast and then have a tendency to overeat the rest of the day and to crave carbohdrate foods. I did suggest that she change her diet and that she increase her physical exercise patterns because she did practically nothing along these lines.

Treatment: After two initial sessions assessing her problems and talking about diet and exercise, Marjorie's treatment consisted of nine sessions of Meditative Therapy. The sessions were very fast-paced and wide-ranging in content. Major themes, psychological, physical and spiritual are given below. Remember when you are reading this material that each person's content in Meditative Therapy is very individualistic and unique. Although general conclusions can be drawn about the workings of Meditative Therapy, specific conclusions about Marjorie are the most reliable. In reading Marjorie's Meditative Therapy experience below, one should be very careful not to draw conclusions about all people who have depressions, or who are homosexual, or who are bisexual, or who have a tendency toward migraines. We all have multiple complaints and there are never two people who show the same constellation or combination of problems.

Another point to remember is that even though examples from her material are presented in the three categories, we should not lose sight of the fact that each has qualities of the other. The psychological category will have some spiritual quality about it, the physical will have some psychological quality about it, and so on. The way it is presented below allows us to categorize the parts, but by doing so something has to be lost because we are not looking at the whole.

Meditative Therapy Themes and Experiences:
A. Examples of Marjorie's physical content
1. **Coldness:** Her Meditative Therapy experiences with coldness occurred throughout her entire nine sessions. In session one she described:
> I'm flying really fast in a superwoman outfit, looking down on everybody. It's cold. I'm kind of trying to land, but can't. Can't get my feet down. Really strange. I see Bishop's Peak, foggy, cold, but pleasant. I smell it. Very relaxing and soothing on top sitting here. Cold, my legs are getting tingly. Strange, really strange. My left foot especially, like the foot is waking up. #1

She continued to describe coldness in session two:

> It's cold in here. The wind comes from the right and it's cold, really cold. Wind is coming right on me and it is cold. I see lights now, but I'm cold, shoulder to elbow is cold. Cold and getting colder. I see snow and it's cold. There is a cold wind in here. #2

By her fourth session she brought a heavy coat with her to wear during the session! She put it on with her hands snugly placed in the pockets. Within ten minues after the session started however she said: "It's cold, I'm very cold right now. It's almost like a hurricane." She wore her coat each time after that, but to no avail because each time she would invariably get cold.

2. **Eye reactions:** Marjorie had eye difficulties as a child including operations and frequent trips to the eye doctor.
> My eyes are going crazy. (vibrating) #1
> My eyes are tightly shut and they hurt. #2
> My eyes are quivering really intensely. #3
> Oh ugh! I'm looking at the eye doctor's building. I'm being placed in the building, placed in the chair. I'm really uptight. Mother there, but father is not. Oh, God! I'm going to get drops in my eyes and they hurt. It smells antiseptic, like a doctor's office. I'm inside and I think I'm throwing a tantrum and now I can't see very well. Now I have to play a stupid game of put the line in the cage. Very frustrating. She knows god damn well I can't see out of that eye. #4

B. Examples of Marjorie's psychological content
1. **Sexuality:** Marjorie's Meditative Therapy content was most heavily weighted toward her sexual functioning, both heterosexual and homosexual. (Some readers may find some of this material offensive. It is presented primarily for clinical purposes and may be omitted if the reader chooses).

> I'm clutching my purse near the woman's building, cold, stark and strange. I feel uncomfortable. Ugly, just ugly. A woman tied up with ropes and labeled a transvestite. Everything is outside written on walls. #1

> See a lobster now with pinchers. Has got me by the hand, and again, so I smash it. See lots of lobsters all in my apartment. They are red and they click,

click, click. Now a giant lobster. I just pushed it over. Chills up my body now (she takes a deep breath.) My neck is really knotted, like a ton. Lobster claw is on my neck. It's being inserted into me. Both of us are standing up. Really strange. I fall on top of him and he shatters. #1 Now something is at my neck - a snake. #1 I see a snake and it bites me. #1 I'm falling, and if I land, I'll land on my back.#2 Oh, she's (mother) hitting me and turning into an animal. Oh no! A cat. I see cats and they go up my neck and she's at my neck. #3 Cat jumped at me from the left side, tearing at my neck, but I'm still walking, etc. #3 Slashed, I kicked someone on the leg (she stretches and fidgets.) Laughter, I'm rolling over and laying on my stomach. Okay, I'm being slammed around the head—a fight. Skeletons all around me. Weirdo, weirdo! #3 I'm walking to the patio through a sand box and swing set, I'm being hit by my mother on the back. Very, very hard, extremely hard. She has no control over herself and I don't know what I've done (she squirms). Oh, that's stupid! What I saw was my father with shorts on. #3

Okay, the last thought was mother and father having intercourse. Two fangs tearing tissue then moving to father and doing the same. Two fangs tearing tissue, really. Okay, I see a child in the jail of the tissue. Bars because of lines - holes caused by the fangs. #4 I'm flashing on an obscene movie I saw. Underground porno. Gross film. #4

I see one couple having sexual relations. The guy has the mask on. They seem to be enjoying themselves and I hear music. The mask is black with a super outline of features. Deep groves. I feel a sharp object coming thru my head. I actually feel it and it hurts. #5

There is a foot standing right by my head and it's a big foot and I moved against the wall and started hitting at it. Two feet now and a huge penis. A huge figure. I'm rolled up into a ball and I'm getting round balls of light especially in my right eye. I see a whole bunch of fleas on my leg. I see a stomach, torn apart, and I see intestines and stomach.and coming out of it is a pipe and something shooting out of it. I think it is hot steaming water. #6

I'm very small and I'm going up a skirt and going up into a woman. And now I'm inside and I'm locked in there behind bars. A snake is wrapped around my stomach and says 'I've got you.' Ohhh, I'm on a mountain and I'm laying with Joe and he's laughing. He's laughing! That's it, I just pulled a switch blade knife on him and say vulgar things to him. I debate either stabbing him or castrating him. He stopped laughing quickly though. #7 Somebody just threw a snake at me. Snake was on a stick. It's biting the right side of my neck and I'm yelling and screaming. It's fangs are in me and it's choking me. #7

I feel major surges at my nose and eyes and chin, like a press. I hear myself scream and Joe is walking toward me and his face changes to an animal and I'm being pushed back into the bedroom. Ugly. I'm being raped and at the same time another image of playing with a bar of soap in the shower together. #8

O.K., I climb down the snake or rope and we sit on a log and talk. I say, O.K., snake what are we going to do? It has put it's arm around me and it is a beige, brown, long coat. It is a person. I just put my head on its shoulder and tell it I'm afraid and it is really ugly, but I look at it. #9 Just had sexual relations with a man and eventually fly off with him. #9

2. **Father:** Marjorie's father died when she was eight. During Meditative Therapy there were scenes presented throughout which dealt with her father and her father's

death. During session number one toward the end she reported that she was at her dad's funeral. Soon after her report of this I had to leave and allow her to continue on her own. She finished the session on her own and left me the following note:

After you left I started crying and talking to my 'Dad.' Continually asked 'why' in a very soft, low voice. I was not afraid of 'it' (a 7 foot ugly creature she'd met earlier in the session) and told my Dad I wasn't afraid of 'it.' I repeated the word why 15 times and then got up.

Subsequent sessions revealed other content dealing with her father which is now given: "Fred in my class. Good looking. Looks like Dad would have looked. 'It' and Dad gave me a big hug." #3

I'm very cold; generates from arms and forearms. A tractor just came over me with snow. Now I'm in a grave. Hmmm, I'm at the grave yard where father's buried. #4

I can smell my Dad's house. I can still smell it on me. A dampness and a ringing and a free. And a very warm, soft blanket being placed on right now. #7

I'm yelling for my father. I feel cold air on my face right now. Oh, I see father and he's chopping up a snake at the cabin and I can see all of his muscles as he's chopping it up. Now I'm talking to a friend, and he's a kid, and I'm telling him my dad's not afraid of anything. #9

C. Examples of Marjorie's spiritual content
  1. **Bright light experiences:**
I see the sun. Now all is going from right to left. A lot of bright, bright lights. #1

Very bright lines now, many, many. Very bright. #3

All kinds of lights and lines. Strobe light effects. Very, very bright. Brighter than I've ever seen. Wavy lines. Bright, psychedelic bright. Very bright. #3

I see a beam of light shining on something. Almost a laser, Starts in a cone type formation, ends up in a point, then into a cone type formation. It is a bright yellow. #9

  2. **The devil:**
Now I see a devil with long fingernails and they are in my left arm and it really hurts and my eyes too. #1

Hmm, I just jumped out of bed and I hide under the bed. I'm scared of something. Giant man-like creature was going to come and get me. Oh, it's got horns, very much like a Devil figure, and has me by the neck. Just clawed me across the stomach, ripped off my pajamas. I'm having that hostile feeling. I'm yelling and screaming inside of me - really hostile. I yell vulgarities. The room I am in is father's room, I used to sleep there. The Devil creature has shrunk. I stomp on it. I'm bigger than it. I'm running now and slamming doors. Oh, I'm on the grass in Chicago and throwing a tantrum. Throwing a major tantrum and my whole family is there. I was picked up by that Devil-like creature. Now all walk away and I'm being hauled by the nape of the neck. Getting colder, from right side, waves and chills. Building. Is an old building. I'm being held by Devil-like creature. Oh ugh! I'm looking at eye doctor building and I'm being placed in the building. Now placed in the chair. ---etc.--- Oh, my Devil-like creature has a small torch next to my left eye. #4

O.K., I see the Devil and I'm in bed and it says, 'I am your father,' and I say, 'No, you're not,' and I pound and scream. #4

3. **Other spiritual material:**
Oh, Poseidon (the Greek god of the sea) threw a fork at me. A three pronged one. Huge. He picked me up and ate me. #1 See a mask, tribal Inca. It is looking at me. I see an Inca god looking at the sun. On top of a pyramid holding up something that was solid and now liquid. Golden jello like. Gloppy and stickey. #1

I hear bells. All kinds of little ones, then Mission bells. Up in choir loft spitting on those below. Now in church singing. Now a nun is correcting us. #2

I'm sitting up in bed watching a tree through the window. Hmm, I see dreams and they are covered with different types of things. A crucifix. Smells like Christmas. It is, the tree is in the other room. #4

I see an old church in Kentucky. Ornate and modernistic. See a Catholic church. I walk upstairs and come across 'it' and 'it' stands there in front of me in full glory. I back down and trip and fall. Now I hear laughter. #6

I'm on a cross being kind of crucified. #6

I hear the song "Go Down Moses, Way Down to Egypt land." #8

I hear "Go Down Moses, Let my People Go." #9

During her ninth and last session with me, Majorie had a series of scenes relating to one topic which I have placed under the spiritual category. The series of scenes was not continuous, that is, they came at various times during the session. The first segment occurred as soon as she closed her eyes:

Hmm, a picture of a lady in waiting during Medieval times. She has a pointed cap, blue dress, beige cap and long sleeves. See the woman I saw this week-end with a purple blouse, long sleeves too of the same type. Back to the Medieval woman. In the sleeve there is a pocket (she takes a deep breath) O.K., inside it is fluctuating between being a handkerchief and being a baby.

I see the shark with me inside and also see the pocket in the Medieval blue world and a child being inside there.

I keep seeing the woman with the baby in her left sleeve pocket with the handkerchief wrapped around it. It is being rocked back and forth and up and down. O.K., she is moving the sleeve up and down to do something and I am being rocked back and forth.

O.K., I come back to the rose bush and cottage. I had sexual relations with a man and went flying off with him. I swam away from the shark and was picked up by a boat. Oh. O.K., the baby was pulled out of the woman's pocket in the sleeve and exposed to the sun and it's growing, up into the air, floating up.

At this point Marjorie opened her eyes and said, That's stupid, I want you to know that's stupid, a bunch of junk. I don't think that is real. I don't know why I am fighting that. I then said, "By now I hoped you would have learned to wait and see." Her reply was, That's too simple. I'll see, but you know, I sure do feel closure and the sun was awfully hot, so hot I was afraid I would get burned.

Remember that I do not spend any time interpreting anyone's Meditative Therapy content. I did not sit down with Marjorie and say to her that "the snake represents this . . . in your life," or that coldness means this . . . about you." There is no need to use interpretation in Meditative Therapy because if one needs to gain an insight the Inner Source knows how to provide for it.

Results of Treatment: Ten months after her ninth session of Meditative Therapy I called Marjorie and asked her if she would complete the evaluation of counseling follow-up form. She said she was glad I had called because she wanted to talk to me about several things. We set up an appointment and discussed some of her concerns which related to the therapy and to certain of her problems. She related that she had been doing the therapy on her own with a close friend, but would have trouble because she would "go off" somewhere, but keep verbalizing and not be consciously aware of it (like sleep talking.) She also said she couldn't stay on the diet I had recommended and that she drank excessive amounts of water, noting that there was a history of diabetes in her family. My mind set, focusing primarily on Meditative Therapy because I had worked with her previously, had caused me to not be thorough enough in my preliminary history taking. I should have discovered these facts through appropriate questioning during the first or second session. I strongly suggested that she go see an M.D. and find out what was causing her remaining difficulties. Before looking at the results of her visit to the doctor let us look at her follow-up ratings and comments:

Complaint	Degree of Improvement
1. Depression	No Improvement
2. Exhaustion (really tired, lack energy, doesn't want to arise in mornings)	Somewhat Improved
3. Major hostility toward self (has suicidal thoughts)	Much Improved
4. Dwelling on thoughts (on death of family)	Very Much Improved
5. Hyperactive (drives self at a high pace, difficult to slow down)	Very Much Improved
6. Upset Stomach (just lately)	Much Improved
7. Weight Problem (gains weight easily, difficult to lose weight	Slight Improvement
8. Sexual Problem (after intercourse, experiences hostility, anger, fear, withdraws and wants to be left alone, is highly emotional.)	"I have had no experience with this yet."
9. Homosexuality	Average Improvement "I have been developing a long term relationship."
10. Menstrual Periods (experience depression, headaches, chills, is emotional.)	No Improvement
11. Sleep Patterns (toss and turn a great deal.)	Much Improved
12. Migraines (about once per year)	No Improvement

When asked to give other changes, positive and negative, which she had observed since beginning counseling she replied:

Positive
Calmer, more assured, peaceful, understand things better.

Negative
1) When listening to a relaxation tape, (right after I had started Meditative Therapy sessions) I was in a small room and I became extremely upset (I wanted to get out of the room: sweated, heavy breathing, acute fear.)

2) Maybe I use Meditative Therapy when I am under pressure. I go into MT when things become difficult. I remove myself from the situation and don't deal with the situation.

To the question, "Do you feel you benefited from dietary suggestions and changes in your diet?," Marjorie stated:

"I would have if I could have stuck to the diet. It is quite difficult because when I am nervous, I eat junk food."

The most outstanding factor of therapy for her was that of, "My experience in Meditative Therapy of re-living my father's death. Also change of perspective, becoming more inner directed. Things that use to control me no longer do, I am much more inner directed."

Marjorie's medical results showed that she was neither diabetic nor hypoglycemic, but that she was anemic. She is presently receiving medical treatment for this condition and it is too early to tell if this treatment will alter significantly her remaining problems.

Evaluation of Therapy: Therapist's View

When asked which therapy was most beneficial Marjorie wrote, "Meditative Therapy, **definitely!**" She stated this so emphatically because she could not stick to her diet and didn't follow my suggestions to exercise regularly. Thus for Marjorie we get a more "pure" look at the effects of the workings of the Inner Source than we had in Kerrie's and John's cases. Meditative Therapy produced some dramatic outcomes in just nine sessions, but still left untouched certain major complaints, for which "outer help" was needed.

This case is also instructive in comparison to Kerrie's and John's cases in terms of complexity. It is obvious that Marjorie's complaints were more psychologically, and perhaps physically, complicated. The content of her sessions was deeper or richer in interpretive material. Yet, by resisting the temptation to interpret, the Inner Source "worked through" much of the material on its own.

Appendix G

PRECAUTIONS FOR AUTOGENIC THERAPY [1]

Table 11. **Non-Indications**
1. Persons with severe mental deficiencies.
2. Children below the age of five (age adapted management for children age 5 and onwards required).
3. When careful and critical control of the patient's training symptoms is not possible.
4. Persons with lack of motivation to apply AT in an adequate manner (e.g., recalcitrant psychopaths.)
5. When a differential diagnostic evaluation of training symptoms (e.g., autogenic discharges versus nature of unrecognized pathologic processes) is not possible (e.g., pain, disturbances of bloodflow, hypoglycemia.)
6. During acute episodes of schizophrenic reaction.

"Contraindication" has been defined as "Any condition, especially any condition of disease, which renders some particular line of treatment improper or undesirable." Generally it is implied that the treatment in question (e.g., AT) may or is known to produce unfavorable reactions, functional changes and sequelae that are detrimental to the patient's health (see Table 12, p. 63.) Consequently, the therapeutic modality (e.g., AT) should not be used.

"Relative Contraindications" are conditions that require particular caution in the application of a therapeutic approach. Such precautions may include modifications in procedure (e.g., not using certain standard formulas) or abandonning the line of treatment (e.g., AT) when undesirable reactions are noticed (see Table 13.)

Table 12. **Contraindications**
7. Persons with **doubtful or impending myocardial infarction** unless monitored (e.g., in Intensive Care Units) and supervised by a physician with AT experience.
8. **During and directly after acute myocardial infarction,** and in the presence of complicating disorders (e.g., arrhythmias, pulmonary embolism, extension of infarct to the endocardial surface with systemic embolism) unless monitored (e.g., Intensive Care Units) * and supervised by a physician with AT expeience.
9. Trainees repeatedly showing significant (paradoxical) **increases in blood pressure** during AT.
10. Diabetic patients (a) lacking reliable collaboration, or (b) in circumstances that do not permit careful clinical control over long periods of time (18-24 months.)
11. Patients with **hypoglycemic conditions:** (a) when the differential diagnostic evaluation has not been completed, (b) when there is a lack of reliable collaboration, (c) when clinical or other circumstances are therapeutically unfavorable.
12. Patients with glaucoma (i.e., **primary;** 1. chronic open angle; 2. acute or chronic angle closure) when weekly tonometric control of intraocular tension is not guaranteed. AT must be discontinued when increases of intraocular tension are noted on two consecutive control measurements (i.e., within 7 days.)
13. **Involutional psychotic reaction** (subacute psychotic outpatients require careful individual evaluation before AT may be used.)

* Based on clinical studies of 35 patients, Koleshao, Savitsky, and Sopchenke[18] insist that AT should be used as an adjunctive approach in the treatment of acute myocardial infarction in intensive care units.

---

1. International Committee on Autogenic Therapy (1977), used by permission.

14. Trainees with **paranoid reaction** showing increase of persecutory or grandiose delusions during or after AT.
15. Dissociative (non-psychotic) reactions (e.g., depersonalization, dissociated personality, stupor, fugue, amnesia, dreamy state, somnanbulism) unless under clinically well supervised conditions.

Table 13. **Relative Contraindications**

16. **Supportive "background" formula "I am at peace."**
    - Persons who are prone to experience unfavorable antithematic reactions(e.g., anxiety, restlessness, massive motor discharges.)
17. **Supportive association of peaceful images.**
    - Persons who have difficulties on finding a "peaceful image."
18. - Persons who have difficulties in holding a "peaceful image."
19. - Persons who report that selected peaceful images assume dynamic (film-like) qualities.
20. - Persons who notice that the selected peaceful images change spontaneously to include disturbing features.
21. - Trainees who frequently report the onset of anxiety or restlessness during and after the exercises should not practice AT without close supervision. They should be instructed to practice long series of exercises (e.g., 20 to 40), each of very short duration (e.g., 5-10 seconds.) If improvement is not observed within about 2 weeks, AT should be discontinued.
22. **First Standard Exercise [heaviness formulas.]**
    - When trainees report strong and largely disagreeable cardiac and vasomotor reactions (e.g., congestion of the cranial region, flushing of face, chest pain, tachycardia, sensations of palpitations), one should proceed slowly with carefully adapted "reduced formulas."
23. **Second Standard Exercise [warmth formulas.]**
    - When the environmental temperature is unusually high.
    - When SE II formulas elicit strong vasomotor reactions (e.g., swelling of training limb, disagreeable pulsating or "pressure", dizziness, feeling of emptiness in the head, initial symptoms of fainting). Such reactions require a step-by-step approach with "reduced formulas" and brief exercises.
24. - Frequent occurrence of disagreeable and disturbing modalities of heart-related autogenic discharges (e.g., anxiety, uneasiness, tenseness, cramp-like pain, precordial pressure, tachycardia.)
25. - Patients with cardiac disorders or others who are unduly "heart conscious" (e.g., "infarctophobia," "cardiac neurosis," "effort syndrome") and show marked apprehensiveness towards their heart (unless very careful and consistent supervision is possible.)
26. - Trainees with a pattern of undesirable reactions during SE I and SE II (e.g., sharp drop in blood pressure, marked decrease of heart rate, disagreeable chest sensations, dizziness, headache, anxiety) may try SE II after all other standard exercises have been practiced and the disturbing reactivity has subsided.
27. - Hypertensive patients reacting with sudden and marked decrease in blood pressure and feelings of uneasiness and anxiety.
28. - Patients on regular hemodialysis treatment when disagreeable cardiac sensations or complaints are reported.
29. - Hyperthyroid conditions.
30. - In children under the age of 10.

Fourth Standard Exercise [respiration.]

31. - Trainees suffering from functional disorders or acute pathological processes of the respiratory system (e.g., bronchial asthma, pulmonary tuberculosis). In many of these cases the fourth standard formula should be postponed till the end of the autogenic standard series.

32. - Trainees who previously practiced methods that included voluntary control of respiratory functions and who find it unusually difficult to relearn a passively oriented attitude while practicing "Breathing calm and regular" - "It breathes me." In these cases SE IV should be postponed until all other standard exercises have been practiced satisfactorily.

Fifth Standard Exercise [solar plexus.]

33. - When the nature and location of the solar plexus cannot be adequately explained, or cannot be adequately understood (e.g., children).

34. - Onset of pain in the abdominal area during SE V.

35. - Trainees with disorders of the digestive tract (e.g., peptic ulcer, duodenal ulcer, acute gastritis, chronic atrophic gastritis, carcinoma of the stomach, hemorrhagic conditions, hypertrophic gastritis, undiagnosed abdominal malignant disease, hyperacidity, inflammatory gastric disorders, portal hypertension, history of gastrointestinal hemorrhage, presence of occult blood in stool.)

36. - Diabetic patients showing a marked decrease in insulin tolerance with frequent episodes of rapid onset of hypoglycemia.

37. - Patients with hyperinsulinism or other forms of hypoglycemia.

38. - Trainees with angina pectoris and frequent disagreeable reactions during SE V.

39. - During pregnancy.

40. - In children below the age of 10.

Sixth Standard Exercise [forehead.]

41. - Trainees who repeatedly report onset or worsening of headache or migraine during or after SE VI.

42. - Trainees with brain injuries: about 50% require a case adapted modification of SE VI or have to stop the formula.

43. - Epileptic patients with marked vasomotor instability affecting the cranial region and other undesirable reactivity.

Partial exercise ["My neck and shoulders are heavy."]

44. - Not during states of sleep deficiency or exhaustion while engaged in potentially hazardous activities (e.g., machinery, driving, supervisory tasks) because of risk of sudden onset of sleep.

45. - Not to be used in a standing or simple sitting posture by patients suffering from narcolepsy, epilepsy, hypotension and marked degrees of vasomotor instability.

Space Exercises

46. - **The First Space Exercise** (i.e., "I imagine the space between my eyes;" ears, shoulders, elbows, etc.) when unduly disturbing reactions (e.g., anxiety, dizziness, vomiting) occur more than twice during or after the exercise and/or when paradoxical increases in heart rate or blood pressure are recorded.

47. - **The Second Space Exercise** (i.e., "My right arm is filled with space," etc.) should not be practiced when frequent control of blood pressure (i.e., before, after exercises) is not possible and when increases in blood pressure are noted on two subsequent occasions (i.e., within 7 days).

References

——————, **Meditation**. Miami, Florida: Mark-Age Brochures, University Life Series, 327 NE20 Terrace (no date given).

Abrahamson, E. and Pezet, A., **Body, Mind and Sugar**. New York: Pyramid Books, 1971 (first published in 1951).

Ahsen, A., **Basic Concepts in Eidetic Psychotherapy**. New York: Brandon House, 1973.

Ahsen, A.,**Psycheye**. New York: Brandon House, 1977.

Alberti, R. and Emmons, M., **Your Perfect Right: A Guide to Assertive Behavior**. San Luis Obispo, California: Impact Publishers, 1970 (second edition, 1974).

Alberti, R. and Emmons, M., **Stand˙Up, Speak Out, Talk Back!** New York: Pocket Books, 1975.

Asher, J., "Whatever happened to psychedelic research?" **APA Monitor**. The American Phychological Association, Vol. 6, No. 11, Nov. 1975, pp. 4-5.

Assagioli, R., **Psychosynthesis**. New York: Viking Press, 1971.

Atkinson, B., **The Writings of Ralph Waldo Emerson**. New York: Random House, 1940, 1950.

Baker, P., **Meditation: A Step Beyond with Edgar Cayce**. New York: Doubleday and Company, Inc., 1973.

Bartlett, L., "What do we really know about psychic phenomena." **Reader's Digest,** 1977.

Benson, Herbert, **The Relaxation Response**. Avon Books, 1976.

Bernstein, M., **The Search for Bridey Murphy**. Garden City, New York: Doubleday, 1956.

Binet, Les, **Alterations de la Personnalite**. Paris, 1892.

Bloomfield, H., et al., **TM [Transcendental Meditation]**. New York: Delacorte Press, 1975.

Boehme, J., **Six Theosophic Points**. Ann Arbor, Michigan: Ann Arbor Paperbacks, The University of Michigan Press, 1958 (written in 1620).

Bonny, H. and Savary, L., **Music and Your Mind**. New York: Harper and Row, 1973.

Breuer, J. and Freud, S., **Studies in Hysteria**. Boston: Beacon Press, 1950 (first published in 1895).

Brown, Barbara, **New Mind, New Body: Biofeedback**. New York: Bantam Books 1974.

Brunton, P., **The Quest of the Overself**. New York: Samuel Weiser, 1975 (original, 1937).

Brunton, P., **The Wisdom of the Overself**. New York: Samuel Weiser, 1970 (original, 1943).

Budge, E. (editor and translator). **Book of the Dead**. New Hyde Park, New York: University Books, 1960.

Budzynski, T., "Some applications of biofeedback-produced twilight states," **Fields Within Fields,** Vol. 5, No. 1, 1972, pp. 105-114.

Budzynski, T., "Tuning in on the twilight zone," **Psychology Today,** Vol. II, No. 3, August 1977, pp. 38-44.

Caldwell, W., **LSD Psychotherapy.** New York: Grove Press, 1968.

Carrington, P., **Freedom in Meditation.** New York: Anchor/Doubleday, 1977.

Cayce, H.,**Gifts of Healing.** Virginia Beach, Virginia: Association for Research and Enlightenment, Inc., 1957.

Cerminara, G., **Many Mansions.** New York: William Sloane Associates, 1950.

Clark, W., Lieff, J., Lieff, C. and Sussman, R., "Psychedelic research: obstacles and values," **Journal of Humanistic Psychology,** Vol. 15, No. 3, Summer 1975.

Corriere, R. and Karle, W., "Neurophysiological measurements of patients undergoing Primal Therapy, in Janov, A., **The Anatomy of Mental Illness.** New York: G. P. Putnam's Sons, 1971, pp. 215-228.

DeBold, R.C., and Leaf, R.C., **LSD, Man & Society.** Middletown, Connecticut: Wesleyan University Press, 1967.

Deikman, A., "Experimental meditation," in Tart, C. (editor), **Altered States of Consciousness.** New York: Anchor Books, 1972, pp. 203-223.

Delboeuf, **Le Magnetisme Animal.** Paris, 1889.

Ditman, K. S., et al., "Nature and frequency of claims following LSD," **Journal of Nervous and Mental Disease,** Vol. 134, 1962, pp. 346-352.

Dodds, James E., **Six Lessons in the Silence.** Santa Barbara, California: J. F. Rowny Press, 1949.

Downing, J. and Wygant, W., Jr., "Psychedelic experience and religious belief," in Blum, R. and Associates, **Utopiates.** New York: Atherton Press, 1964, pp. 187-204.

Editors, "Interview: Ingo Swann," **Psychic Magazine,** Vol. IV, No. 4, April 1973.

Embler, W., "The metaphors of mysticism," **ETC: A Review of General Semantics,** Vol. 31, No. 3, Sept. 1974, pp. 272-287.

Forem, Jack, **Transcendental Meditation.** New York: E. P. Dutton, 1973.

Frank, L., **Affektstoerungen.** Berlin: Springer, 1913.

Frankl, V., **The Will to Meaning.** New York: The New American Library, Inc., 1969.

Frankl, V., **The Doctor and the Soul: From Psychotherapy to Logotherapy** (Second Edition). New York: Alfred A. Knopf, 1960.

Fredericks, C. and Goodman, H., **Low Blood Sugar and You.** New York: Constellation International, 1969.

Frederking, W., "Deep relaxation with free ideation," **Psyche,** Vol. 2, 1949, p. 211.

Frekerking, W., "Intoxicant drugs (Mescaline and Lysergic Acid Diethylamide) in psychotherapy," **Journal of Nervous and Mental Disordes,** Vol. 121, No. 3, 1955, pp. 262-266.

Fretigbny, R. and Virel, A., **L'Imagerie Mentale: Introduction a l'onirotherapie.** Geneva: Mont Blanc, 1968.

Freud, S., **A General Introduction to Psychoanalysis.** New York: Washington Square Press, 1952 (original, 1924).

Freud, S., **Therapy and Technique.** New York: Collier Books, 1963.

Gaskell, G., **Dictionary of All Scriptures and Myths.** New York: Julian Press, 1960.

Goldsmith, J., **The Art of Meditation.** New York: Harper and Row, 1956.

Goleman, D., "Meditation as methatherapy," in White, J. (editor), **What is Meditation?** New York: Anchor Books, 1974 (a) pp. 181-198.

Goleman, D., "Meditation and psychic phenomena," in White J. (editor), **What is Meditation?** New York: Anchor Books, 1974 (b), pp. 209-224.

Goleman, D., **The Varieties of the Meditative Experience.** New York: E. P. Dutton, 1977.

Green, A. and Green, E., **Beyond Biofeedback.** New York:Delacorte, 1977.

Green, A., et al., "Psychophysiological Training for Creativity," **The Menninger Foundation,** Topeka, Kansas, 1971.

Grof, S., **Realms of the Human Unconscious.** New York: The Viking Press (an Esalen Book), 1975.

Hannah, F., et al., "Sex Differences and Relationships Among Neuroticism, Extraversion, and Expressed Fears," **Perceptual and Motor Skills,** Vol. 20, 1965, pp. 1214-1216.

Hart, J., et al., "Feeling Therapy," **Personal Growth,** No. 22, 1974, pp. 3-12. Berkeley, Explorations Institute, P. O. Box 1254.

Hart, J., et al., **Going Sane: An Introduction to Feeling Therapy.** New York: Behavioral Publications, 1975.

Hesse, H., **Steppenwolf.** New York: Holt and Company, 1929.

Hesse, H., **Siddhartha.** New York: New Directions, 1951.

Houston, J. and Masters, R., "The experimental induction of religious-type experiences," in White, J. (editor), **The Highest State of Consciousness.** New York: Anchor Books, 1972, pp. 303-321.

Hubbard, L. R., **Dianetics.** New York: Hermitage House, 1950.

Humphreys, C., **Concentration and Meditation.** Baltimore, Maryland: Penguin Books, Inc., 1973 (first published in 1935).

Huxley, A., "Visionary Experience," in White, J. (editor), **The Highest State of Consciousness.** New York: Anchor Books, 1972. pp. 34-57.

Huxley, A., **Doors to Perception.** London: Chatto and Windus, 1968.

Huxley, A., "Introduction to F.W.H. Meyers," in Smith, S. (editor), **Human Personality and Its Survival of Bodily Death,** Smith, S. (editor). Hyde Park, New York: University Books, 1961 (original, 1903).

Jacobson, E., **Progressive Relaxation.** Chicago: University of Chicano Press, 1938.

James, W., **The Varieties of Religious Experience.** Hyde Park, New York: University Books, 1963 (original, 1902).

Janet, **L'Automatism Psychologigue.** Paris, 1889.

Janov, A., **The Primal Scream.** New York: G. P. Putnam's Sons, 1970.

Janov, A., **The Anatomy of Mental Illness.** New York: G. P. Putnam's Sons, 1971.

Janov, A., **The Primal Revolution.** New York: Simon and Schuster, 1972.

Janov, A., "Prototypic pain and primal theory," **The Journal of Primal Therapy,** Vol. 1, No. 1, Summer 1973, pp. 64-67.

Janov, A., "Further implications of 'levels of consciousness' on suicide," **The Journal of Primal Therapy,** Vol. 1, No. 3, Winter 1974 (a), pp. 197-200.

Janov, A., "The dangers in the misuse of Primal Therapy," **The Journal of Primal Therapy,** Vol. 1, No. 4, Spring 1974(b), pp. 283-312.

Jung, C. G., "The psychological aspects of the Kore," in **The Collected Works of C. G. Jung.** New York: Bollingen Foundation, Series XX, Vol. 9, Part 1, 1958, pp. 190 and 193.

Jung, C. G., "The concept of the collective unconscious." in **The Collected Works of C. G. Jung.** New York: Bollingen Foundation, Series XX, Vol. 9, Part 1, 1958, p. 49, (a).

Jung, C. G., "The phenomenology of the spirit in fairytales," in **The Collected works of C. G. Jung.** New York: Bollingen Foundation, Series XX, Vol. 9, Part 1, 1958, p. 215, (b).

Jung, C. G., "A study in the process of individuation." in **The Collected Works of C. G. Jung.** New York: Bollingen Foundation, Series XX, Vol. 9, Part 1, 1958, p. 352, (c).

Jung, C. G., "Two essays on analytical psychology," in **The Collected Works of C. G. Jung.** New York: Bollingen Foundation, Series XX, Vol. 7, 1958, p. 220, (d).

Jung, C. G., "Psychology and religion," in **The Collected Works of C. G. Jung.** New York: Bollingen Foundation, Series XX, Vol. 11, 1958, p. 496, (e).

Kapleau, P., **The Three Pillars of Zen.** Boston: Beacon Press, 1967.

Karagulla, S., **Breakthrough to Creativity.** Santa Monica, California: Devorss, 1967.

Keyes, Ken, Jr., **Handbook to Higher Consciousness.** Berkeley: Living Love Center, 1974.

Kitselman, A. L., **E-Therapy.** La Jolla, California: Institute of Integration, (5939 Camino de la Costa), 1950.

Kretschmer, W., "Meditative techniques in psychotherapy," in Tart, C. (editor), **Altered States of Consciousness.** New York: Anchor Books, 1972, pp. 224-233.

Krishna, Gopi, **Kundalini: The Evolutionary Energy in Man.** Boulder, Colorado: Shambhala Publications, Inc., 1967.

Krishna, Gopi, **The Awakening of Kundalini.** New York: E. P. Dutton and Company, 1975.

Krishnamurti, J., **Commentaries on Living** (third series), Rajagopal, D. (editor). Wheaton, Illinois: The Theosophical Publishing House, 1960.

Krishnamurti, J., **The First and Last Freedom.** New York: Harper & Row, In., 1975.

Kubler-Ross, E., **On Death and Dying.** New York: Macmillan, 1969.

Kubler-Ross, E., **Death, The Final State of Growth.** Englewood Cliffs, New Jersey: Prentice-Hall, Inc., 1975.

Leary, T., "Introduction," in Solomon, D. (editor), **LSD, The Consciousness Expanding Drug.** New York: G. P. Putnam's Sons, 1964, pp. 1-19.

Leary, T., **The Psychedelic Experience, A Manual Based on the Tibetan Book of the Dead.** New Hyde Park, New York: University Books, 1964.

Leary, T., et al., "Rationale of the Mexican psychedelic training center," in Blum, R. and Associates, **Utopiates.** New York: Atherton Press, 1964, pp. 178-186.

Leary, T., "The religious experience: its production and interpretation," in Weil, G., et al. (editors), **The Psychedelic Reader.** New York: University Books, 1965, pp. 191-213.

Lecomte du Nouy, P., **Human Destiny.** New York: Longmans, Green and Company, 1947.

LeShan, L., **How to Meditate.** Boston: Little Brown and Company, 1974.

Lilly, J., **The Deep Self.** New York: Simon and Schuster, 1977.

Luthe, W. (editor), **Autogenic Therapy.** New York: Grune and Stratton, Inc., 1969 (a).

Luthe, W. (editor), **Autogenic Therapy, Volume 1: Autogenic Methods,** by Schultz, J. and Luthe, W. New York: Grune and Stratton, Inc., 1969 (b).

Luthe, W. (editor), **Autogenic Therapy, Volume II: Medical Applications,** by Schultz, J. and Luthe, W. New York: Grune and Stratton, Inc., 1969 (c).

Luthe, W. (editor), **Autogenic Therapy, Volume III: Applications in Psychotherapy,** by Schultz, J. and Luthe, W. New York: Grune and Stratton, Inc., 1969 (d).

Luthe, W. (editor), **Autogenic Therapy, Volume IV: Research and Theory,** by Luthe W. New York: Grune and Stratton, Inc., 1970 (a).

Luthe, W. (editor), **Autogenic Therapy, Volume V: Dynamics of Autogenic Neutralization,** by Luthe, W. New York: Grune and Stratton, Inc., 1970 (b).

Luthe, W. (editor), **Autogenic Therapy, Volume VI: Treatment With Autogenic Neutralization,** by Luthe, W. New York: Grune and Stratton, Inc., 1973.

MacHovec, F., "Hypnosis before mesmer," **The American Journal of Clinical Hypnoosis,** Vol. 17, No. 4, April 1975, pp. 215-220.

McInery, B., "Research with primal patients--vital signs," **The Journal of Primal Therapy,** Vol. II, No. 1, Summer 1974, pp. 51-63.

Masters, R. and Houston, J., **Mind Games: The Guide to Inner Space.** New York: Viking Press, 1972.

Masters, R. and Houston, J., **The Varieties of Psychedelic Experience.** New York: Holt, Rinehart and Winston, 1966.

Maupin, E., "Individual differences in response to a Zen meditation exercise," in Tart, C. (editor), **Altered States of Consciousness.** New York: Anchor Books, 1972, pp. 191-202.

Maupin, E., "On meditation," in Tart, C. (editor), **Altered States of Consciousness.** New York: Anchor Books, 1972, pp. 181-190.

Menninger, K., **Theory of Psychoanalytic Technique.** New York: Harper and Row, 1958.

Mishra, R. S., **Yoga Sutras.** New York: Anchor Books, 1973.

Missildine, W. H., **Your Inner Child of the Past.** New York: Simon and Schuster, 1963.

Moody, R. A., **Life After Life.** Atlanta: Mockingbird Books, 1975.

Moser, L., "Hypnotism in Germany," in Dingwall, E. (editor), **Abnormal Hypnotic Phenomena, Volume II.** London: J. and A. Churchill, Ltd., 104 Gloucester Place W.I., 1967.

Mowrer, O. H., **The Crisis in Psychiatry and Religion.** Princeton, New Jersey: D. Van Nostrand, 1961.

Naranjo, C. and Ornstein, R., **On the Psychology of Meditation.** New York: The Viking Press, 1971.

Nelson, H., "The Army's LSD guinea pigs and a new research bind," **San Francisco Sunday Examiner and Chronicle,** Sunday Punch Section, Aug. 24, 1975, p. 2.

Osis, K., **Deathbed Observations by Physicians and Nurses.** New York: Parapsychology Foundation, 1960.

Osis, K., et al., "Dimensions of the meditative experience," **The Journal of Transpersonal Psychology,** No. 2, 1973, pp. 109-135.

Pahnke, W., "LSD and Religious Experience," in DeBold, R. and Leaf, R. (editors), **LSD, Man and Society.** Middletown, Connecticut: Wesleyan University Press, 1967, pp. 60-84.

Pixa, B., "A psychic approach to psychiatry," **San Francisco Sunday Examiner and Chronicle,** Sunday Scene, Feb. 23, 1975, p. 4.

Read, A., et al., **Edgar Cayce on Diet and Health.** New York: Paperback Library, 1969.

Reyher, J., "Free imagery: an uncovering procedure." **Journal of Clinical Psychology,** Vol. 19, 1963, pp. 454-459.

Reyher, J. and Smeltzer, W., "The uncovering properties of visual imagery and verbal association: a comparative study," **Journal of Abnormal Psychology,** Vol. 73, 1968, pp. 218-222.

Reyher, J. and Morishige, H., "EEG and rapid eye movements during free imagery and dream recall," **Journal of Abnormal Psychology,** Vol. 74, 1969, pp. 576-582.

Reyher, J., "Emergent uncovering: a method for producing and objectifying psychopathology, depression, and other psychodynamic processes," Unpublished Paper, Michigan State University, East Lansing, Michigan.

REFERENCES

Rhine, J. and Pratt, J., **Parapsychology, Frontier Science of the Mind.** Springfield, Illinois: Charles C. Thomas, 1957.

Rogers, C. R., **On Becoming A Person.** Boston: Houghton Mifflin, 1961.

Rogers, C. R. "Some new challenges." **The American Psychologist,** Vol. 28, 1973, pp. 379-387.

Rogo, D. S., "Strange journeys of the mind," **Human Behavior,** April 1976, pp. 56-61.

Samuels, M. and Samuels, N., **Seeing With the Mind's Eye.** New York: Random House: Berkeley, California: The Bookworks, 1975.

Sannella, L., **Kundalini--Psychosis or Transcendence?** San Francisco, California: H. S. Dakin Company, 1976.

Sargent, J. D., Green, E. E. and Walters, E. D., "Preliminary report on the use of autogenic feedback techniques in the treatment of migraine and tension headaches," **The Menninger Foundation,** Dec. 1971.

Schultz, J. H., **Das Autogene Training.** Leipzig: G. Thieme Verlag, 1932.

Seachrist, E., **Meditation, The Art of Listening,** Audio Tape No. 1021, Side 1. Virginia Beach, Virginia: The Association for Research and Enlightenment, Inc.

Smith, G. (editor), **Letters of Aldous Huxley.** London:Chatto and Windus, 1969.

Smith, H., "Do drugs have religious import?" in Solomon, D. (editor), **LSD, The Consciousness Expanding Drug.** New York: G. P. Putnam's Sons, 1964, pp. 152-167.

Smith, S., "Introduction", in Myer, F. W. H., **Human Personality & Its Survival of Bodily Death.** Secaucus, N. J: University Books, 1961.

Stanford, A. (translator), **The Bhagavad Gita.** New York: Seabury Press (Copyright 1970 by Herber & Herber, Inc.)

Stapleton, R. C., **The Gift of Inner Healing.** Waco, Texas: Word Books, 1976.

Steinkirchner, A., **Self Psychotherapy.** Venice, California: Aguin Publishing Company, 1974.

Stevenson, I., **Twenty Cases Suggestive of Reincarnation.** New York: American Society for Psychical Research, 1966.

Sutich, A., "Transpersonal therapy," **The Journal of Transpersonal Psychology,** No. 1, 1973, pp. 1-6.

Swami Rami, Ballentine, R. and Swami Ajaya, **Yoga and Psychotherapy.** Glenview, Illinois: Himalayan Institute, 1976.

Szent-Gyoergyi, A., "Drive in living matter to perfect itself," **Synthesis,** Vol. 1, No. 1.

Tart, C. (editor), **Altered States of Consciousness.** New York: Anchor Books, 1972.

Timmons, B. and Kanellakos, D. P., "The psychology and physiology of meditation and related phenomena: bibliography II," **Journal of Transpersonal Psychology,** No. 1, 1974, pp. 32-38.

Timmons, B. and Kamiya, J., "The psychology and physiology of meditation and related phenomena: a bibliography," **Journal of Transpersonal Psychology,** No. 2, 1970, pp. 41-59.

Trungpa, Chogyam, **Cutting Through Spiritual Materialism.** Berkeley, California: Shambhala Publications, Inc., 1973.

Turner, G. D. and St. Clair, M. G., **Individual Reference File of Extracts From the Edgar Cayce Records.** Virginia Beach, Virginia: The Association for Research and Enlightenment, Inc., 1970.

Underhill, E., **Mysticism.** New York: E. P. Dutton and Company, 1961 (original, 1911).

Unger, S., "Mescaline, LSD, Psilocybin, and personality change," in Solomon, D. (editor), **LSD, The Consciousness Expanding Drug.** New York: G. P. Putnam's Sons, 1964a, pp. 200-228.

Unger, S., "LSD and psychotherapy: a bibliography of the English language literature," in Solomon, D. (editor), **LSD, The Consciousness Expanding Drug.** New York: G. P. Putnam's Sons, 1964b, pp. 257-266.

Walker, K. A., **A Study of Gurdjieff's Teaching.** London: Jonathan Cape, 1969.

Wambach, H., "Life before life," **Psychic Magazine.** Jan/Feb. 1977, pp. 8-13.

Watkins, M. M., **Waking Dreams.** New York: Gordon and Breach, 1976.

Watts, Alan W., **Meditation.** Celestial Arts, 1974.

Watts, Alan W., **The Way of Zen.** Vintage Books, Pantheon Books, 1957.

Wescott, R., **The Divine Animal.** New York: Funk and Wagnalls, 1969.

White, J. (editor), **What is Meditation?** New York: Anchor Books, 1974.

White, J. (editor), **The Highest State of Consciousness.** New York: Anchor Books, 1972.

White, J. (editor), **Frontiers of Consciousness.** New York: Avon Books, 1974.

Wilhelm, R. (translator), **The Secret of the Golden Flower.** New York: Harcourt Brace Jovanovich, Inc. (Harvest Book), 1962.

Windsor, J. C., "A holistic theory of mental illness," **The A.R.E. Journal.** Virginia Beach, Virginia: Association for Research and Enlightenment, Inc., Vol. IV No. 4, Autumn 1969, p. 188.

Wolman, B., **Handbook of Parapsychology.** 1977.

Wolpe, J., **Psychotherapy by Reciprocal Inhibition.** Stanford, California: Stanford University Press, 1958.

Wolpe, J., **The Practice of Behavior Therapy.** New York: Pergamon Press, 1969, 1973.

Zaehner, R., **Mysticism, Sacred and Profane.** New York: Oxford Galaxy Books, 1961.

Index

A

Abreaction, 7, 8, 23.
Active imagination, 35, 44.
Ahsen, A., 232.
Alberti, R., 151, Acknowledgements.
Alpert, R., 222.
Ammenorrhea, 11.
Anxiety, 6, 11, 13.
Archetypes, 37.
Assagioli, R., 50, 233.
Assertiveness, 48, 150, 151, 156, 157, 158, 161, 163, 171, 249, Appendix E.
Astral plane, 131, 132.
Autogenic training, 6, 41-43, 239-245.
    Autogenic Abreaction, 36, 41-43, 55, 103, 149, 184, 188, 198, 206-209, 214, 239-245.
    Autogenic discharges, 6, 42, 43.
    Precautions for, 249, Appendix G.
    Standard exercises, 42, 48-49, 167, 184, 239-245.

B

Baker, P., 100, 117, 118, 133.
Bartlett, L., 116.
Behavior Therapy, 13, 44, 150, 151, 248.
Bernstein, M., 120.
Bhagavad Gita, 39, 98.
Bible, 97, 98, 179.
Binet, 218.
Biofeedback, 3, 42, 176, 232, 233.
Biological wisdom, 4, 6, 176.
Bloomfield, H., 82, 83.
Boehme, J., 100.
Bonny, H., 100.
Brain, 43, 44, 48, 113, 141, 176, 209, 226, 229, 240.
Breuer, J., 23, 218.
Brown, B., 176.
Brunton, P., 177.
Buddhism, 22, 38, 79, 80, 85, 177, 179.
Budge, E., 99.
Budzinski, T., 232.

C

Caird, W.K., 142.
Caldwell, W., 223.
Carrington, P., 168, 169.
Cayce, E., 99, 100, 117, 118, 133, 149, 179.
Cerminara, G., 120.
Christ-consciousness, 4, 33 100.
Clairvoyance, 116, 119.
Clark, W., 225.
Client-centered therapy, 151.
Collective unconscious, 37, 50.
Communication with discarnate entities, 116, 117, 124-128.
Consciousness
    A balanced view, 4.
    Altered consciousness, 19, 20, 45, 169, 232.
    Awakening of memories, 23.
    The subconscious, 4-5, 30, 31, 32, 219.
    The superconscious, 4, 5, 50.
    The unconscious, 4, 5, 25, 36, 50.

D

Darkness, 99, 100, 103.
Death, 43, 52.
Deep relaxation with free ideation, 35, 37, 234-239.
Deep-self, 4, 28, 38, 233.
Deikman, A., 82.
Delboeuf, 218.
Dianetic Therapy, 22-26, 28, 39.
Dietary considerations, 137, 147, 148, 154, 158, 161, 163, Appendix E, Appendix F.
Directive, 20, 21, 30-33, 44, 55, 151, 186, 217, 233.
Downing, J., 220.
Dreams, 3, 11, 36, 37, 53, 208, 209, 229, 233.

E

Eccles, Sir John, 176.
Eclectic, 150, 151, 157.
Embler, W., 93, 94.
Emergent uncovering, 23.

NOTES

NOTES

NOTES

NOTES

NOTES

NOTES

NOTES